"These thoughtful essays off[...] experience from the inside, v[...] edy and hope, and lessons fr[...] and insight." —Noam Chomsk[y...]

"The history of Yugoslavia is of global relevance, and there's no one better placed to reveal, share, and analyze it than Andrej Grubačić. From the struggle of the Roma to the liberating possibilities of 'federalism from below,' this collection of essays is required and radical reading." —Raj Patel, author of *Stuffed and Starved: Markets, Power and the Hidden Battle for the World's Food System*

"This book of essays shows a deep grasp of Yugoslav history and social theory. It is a groundbreaking book, representing a bold departure from existing ideas, and an imaginative view to how a just society in the Balkans might be constructed." —Howard Zinn, author of *A People's History of the United States*

"*Don't Mourn, Balkanize!* is a powerful and courageous book refusing to let the memory of a long history of colonization of the Balkans by the states-architects of Europe be erased or lead to a politics of resignation. Its vision of a 'federalism from below' sustained by networks of autonomous, culturally diverse communities has a significance that transcends the Balkans." —Silvia Federici, author of *Caliban and the Witch: Women the Body and Primitive Accumulation.*

"I cannot think of another work that even tries to accomplish what Andrej Grubačić has artfully undertaken in this volume. *Don't Mourn, Balkanize!* is the first radical account of Yugoslav history after Yugoslavia. Surveying this complex history with imagination and insight, Grubačić's book provides essential information and perspective for all those interested in the recent history of this part of the world." —Michael Albert, author of *Parecon: Life After Capitalism*

"Andrej Grubačić is a rare genuine authority on the recent history and politics of the Balkans. I have known him for a decade, have followed and read his work with profit, and corresponded with him on matters which I found difficult in doing my own writing in this field." —Edward S. Herman, Wharton School, University of Pennsylvania

"I can think of no better person than my close friend Andrej Grubačić to put the shattered pieces of a broken region back together again in a book that illuminates the abuses of rulers over the ruled. Grubačić is a native of the former Yugoslavia, an academic, and an anarchist historian; his encyclopedic knowledge make him a crucial commentator for all interested in this often under-reported part of the world. Turning a tragic past upside down while agitating for a new emancipatory future, *Don't Mourn Balkanize!* is the perfect remedy for the elite narrative of domination." —Chris Spannos, ZNet, author of *Real Utopia: Participatory Society for the 21st Century*

"Andrej Grubačić returns with another magnificent book that in the finest tradition of Yugoslav Zenitism reinvents a concept of the Balkan barbaro-genius and its prefigurative adventure into new and authentic political structures and praxis. *Don't Mourn, Balkanize!* shouldn't be read solely as a hidden history of the Balkans and inspiring political struggles of the (newest) social movements in the region, but also as a much needed epistemological and methodological manual how to write such a history. Peranalogiam with Boaventura de Sousa Santos, Eduardo Restrepo, and Arturo Escobar, Grubačić develops other histories/history otherwise that builds on a new epistemological paradigm in attempt to visualize the hidden, and, above all, to give credit to all those ideas, practices, and subjects that have been for too long marginalized, trivialized, and excluded. Finally, we have a book that documents the Balkan anarchist movements and their share in a global struggle for another, better world, and their important contribution to win, ergo balkanize it!" —Ziga Vodovnik, author of *Anarchy of Everyday Life* and *Notes on Anarchism and Its Forgotten Confluences*

"It's wonderful to read something on the Balkans that goes beyond doom and gloom. Andrej Grubačić turns the world on its head, especially with his notion of Balkanisation from below—a return to 'what is the most precious part of our history . . . a pluricultural vision of multiethnic, indeed transethnic, antiauthoritarian society,' from which he can convincingly call for a Balkanisation of Europe and of the world. A delight." —John Holloway, author of *Change the World Without Taking Power: The Meaning of Revolution Today*

"Here are two books. The first book is a searing critique of U.S. imperialist aggression and official hypocrisy. Consider: At a time when the United States demanded of other, smaller countries that they approve bilateral agreements shielding U.S. citizens from extradition to an international criminal court, the United States compelled the extradition to just such a court of the president of Serbia, a sovereign nation. Further, the U.S. government, unable to obtain approval from the United Nations, misused a network of states created for another purpose (NATO) to approve the bombing of Serbia. For three months bombs were dropped from 40,000 feet on ancient bridges and innocent civilians without the loss of a single American pilot. Thereafter the United States created in its new southeastern Europe protectorate a huge new military base and, apparently, sites for the interrogation and torture of so-called enemy combatants, while insisting on structural adjustment and privatization that smoothed the way for investment by multinational corporations. These were the elements of the 'shock and awe' template that the United States then sought to impose on Iraq and Afghanistan. After preliminary invasions of Grenada and Panama, the Balkans thus served to launch what has come to be called America's Long War against terrorism. The second book-within-a-book looks at the small green shoots of new life that have begun to come up through the floor of this fire-blackened forest. The courageous, persistent opposition to privatization by workers at the pharmaceutical plant Jugoremedija has prompted the federation of workers of a number of enterprises into a broader resistance front. Meanwhile, survivors of these hard times have begun to dream dreams that go beyond illegal diplomatic recognition of Kosovo as an independent nation or partition of Kosovo into Albanian and Serbian components. The hope is that the Balkans, precisely because of the many ethnic groups—including the Roma, or Gypsies—that have sought to find ways to live together there over the centuries, might pioneer for us all a model of regional community that avoids the concentration of all the means of compulsion in one centralized state and instead seeks horizontal bonds of mutual aid." —Staughton Lynd, historian, attorney, labor activist, and pacifist, co-author of *Wobblies and Zapatistas: Conversations on Anarchism, Marxism and Radical History*

DON'T MOURN, BALKANIZE!
ESSAYS AFTER YUGOSLAVIA

By Andrej Grubačić

Don't Mourn, Balkanize! Essays After Yugoslavia
By Andrej Grubačić
© Andrej Grubačić

This collection © PM Press 2010
All rights reserved. No part of this book may be transmitted by any means
without permission in writing from the publisher.

Earlier versions of these essays and interviews
were first published on Znet, 2002–2010

Published by:
PM Press
PO Box 23912
Oakland, CA 94623
www.pmpress.org

Cover by John Yates/Stealworks
Interior design by briandesign

ISBN: 978-1-60486-302-4
Library of Congress Control Number: 2010927780
10 9 8 7 6 5 4 3 2 1

Printed in the USA on recycled paper

Dedicated to my grandparents

Contents

II. BALKANIZATION FROM BELOW

Preface

Over the many years I have spent writing about Yugoslavia, I have been accused of almost everything. Serbian nationalists have accused me of treason (presumably against Serbia), or even of being a covert agent (presumably of the United States). Serbian and other post-Yugoslav pro-Europeans have accused me of nationalism (presumably Serbian), or again of being a covert agent (presumably of the Serbian state). Distinguished British and American liberals and Leftists, after reading my commentaries, have referred to my writings as typical of that "stubborn, unapologetic Balkan mindset." Some of this is true. I am a stubborn, unapologetic Balkanite. I suppose that if one wishes to insist on using the word, I am also a "traitor": both to the ethno-nationalist cause and of the European one.

I grew up in Belgrade—or, more precisely, between Belgrade and Sarajevo—but I always considered myself Yugoslav. I do not see any reason to stop doing so now. Yugoslavia might not exist anymore (after all, this collection includes, as its subtitle, the words "after Yugoslavia"), but Yugoslavia for me, and for people like me, was never just a country—it was an idea. Like the Balkans itself, it was a project of interethnic coexistence, a transethnic and pluricultural space of many diverse worlds.

The Balkans I know is the Balkans from below: a space of *bogoumils*—those medieval heretics who fought against Crusades and churches—and a place of anti-Ottoman resistance; a home to *hajduks* and *klephts*, pirates and rebels; a refuge of feminists and socialists, of antifascists and partisans; a place of dreamers of all sorts struggling both against provincial "peninsularity" as well as against occupations, foreign interventions and that process which is now, in a strange inversion of history, often described with that fashionable phrase, "balkanization."

My family was a microcosm of this deeper Balkan reality. My grandparents were socialists, partisans and antifascists—dreamers who believed in self-management and the Yugoslav "path to socialism." This idea—and especially the Yugoslav and Balkan dream of an interethnic, pluricultural space—was dramatically dismantled in the 1990s, when I found myself living in a country that was no longer my own. It was ruled by people to whom I could not relate, local tyrants that we used to call *aparatciki*, bureaucrats of ideas and spirit. That was the beginning of my struggle to understand my own identity and the problem of Yugoslav socialism. I went on to look for another path toward what my grandparents understood as communism. It seemed to me that the Marxist-Leninist way of getting "from here to there"—the project of seizing the power of the State, and functioning through a "democratically" centralized party-organization—had produced not a free association of free human beings, but a bureaucratized expression of what was still called, by the official ideology of a socialist state, Marxism.

Given my distrust of bureaucratic Marxism, I became an anarchist very early on. Anarchism, in my mind, meant taking democracy seriously and organizing prefiguratively—that is, in a way that anticipates the society we are about to create. Instead of taking the power of the state, anarchism is concerned with socializing power—with creating new political and social structures not after the revolution, but in the immediate present, in the shell of the existing order. The basic goal, however, remains the same. Like my grandparents, I too believe in and dream of a region where many worlds fit, and where everything is for everyone.

I survived the violence of the Yugoslav wars and NATO interventions, but in the end it was my political work in Belgrade—in the country that I still refuse to call by any other name but Yugoslavia—that made it difficult for me to stay there. With the kind help of many generous friends, especially those from Z Communications, I found refuge in the United States. Although I moved to the United States in 2005, I was already a foreigner well before that moment. I became a foreigner in the early 1990s, when the political ideas of interethnic cooperation and mutual aid as we had known them in Yugoslavia were destroyed by the combined madness of ethno-nationalist hysteria and humanitarian imperialism.

Being here, on the other side of the world, away from home and reading news from Yugoslavia—or whatever other name local elites and foreign embassies now use to describe it—was then and remains now equally disconcerting. The new, former state-socialist republics were neoliberalized, privatized or colonized and caught in an uneasy tension between sclero-nationalism and neoliberalism. A foreigner with papers to prove it, I remain an outsider trying to make sense of what has happened to the idea of the Balkans and to the country I came from. At the same time, I have and continue to find myself to be a Yugoslav, a man without a country but also, as an anarchist, a man without a state.

I feel absolutely no loyalty to Serbian, Croatian, or Bosnian national causes. I have no other emotion but utter contempt for people who helped destroy Yugoslavia, and I feel the same about the people who are now selling what is left of it. I stand equally distant from the traditionalists and from so-called transitionalists. During the 1990s, some of us in Belgrade used to say "Neither Milošević nor NATO." I still believe in this. As you will hopefully discover through reading this book, I believe that the obligations and responsibilities that stand before us (all of us who believe in this deeper conception of the Balkans) are to restore and to revive the idea of Balkan federalism; to infuse it with a new, contemporary meaning; and to fight against the interconnected impositions

of Euro-American imperialism and provincial ethno-nationalism. In other words, we must simultaneously and passion-
ately struggle for another, balkanized Europe and a different,
balkanized world. The future of Europe, should there be one,
is in the Balkans, not the other way around.

This book is a chronological selection of various commentaries, interviews and essays written for ZNet and *Z Magazine*
"after Yugoslavia" and between 2002 and 2010. Some of these
essays and conversations were written in Yugoslavia, others
in the United States. All the essays have been originally written in Yugoslav languages and were translated by different
people. It is important to read these essays chronologically so
as to see how movements and ideas mature. The reader will
find me contradicting myself, as well as making mistakes and
trying to correct them, all of which reflects my own development as a protagonist, propagandist, and essayist.

The reader will notice that I carefully avoided using cita-
tions and footnotes. This book is not a scholarly volume, it is
not a piece of investigative journalism, and most emphati-
cally it is not a work of theory. It is a selection of commentaries and conversations in the long tradition of Balkan socialist propaganda. However, I reference some of the literature I
find useful in my introduction to each section, and include a
timeline of relevant historical events.

The first part, "Balkanization from Above," follows the far-
cical trial of Slobodan Milošević; the assassination of Zoran
Djindjić; the "humanitarian" occupations of Bosnia and
Kosovo by the "international community"; and the privatization and neoliberalization of the Serbian part of Yugoslavia.
While writing these essays, I learned and generously bor-
rowed from many writers and magazines on the left, right,
and center from Serbia and other Yugoslav countries. I used
insights and facts that I discovered in the writings of Trivo
Inđić, Slobodan Antonić, Aleksa Djilas, Dusan Kecmanovic,
Ljiljana Smajlović, Miljenko Jergović, and Boris Buden as
well as in local anarchist literature and mainstream journals
such as *Reporter, Politika, Oslobodjenje, Vesnik, Rec, Balkanika,*

Republika, and many others. The other part of the book, "Balkanization from Below," consists of essays and conversations related to the possibilities of anticapitalist, pluricultural resistance in post-Yugoslavia. This section also includes an excerpt from my debate with Dragan Plavsic (who is one of the most reasonable regional commentators and one of the most pleasant Trotskyists with whom to disagree), as well as a part of my conversations with Michael Albert, the American theorist of participatory economics, who spent many years engaging seriously with the fascinating and understudied project of Yugoslav self-management. The second interview with members of Freedom Fight was a collective work of the Global Balkans Network, though mostly the work of my comrade Kole Kilibarda. The last essay, from which the book takes its title, was a talk given at the assembly of the Greek Anti-Authoritarian movement; it was later republished on ZNet.

I am very grateful to my friend and editor Romy Ruukel for all her valuable suggestions. I am very grateful to Larisa Mann for all her insightful comments, and to Roxanne Dunbar-Ortiz for her generous introduction. It is hard for me to find words to express sufficient gratitude to Staughton Lynd, my mentor, co-conspirator, and friend, who worked with me on this manuscript as a "guerrilla editor."

Lastly, special gratitude goes to my friends and comrades Ziga Vodovnik, Sani Rifati, Milenko Sreckovic, Ivan Zlatic, Marija Ivet, Tamara Vukov, Irina Ceric, and Spencer Rangitsch: balkanotopians, co-conspirators, and dreamers of another Balkans. *Borba se nastavlja.*

San Francisco, May 2010

Introduction
By Roxanne Dunbar-Ortiz

Like many people in the United States, I first heard of Yugoslavia in 1957, when I read *The New Class*, a slim, readable volume by a communist dissident denouncing Yugoslavia and communism in general. Milovan Djilas had joined the Communist Party as a student in the 1930s, and then fought alongside Tito in the Partisan Resistance against Nazi occupation of Yugoslavia. The Partisans took power at the end of the war but soon after, the Yugoslav Communist Party broke with the Soviet Union and became an independent socialist government. Although Djilas served as vice president and was headed toward future leadership of the federated Republic, he began to be a vocal critic of the Yugoslav system for becoming bureaucratic and creating a "new class" of privileged bureaucrats to replace capitalists. He was expelled from the Party, then arrested and imprisoned when he denounced Yugoslavia for remaining neutral when the Soviets invaded Hungary in 1956, suppressing an anticommunist uprising there. His book was published at that dramatic moment, becoming a best seller in the United States; Djilas became a household name, even in my working-class provincial world of Oklahoma. This reflected the ubiquity and pervasiveness of anticommunist propaganda in the United States during the Eisenhower administration, when the Central Intelligence Agency was used to overthrow democratic governments and install dictatorships in Guatemala, Guyana, and Iran under the guise of preventing the spread of communism. A decade later, I would understand that what the U.S. ruling class (as the carrier of European capitalist/imperialist domination) feared was not the spread of Soviet communism, but rather nationalism and the rise of the former colonies in Africa, Asia, Latin America, the Pacific, and Caribbean—well over half of the world's population—to a unified bloc or regional federations.

Yet, what I gleaned from Djilas's *The New Class* was advocacy for Yugoslav-style socialism. Unlike the wildly popular work of Russian émigré writer Ayn Rand, his book was not a call for capitalism but a criticism of the corruption of socialism. At the time, there were few opportunities in "Middle America" to hear something positive about socialism. I knew that my esteemed grandfather, who died before I was born, had been a member of the U.S. Socialist Party as well as the Industrial Workers of the World (IWW) in Oklahoma for two decades, in the organization's heyday of the early 1900s. I had heard my father's stories about his father's dream of a Socialist Commonwealth, a dream of a critical mass of the population of Oklahoma, and the United States, not something weird or marginal. He spoke of this as people working together in mutual assistance, so that there would no longer be poor people or rich parasites. At age eighteen, I thought that Djilas was condoning such a reality and warning of its loss in his country.

My next encounter with Yugoslavia took place at San Francisco State College (now University) where I began working for a degree in history in 1961. My required introduction to European history was taught by Peter Christoff—a Yugoslav, more precisely a Macedonian, as he made clear. The other history majors considered Christoff to be a joke, because he only lectured about the history of Macedonia. It was true, but as I knew nothing about European history other than what I had read about the Third Reich, studying it from the perspective of the Balkans was not alien to me. From Christoff, I learned that peoples and nations and states were different entities, and that the "state" was controlled by a ruling class, often representing and benefiting a small minority of the population under its rule. I date my interest, even obsession, with the "national question," to Christoff's course.

Subsequently, I began to specialize in Western Hemisphere and Indigenous histories and studied Europe through the lens of colonization and decolonization. I returned to thinking about Yugoslavia in the mid-1970s, when I became involved with a project to form a lobby for advocating human rights and decolonization for Indigenous peoples of the Western Hemisphere at the United Nations, a project that emerged out of the American Indian Movement's dramatic resistance at Wounded Knee in 1973, following a decade of recharged Indigenous resistance. At this time, American Indian Movement (AIM) leaders already had forged relationships with representatives of national liberation movements, six of which held special status as non-voting observers in the United Nations General Assembly and all its subsidiary bodies, as well as in the Non-Aligned Movement. These organizations were Palestine Liberation Organization, African National Congress, Pan-African Congress, Southwest African People's Organization, Zimbabwe African Peoples Union and the Zimbabwe African National Union (until Zimbabwe won its independence in 1980). Through those ties, the Indigenous movement had friendly relations with states-members of the Non-Aligned Movement and enthusiastic support of some, such as the newly liberated Angola and Mozambique, as well as Algeria and Yugoslavia. The Non-Aligned states make up the majority of the membership of the UN, so if they vote as a bloc, which they often do, a resolution passes or fails accordingly. When the Socialist bloc existed, it did not always agree with the Non-Aligned Movement positions, but on principle would never vote against them. This then isolated the minority of Western European and Anglo states along with the U.S. client states mainly in Latin America.

The Non-Aligned Movement may have never developed into a viable body without Yugoslavia and its principled and fierce neutrality. Founded in 1961 by the heads of four states—Nasser of Egypt, Nehru of India, Nkrumah of Ghana, and Tito of Yugoslavia—most of the member-states had ties either closer to the West or to the Socialist bloc. They varied in forms of government from electoral democracy to dictatorship; some were even at war with each other at times. Through it all, Yugoslavia remained democratic and refused to become embroiled in the USSR-U.S. divide. During the second decade of the Non-Aligned Movement in the 1970s, its demands for development aid were reframed as "transfer," actually a form of reparations for the arrested development of peoples under Western colonialism. Transfer of wealth and technology took the form of the New International Economic Order, which was linked with the New International Information Order. The UN passed resolutions to that effect, and the Independent Commission on International Development Issues was established, chaired by Willy Brandt. His 1980 report (later published as *North-South: A Program for Survival*) reflected the work and demands of the Non-Aligned Movement and was widely accepted as not only necessary for the Third World (as Africa, Asia, Latin America, the Caribbean, and Pacific were called) but also for to benefit the peoples of the rich countries. The UN planned a special General Assembly session in August 1980 to accept the Brandt Report and to establish mechanisms for its implementation. However, the Carter administration abruptly withdrew its support and demanded that the Socialist bloc assume an equal economic burden as the capitalist states with much higher GNP. It was at this time that the idea of the "two superpowers" was conceived and became currency for describing geopolitics and economies. No such initiative could possibly have taken place without the participation of the wealthiest country. In 1980, an election year, Ronald Reagan roused a new wave of fear and hatred of the United Nations that had first taken hold in the 1950s under the influence of the John Birch Society.

President Tito died the same summer as the UN Special Session in 1980. Most Western "experts" attribute the 1990s conflict in the Balkans to the loss of the strong leader-founder of Yugoslavia. Although certainly the peoples and people of Yugoslavia must have mourned the death of Tito and had to make adjustments in governance, the argument that Yugoslavia's demise was afterwards inevitable is not at all obvious. From what I observed, Yugoslavia's construc-tive role in the world—respect for and full participation in the UN; a model of political independence within a frame-work of interdependence and mutual assistance; promotion of nuclear disarmament; and leadership in the Non-Aligned Movement, though much more difficult after the failure of the New International Economic Order—continued seamlessly and dynamically after Tito's death. Each of the six republics of Yugoslavia—Bosnia and Herzegovina, Croatia, Macedonia, Montenegro, Slovenia, and Serbia (including the autonomous provinces of Vojvodina and Kosovo that after 1974 were largely equal to the other members of the federation)—rotated in the presidency of the Federal Republic, and the diplomatic corps included representative from each of the republics. Yugoslavia was uniquely stable among nation-states, because it viewed social interaction as endlessly prone to conflict, not just among individuals but the in the divisions along national, reli-gious, ethnic, and linguistic lines. It took such care that equity reigned. Its approach to governing recalls the Six Nations of the Iroquois Confederacy in what is now the United States. In all these respects, the Indigenous representatives doing inter-national networking were impressed with Yugoslavia's model.

Indigenous lobbying and building relationships within the UN bore fruit in 1981 with the establishment of the Working Group on Indigenous Populations, a body of independent experts nominated by states, which met for the first time in 1982. Yugoslavia nominated Ivan Tosevski, a Macedonian and international law professor at Skopje. He employed his ample skills of persuasion and meticulous knowledge of the inter-national law of self-determination to advance the visibility of the Indigenous at the UN and to develop protective measures in international law.

When the international Indigenous movement burst into visibility in 1992 on the occasion of the Columbus quincentenary, many even on the Left were surprised at and had no previous knowledge of the groundwork being laid during the previous fifteen years, much of which was made possible by the solidarity formed within the Non-Aligned Movement, particularly with Yugoslavia (as well as Algeria, Cuba, and, of course, the liberation movements). Unfortunately, few in the U.S. Left have learned about that connection or about the crucial importance of the Non-Aligned Movement and of Yugoslavia as a key state, both as a model of regional federation as well as its internal socioeconomic relations. So, when conflict developed in the Balkans in the period of the collapse of the Soviet Union, which led to the dissolution of Yugoslavia, only the hardcore anti-imperialists saw the hand of the United States and Western European countries, particularly Germany, at work. This left a vacuum for Western-based human rights groups, especially in the U.S. and France—a vacuum to fill with their calls for "humanitarian intervention," which made the U.S. and NATO military actions much easier, in the process guaranteeing a future existence for NATO that had no reason for continuing following the disbanding of the Soviet organized Warsaw Pact. The stage was also set for the military interventions and occupations in Iraq and Afghanistan.

Why the U.S./NATO determination to destroy Yugoslavia? Western European and North American colonialist imperialist states are notorious for using the strategy of "divide and rule" in pitting against each other national, ethnic, religious, and linguistic groups that prior to colonialism had developed institutions and traditions that allowed them to coexist symbiotically and often merge through intermarriage or alliances. Colonial states, by favoring one group or another, can easily create conflict and even genocide. Consequently, such states develop a strong adversity to any signs of regional coalitions or to alliances that they cannot control. Four centuries of resistance by colonized peoples culminated in freedom movements following World War II that the colonizing states could not prevent, and the United States had a neoliberal, neocolonial strategy to replace. That included, and still includes, the prevention of the formation of autonomous regional blocs and alliances, first fought out on the Korean peninsula, then Southeast Asia, then Africa, Latin American, the Caribbean, the Middle East, the Socialist bloc, and Yugoslavia.

Although I had more direct political interaction and experience with Yugoslavia than most people in the U.S. did, and I am a scholar and historian, I never undertook a formal study of Yugoslavia. It was not until 2002, when I began reading Andrej Grubačić's essays and interviews on Z Communications that I began making sense of my own direct observations. This indispensable collection contains those very essays. Then, I had the pleasure of meeting the writer in 2007, when he moved to San Francisco, and we became friends and collaborators on a number of projects. He had moved to the United States in 2005 at age twenty-nine but was already deeply involved in a doctoral dissertation at SUNY Binghamton on utopian moments in U.S. history. I am a historian and university professor nearly twice his age, but I learn from him, not only due to his comprehensive command of historical and theoretical works, but also due to the depth of his wisdom. As could be expected, although the essays in this collection focus on the Balkans, they also hold lessons and truths about larger questions, particularly about the actual effects of U.S. imperialism and capitalism.

Andrej Grubačić was born to a revolutionary family. His grandparents were socialists, and his grandfather represented Yugoslavia in the founding and affairs of the Non-Aligned Movement. He grew up nourished on the ideas and reality of workers' self-management and a particular path to socialism that was democratic and put people first, celebrating the particularity of every person, and the complementariness of collectivity and individuality. These qualities are present in Grubačić's writing and his persona as an anarchist, or "libertarian socialist" as he prefers to be known. He has brought a new hope of unity in struggle, and the old-fashioned principle of "an injury to one is an injury to all" to the scattered movements in the United States.

Soon after the beginning of the destruction of the Yugoslav dream in the early 1990s, Grubačić found new life and hope in the uprising of the Maya communities in Chiapas, Mexico. The Maya, who make up the majority of the population of Chiapas (a part of their ancient homeland of Mesoamerica, now divided among three Mexican states and three other modern states) made themselves visible under the banner of the EZLN (Zapatista National Liberation Army). The immediate cause of their uprising at just after midnight on January 1, 1994, was the North American Free Trade Agreement (NAFTA), which went into effect at that moment. Grubačić, like many others, directed his skills and energy to what came to be called the anti-globalization movement, traveling to Zapatista-controlled villages in Chiapas and to social centers in Italy. At the time, he was a nineteen-year-old a university student. He was involved in World Social Forum (WSF) from its conception, at the first meeting in Porto Alegre, Brazil, in early 2001 to protest the concurrent World Economic Forum (WEF) held in Davos since 1971 to produce and promote neoliberal policies throughout the world. Some twenty thousand people from 117 countries attended the first WSF gathering. The World Social Forum has continued to meet throughout the decade in global and national locations, and Grubačić serves on its international committee.

After Grubačić moved to the United States, first to New York, he happened to read a book by the venerable Staughton Lynd, one of the most important radical activists and thinkers of the second half of the 20th century and beyond. Staughton is most famous for his work in Mississippi with the Freedom School, established in 1964 by the Student Nonviolent Coordinating Committee (SNCC), and for his opposition to the Vietnam War, which took him to Hanoi and resulted in his being fired from his position as professor of history at Yale University. He and his wife Alice studied law and moved to Youngstown, Ohio, to provide assistance to industrial workers, and they have remained there while most of the jobs have left. Like Grubačić, Staughton and Alice had also been inspired by the Zapatistas, as they had been by the Sandinistas in the in the 1980s. Grubačić and Staughton began a dynamic conversation, eventually captured in the 2008 book *Wobblies and Zapatistas: Conversations on Anarchism, Marxism, and Radical History,* and found they were on a road to discovering what Grubačić calls a "libertarian socialism for the 20th century"—rekindling the early-20th-century dream, among U.S. workers and farmers through the IWW and Socialist Party, of a "socialist commonwealth."

Grubačić has adopted the Lynds' practice of "accompaniment," which they had learned from the Zapatistas. Accompaniment means walking side by side with another to a destination. One side is rich in experience but lacking in formal skills; the other side has those skills, and each contributes something vital to the process. Grubačić realized that he had experienced accompaniment in Yugoslavia. There, he and other university students had recognized that the only organized resistance to the encroaching tide of privatization and neoliberalism was taking place among workers in the Serbian countryside. They decided to go there and approach the workers who were distinctly different from the students. Some had fought in the recent Yugoslav wars and most were conservative, patriarchal, and traditional. The students offered to them their skills in foreign languages, writing, law, knowledge of and access to the internet, and connections to workers and movements outside Serbia. Students and workers started working together and learning from each other, and both changed. After a decade of accompaniment, which Grubačić continues through the internet and frequent visits, the same group of students plays an important role in the Coordinating Committee for Workers Protests in Serbia. This, too, parallels the Zapatista process, which also continues; non-Indigenous university students went to live in the Maya villages in the 1970s, forging a relationship of struggle through accompaniment.

Most of the essays here were written during the period of 2002–2007, spanning most of the two terms of the Bush administration. Grubačić could have worked the material of these essays into an academic tome, but that would have robbed us, the readers, of the effects of their dynamic rawness.

Balkan history, as written in the West, has so far defied most readers and even historians. Grubačić demonstrates the reasons why, the main one being that they begin with a false premise that is racist at its core. Historical and current examples of Balkan stereotyping continue to form a thread throughout his essays. In his brief but brilliant "Eisenhower's Mistake: A Tale of an Astonishing Letter to the Former German Chancellor" (2007), Grubačić gives one little-known example:

> The first time I heard of Willy Wimmer was during the NATO "freedom through bombs" campaign in Serbia in 1999. "Never before so few lied so thoroughly to so many, as in connection with the Kosovo war," he famously observed. "People died for this." Wimmer, then a member of the Christian Democratic Union party in the German Bundestag, was referring to the organized media's attempt to convince the population of Germany that there was indeed a humanitarian catastrophe in Kosovo, one that would necessitate a humanitarian intervention.
>
> The attempt was, as we know, all too successful. NATO spokesman Jamie Shea said at the time that, "The political leaders played the decisive role with regard to public opinion." He was referring to German politicians, those "democratically elected representatives," who "knew which news was important for public opinion in their country . . ."
>
> A well-informed Serbian conservative weekly published a translation of the letter from Wimmer to the German Chancellor Schroeder. The letter is a report from a conference held in the Slovakian capital of Bratislava, organized by the State Department and

the American Enterprise Institute. The subject of this conference, attended by numerous prime ministers "from Baltic to Macedonia," was the Balkans and expansion of NATO.

Wimmer had heard many interesting things in Bratislava. For instance, that "Operation Horseshoe"— the plan allegedly conceived by the Serbs to drive the Albanian population out of Kosovo in 1999—was a propaganda invention; that the purpose behind the Kosovo war was to enable the USA to correct an oversight of General Eisenhower's in the Second World War and to establish a U.S. military presence in the Balkans with a view to controlling the strategically important peninsula. He heard a high-ranking American official saying that the American aim was to draw a geopolitical line from the Baltic Sea to Anatolia and to control this area as the Romans had once controlled it. One would suppose that the American *mare nostrum*, or "our sea," is not the Mediterranean but the Atlantic. Wimmer had a distinct impression that everyone agreed (and could have cared less) about the fact that NATO humanitarian attacks are illegal under international law and were done very deliberately, in order to establish the precedent for future "humanitarian" actions without a UN mandate.

Beneath such imperialist opportunism, as well as a justification for it, is a long time Western "othering" of the people of the Balkans. In a March 2007 essay, "The Balkans: The Independence Will Be Supervised," Grubačić identifies some contemporary Western officials and commentators (some of whom pretend to be journalists). Grubačić writes:

I was reading an EU journal today, I think it was the *Frankfurter Rundschau*, when a curious article attracted my attention ... [It] ended with a rather grim prediction of difficult times ahead for state-building in the Western Balkans. ...

The label "Western Balkans" is the latest in a line of attempts to deflect the subversive anticolonial connotations of this misbehaving peninsula. Renaming the Balkans has a long and fascinating history. From Austro-Hungarian balkanologists to State Department experts of today, from Southeast Europe to the Western Balkans, the idea was always the same: to debalkanize the Balkans, for which purpose a more neutral language is useful. U.S. President Clinton was very clear about the fact that "Europe has no other option but to bring the entire area of Southeast Europe into the European family ... and debalkanize the Balkans once and for all," even if this takes "bomb[ing] the fuckers" (Richard Holbrooke).

One could ask why this attention is so necessary. Experts seem to be in agreement that it is because of the savage and barbarian ways of the people in the Balkans, ways that need to be tamed and civilized. However, they disagree about the source of this "'innate savagery.'" According to Robert Kaplan, author of the *Balkan Ghosts*, it is the absence of light: "[The Balkans] was a time-capsule world: a dim stage upon which people raged, spilled blood, experienced visions and ecstasies. Yet their expressions remained fixed and distant, like dusty statuary."

Others, like one famous British journalist, blame table manners:

> The ferocity of the Balkan peoples has at times been so primitive that anthropologists have likened them to the Amazon's Yanamamo, one of the world's most savage and primitive tribes. Up until the turn of the present century, when the rest of Europe was concerned as much with social etiquette as with social reform, there were still reports from the Balkans of decapitated enemy heads presented as trophies

on silver plates at victory dinners. Nor was
it unknown for the winners to eat the loser's
heart and liver.... The history books show it as
a land of murder and revenge before the Turks
arrived and long after they departed.

Vesna Goldsworthy, author of the wonderful book
Inventing Ruritania, calls this line of argument "racism
of nuance." I agree with the racism part, but have to
say that I don't see a nuance. Goldsworthy cites one
former UN representative in Kosovo who wrote in
the *Guardian* that governing Kosovo is like "dressing
a child: you give it the trousers of economy, the shirt
of education, the jacket of democracy, etc. And all the
while, the child wants to run out and play outside in
its underpants. If we let it, it could hurt itself." Could
the underpants be at the root of the Balkan problem?

Simon Winchester would disagree. He thinks
it is something that has to do with the mountains:
"Just what was it that had marked out this particular
peninsula, this particular gyre of mountains and
plains, caves and streams, and made it a byword, quite
literally, for hostility and hate? What forces were really
at work here? ... The two [mountain] chains smashed
into one another to create a geological fracture zone
that became a template for the fractured behavior
of those who would later live upon it." And just
like "these strange and feral Balkans" are outlandish
and unlike the rest of Europe, its inhabitants, "the
wild and refractory peoples of the Balkans," are
fundamentally (and anthropologically) different: "One
might say that anyone who inhabited such a place for
a long period would probably evolve into something
that varied substantially, for good or for ill, from
whatever is the human norm." Sounds convincing.

Beyond these blunt musings, however, is the deeper truth
as summed up by the venerable George Kennan, the father

of the U.S. policy of containment since the beginning of the Cold War, who also considered himself a Balkan expert. Grubačić quotes Kennan:

> What we are up against is the sad fact that developments of those earlier ages, not only those of the Turkish domination but of earlier ones as well, had the effect of thrusting into the southeastern reaches of the European continent a salient of non-European civilization that has continued to the present day to preserve many of its non-European characteristics, including some that fit even less with the world of today than they did with the world of eighty years ago.

Thus we see here the so-called Western Civilization's seemingly instinctive mistrust and fear of the dark and menacing East. Grubačić acknowledges that Kennan

> is quite right to point out two factors: one is the ethnic and cultural mix of the Balkan peoples—a "Macedonian salad," a peninsula always much more diverse and tolerant of diversity then the (rest of) Europe. The other factor is its stubborn refusal of what is forced upon us as "Europe" and "civilization." If we are to try to identify some of the most important aspects of the history of the Balkans, we cannot but point out the persistent vision of a surprisingly consistent utopia, of a decentralized communal society, in perpetual struggle against centralization, colonization, and cultural norms imposed by its civilized Western "Other." Debalkanization of the Balkans assumes the attempt to eradicate the history of this world turned upside down, a decentralized and fragmented world of anticolonial struggles, heretics (*bogumili*), maritime and land pirates (*hajduci* and *uskoci*), rebels and revolutionaries, anti-authoritarians, Romanis, self-governed communities, socialist federations, partisans, and antifascists. Balkanization

is indeed all about fragmentation, but it is not (only)
ethnic fragmentation: balkanization implies resistance,
and a decentralized and federated alternative to the
violent centralization of states and empires. This
is why balkanization needs to be arrested and the
Balkans need to be renamed and "debalkanized."

Grubačić does not believe that integrating the Balkans
into Western Europe is desirable; on the contrary, he states
that "we need to get Europe into the Balkans." He sees the
need to challenge the contradiction of Western universalism,
the one between civilizers and savages, and to offer an alternative as old as the Balkans itself, an alternative to nationalism, colonialism, and capitalism. "In this idea, Balkan people
need to find the strength and orientation for a new politics for another Balkans. It should be a politics of a Balkan
Federation. A participatory society, built from the bottom up,
through struggles for the creation of an inclusive democratic
awareness, participatory social experiments, and an emancipatory practice that would win the political imagination of all
people in the region. It is a politics that says unequivocally
to the European Union and its state-architects in Bosnia and
Kosovo: get the hell out of here."

The most recent essay in the collection, "Don't Mourn,
Balkanize! A Vision for the Balkans," provides more discussion of what Grubačić calls "political Balkan-phobia," which in
turn justifies, "humanitarian imperialism," particularly une-
quivocal as enunciated by international human rights deni-
zen Michael Ignatieff:

> Bosnia, Kosovo, and Afghanistan ... are laboratories
> in which a new imperium is taking shape, in which
> American military power, European money and
> humanitarian motive have combined to produce
> a form of imperial rule for a post-imperial age ...
> Bosnia after Dayton offered laboratory conditions
> in which to experiment with nation-building ...
> the reconstruction of the Balkans has not been an

exercise in humanitarian social work, it has always
been an imperial project ... because nation-building is
the kind of imperialism you get in a human rights era.

Taking a historical view, Grubačić identifies a longtime
"elite fear of autonomous spaces," because European colonial modernity arose, in no small part, as a result of successful fights for the formation and territorial unification of a
regional identity. The state-architects of Europe of that time
were, in fact, obsessed with the demon of the Balkans, balkanization being taken here in the sense of a "balkanization
from below," an alternative process of territorial organization,
decentralization, territorial autonomy, and federalism.

He dates the invention of "Balkanity as a political and
geocultural concept" to the Congress of Berlin, organized
by Otto von Bismarck. Carving up the Balkans led to a later
Congress that carved up Africa and created the "scramble for
Africa," which in turn led to World War I following an incident
in the Balkans. Grubačić cites Maria Todorova, who suggests
that the adjective "Balkan" ceased to be "a vague geographical concept and was transformed into one of the most consistently pejorative epithets in Western political discourse."
Grubačić adds,

It is interesting to note that the term "Balkans,"
with its "race of brigands," was barely used during
the Communist period. Four of the countries were
subsumed into the phrase "Eastern Europe" while
Greece and Turkey were "NATO's southern flank." It
is no accident that when Yugoslavia collapsed in 1991,
the term Balkans came back. At the same time as the
"savage Balkans" was reintroduced, the propaganda
myth of the artificiality of now former Yugoslavia, and
its "dark Balkan origins," emerged from the woodwork
of metropolitan academia.

Most interesting and thought-provoking in the final essay is
Grubačić's offering of the idea of a "collective and emancipa-

tory research project" that would benefit all who struggle for profound structural socioeconomic change and a new vision of life after the capitalist/imperialist state. He argues that the Balkans is one place to begin such a project, a "balkanology from below." He writes:

> [I]n unlocking the radical potential for thinking from difference and towards the constitution of alternative local and regional worlds, and taking seriously the epistemic force of local histories and thinking theory through from the political praxis of subaltern groups, radical balkanologists would do well to follow in the steps of Peter Linebaugh, Marcus Rediker and other historians from below who have been adventuring for traces of the "many-headed hydra" of rebels and revolutionaries, and hidden stories of popular struggles across the proletarian Atlantic. The beautiful, dazzling history of anti-authoritarian Balkans is replete with struggles of pirates and land pirates; *hajduks, uskoci, and klephts*; *bogumils* and partisans; heretics; and agrarian rebels of all kind, all misunderstood by communist and nationalist historians alike.

Grubačić finds historical precedents of expressions of Balkan federalism prior to the founding of Yugoslavia in the 20th century. Before he proceeds to propose a new kind of federation of autonomous peoples, he feels compelled to deal with the dark side of nationalism:

> The history of the Balkans is not only a history of interethnic cooperation. It is also a bloody history of nationalist atrocities that we are responsible for, that are self-inflicted. Not more than anywhere else in Europe, perhaps, and not without encouragement from outside, but nevertheless very real. The authoritarian Left in the Balkans, with its stubborn insistence on "national sovereignty," and support

for nation-state form as a necessary stage in social liberation, played a negative role in defining a position on nationalism. I would not like to be misunderstood here. When I say that I advocate regionalism and pluriculturalism, or that I criticize a Jacobin model of a monocultural state, I do not mean to say that we can evade the violent aspects of our brutal nationalist past. We have to confront in the same breath the terror visited upon us by Euro-colonial violence and our own self-inflicted brutalities. For the past to become a principle of action in the present we have to stop living in the past and instead integrate it into the present in an emancipatory way. In order to build a pluricultural Balkans the present has to be liberated from the past. It should be clear that I am not advocating an erasure of the past, but a work of remembrance as part of the work of freedom.

The question Grubačić poses and answers is: "But how can a national issue be dealt with in a more programmatic sense? I believe that nationalism can only be answered within a regional framework, and I believe that the Balkans can provide a model for another Europe, a balkanized Europe of regions, as an alternative to both transnational European super—state and nation—states. A balkanization of Europe would be premised on the politics of autonomous regions and a plurality of cultures."

Visualizing this regionalization, he sees a Balkans that is neither capitalist nor bureaucratic-socialistic, but rather a transethnic society with a pluriculturalist outlook, "an outlook which previously existed but was lost in its incorporation into nation-state frameworks, an outlook that recognizes multiple and overlapping identities and affiliations characterized by proliferation and multiplicity, an outlook that recognizes the unity produced out of difference." In a historical turnaround, Grubačić calls for an understanding that "the scandal borne by the word Balkans" can lead to redefining the power of its idea: "The kind of society we are talking about is possible only within the framework of a Balkan Federation, with no state, and beyond nation. A world where many worlds fit. If this is not our reality today, it follows that our duty, our only duty, is to fight to make it our reality tomorrow."

Roxanne Dunbar-Ortiz
San Francisco, 2010

The Dismantling of Yugoslavia: A Timeline

1991–1992 By 1992 the Yugoslav Federation, formed as a socialist state after World War II, is falling apart. The constitution establishes six constituent republics in the federation: Bosnia-Herzegovina, Croatia, Macedonia, Montenegro, Serbia, and Slovenia. Serbia also has two autonomous provinces: Kosovo and Vojvodina. Imperialism combined with local ethnic nationalism leads Slovenia and then Croatia to leave the socialist federation, with the encouragement of the international community eager to dismantle an independent socialist state. The war in Croatia leads to a conflict with other Yugoslav republics, a war resulting in hundreds of thousands of refugees and reawakening memories of the Croatian Nazi brutality of the 1940s. By 1992, a further conflict breaks out in Bosnia, which had also declared independence. The Serbs who live there are determined to remain within Yugoslavia. Yugoslavia finds itself under a UN embargo. Food and medicine become scarce. By 1993, the Bosnian Muslim government is besieged in the capital city, Sarajevo, surrounded by Bosnian Serb forces who control around 70 percent of Bosnia.

In Central Bosnia, the mainly Muslim army fights a separate war against Bosnian Croats who wish to be part of Croatia. The international community, spearheaded by the United States, makes it impossible for warring sides to reach any kind of peace agreement.

1995   Americans succeed in imposing the Dayton agreement of November 1995, which creates two self-governing entities within Bosnia—the Bosnian Serb Republic and the Muslim-Croat Federation—with their own governments, parliaments and armies. A NATO-led "peacekeeping force" is charged with implementing the military aspects of the peace agreement with extensive additional powers. This is the beginning of the European occupation of Bosnia. In the meantime, Croatia takes back most of the territory earlier captured by Serbs through ethnic cleansing during U.S.-backed military campaigns in 1995. This operation results in the mass exodus of at least two hundred thousand Serbs from Croatia.

1998–1999   In 1998, the Albanian Kosovo Liberation Army instigates a civil war in Serbian part of Yugoslavia. The international community again supports further disintegration of Yugoslavia. Serbian President Slobodan Milošević sends the army to Kosovo. The international imperialist community responds by launching NATO air strikes against Yugoslavia in March 1999, the first attack on a sovereign European country in the alliance's history. The strikes focus primarily on civilian targets in Serbia and Montenegro. This operation, with the Orwellian name "Merciful Angel," kills thousands of civilians, including a journalist and

technicians working for the Serbian national
TV station, and destroys much of the Yugoslav
infrastructure.

2000   Serbian opposition to Milošević becomes more
and more serious. After the elections, opposition
claims victory and Vojislav Koštunica declares
himself the "people's president." Federal Election
Commission calls for a second ballot, saying
that neither candidate won an outright majority.
Hundreds of thousands of opposition supporters
take to the streets of Belgrade to demand that
Milošević stand down. Students are organized
by a group called OTPOR. In October, a general
strike begins as Milošević remains defiant. Tens
of thousands of opposition supporters capture
the parliament building and take over the state
TV station. This event becomes known as
the October 5th revolution. The international
community acknowledges the legality of
Koštunica's victory.

2001   Former president Milošević is placed under
twenty-four-hour police surveillance in Belgrade.
Soon after, Milošević is arrested in the early
hours after a standoff in his home. He is taken
to Belgrade's main prison and charged with
misappropriation of state funds and abuse of
his official position. However, U.S. President
Bush demands that Yugoslavia hand Milošević
over to the international war crimes tribunal in
The Hague, lest the country not receive any U.S.
aid. As a result of this blackmail, Serbian Prime
Minister Zoran Djindjić overrules Constitutional
Court and authorizes Milošević's extradition to
the tribunal. This is the beginning of the conflict
between Djindjić and Yugoslav President Vojislav

Koštunica, a supporter of a Belgrade trial for Milošević. Koštunica's Democratic Party of Serbia pulls out of Serbian government. UN lifts the arms embargo against Yugoslavia, three years after it was imposed over the treatment of ethnic Albanians in Kosovo. Ibrahim Rugova, president of the nationalist Albanian Democratic League, becomes president of Kosovo.

2002 The trial of Slobodan Milošević, on charges of genocide and war crimes, begins in The Hague. In Serbian part of Yugoslavia, all forty-five deputies belonging to Yugoslav President Vojislav Koštunica's Democratic Party of Serbia walk out of Serbian parliament. Montenegro moves closer to independence after President Milo Đukanović takes on the more powerful job of prime minister.

2003 Serbian and Montenegrin parliaments approve a constitutional charter for new union of Serbia and Montenegro. On February 4, Yugoslavia ceases to exist. A new state—a union of Serbia and Montenegro—is proclaimed, with Svetozar Marović as president. In March of the same year, Serbian Prime Minister Zoran Djindjić is assassinated in Belgrade. A state of emergency is declared, with many dissidents arrested. Slobodan Milošević is indicted in Serbia for the murder and attempted murder of two key political opponents, Ivan Stambolić and Vuk Drašković respectively, in 2000.

2004 In March, former Yugoslav President Vojislav Koštunica becomes prime minister of Serbia in a center-right coalition government. There are new clashes between Serbs and ethnic Albanians in Kosovo after an Albanian attack on Kosovo Serbs in the divided town of Mitrovica. NATO sends more soldiers. Democratic Party president and pronounced pro-European politician Boris Tadić is elected Serbian president. His defeated opponent is Radical Party nationalist Tomislav Nikolić.

2005 Talks began on a Stabilization and Association Agreement with the European Union.

2006 Kosovo's President Ibrahim Rugova dies. Fatmir Sejdiu succeeds him, and UN sponsored talks on future status of Kosovo begin. Prime Minister Kosumi resigns and is succeeded by former KLA commander Agim Çeku. Slobodan Milošević is found dead in his cell in The Hague, under suspicious circumstances. He is buried in his hometown of Požarevac. At the same time, European Union calls off talks on closer ties because of Belgrade's failure to arrest war crimes suspect Ratko Mladić. After a referendum to separate from Serbia, Montenegro declares independence.

2007 United Nations envoy Martti Ahtisaari presents a plan for independent Kosovo. The plan is immediately welcomed by Kosovo Albanians and immediately rejected by Serbia. In Kosovo, another former KLA member, Hashim Thaçi, emerges as the winner in general elections. Serbs seize a UN building in Mitrovica. More than a hundred people are injured.

2008 Kosovo declares independence. Serbia says that the declaration is illegal. The international community immediately recognizes supervised independence. Serb opponents of independence seize a UN courthouse in Mitrovica, and more than a hundred people are injured in subsequent clashes with UN and NATO forces. A UN police officer is killed. Kosovo Serbs set up their own rival assembly in Mitrovica. Roma and other Kosovo people are unrepresented. The UN General Assembly votes to refer Kosovo's independence declaration to the International Court of Justice. European Union mission (EULEX) takes over police, justice and customs services from the UN. New "multiethnic" Kosovo Security Force launches under NATO supervision. The occupation of Kosovo by international forces properly begins. This happens much to the dismay of ordinary Albanians, Serbs, and Roma.

2009 Serbian President Boris Tadić and his government submit arguments to the International Court of Justice on the dubious legality of Kosovo's declaration of independence. Ethnic clashes break out in Mitrovica. After the local elections in two Serb-controlled districts in northern Kosovo, violent protests engulf the divided town of Mitrovica.

2010 The International Court of Justice in The Hague decides that Kosovo's declaration of independence is legal.

I. BALKANIZATION
FROM ABOVE

Introduction

> *The Serbs are two-dimensional people with a craving for*
> *simplicity and an ideology so basic it can be understood*
> *without effort. They need enemies, not friends, to focus*
> *their two-dimensional ideas. Life for them is a simple*
> *tune, never an orchestration, or even a pleasant harmony.*
> *Animals make use of their resources with far greater*
> *felicity than these retorted creatures, whose subscription*
> *to the human race is well in arrears.*

The above quote does not belong to the days of German prop-
aganda and struggle of the Nazis against Yugoslav partisans.
It is a recent statement of British humanitarian Sir Peter
Alexander Ustinov, who, according to the journal aptly named
The European, "had a magical way with children."

The sentence is not altogether surprising. Karl Marx
referred to the Balkan Slavs as "unhistorical people." They
were, in his view, and the one of Engels, "the racial dregs
of a thousand years confused development," who "although
pretending to fight for liberty, they were inevitably found on
the side of despotism and reaction." They "lack the primary
historical, geographical, and economic prerequisites of independence and ability to exist."

This deep-seated cultural derision of the Balkan peoples is the crucial aspect of what I am here calling "balkani-

zation from above." I use this expression to describe a project, remarkably consistent in history, of breaking Balkan interethnic solidarity and regional socio-cultural identity; a process of violently incorporating the region into the system of nation-states and capitalist world-economy; and contemporary imposition of neoliberal colonialism. Both Europeans and local self-colonizing intelligentsia have in common a contempt for everything that comes from this "wretched peninsula." The events described in the following chapter are nothing but the most recent phase in colonial ordering of the Balkans and its "retorted creatures." The history of the Balkan peninsula is written in blood of the Great Powers' attempts to prevent movements towards Balkan unity. Although essays in this chapter cover only the latest manifestations of elite balkanization, my contention is that the destruction of state-socialist Yugoslavia was a project of the same century-long process of balkanization from above. In contrast, Socialist Yugoslavia was a result of a long tradition of movements for Balkan unity, a manifestation of balkanization from below. After the defeat of real existing socialism, the Yugoslav state, with its indigenous socialism, and its global south, nonaligned orientation, could no longer be tolerated. Through the historically well-established pattern of imperialist intervention and local collaboration, this typically Balkan experiment has been destroyed in a series of bloody ethnic wars. Europeans and Americans have successfully blocked every peace initiative during the conflict. Balkanophobic racism in "the civilized world" has diverged into "paternalistic balkanism," reserved for the help-less and childlike Bosnians and Kosovars, and "raw balkanism," exemplified in Sir Peter's quote, meaning the evil Serbs. Former Yugoslav republics were immediately transformed into veritable laboratories of "state-building," "multiculturalism," "truth and reconciliation," "democracy-promotion," and economic privatization. Political choices became restricted to local chauvinist and pro-European options. Alternatives were declared non-patriotic or anti-European. The so-called non-governmental organizations and other organs of civil society, that monstrous creation of American democracy- promotion, joined hands with nationalists and outright fascistic extremists against the pro-Balkan Left.

The International Tribunal in The Hague was established in order to promulgate and further refine the official (European and American) truth of humanitarian ideology. Intervention on behalf of this ideology ("humanitarian intervention") was wildly popular among Euro-American elites, and subsequently used as a justification in every imperialist adventure from Iraq to Afghanistan.

The essays in the following section hold up for ridicule the almost hysterical tone directed primarily against the Serbs, especially extreme in British and French newspapers, in many ways paralleling American public discourse on the Middle East. This is not to say Americans are innocent of defaming the Balkans: Clinton's advisor Robert D. Kaplan, a self-styled philosopher, wrote *Balkan Ghosts: A Journey Through History*, a spectacularly vicious book having less to do with Balkan reality than the movie *Ghostbusters*. An official in President Obama's administration, Samantha Powers, perpetuates this fantastical approach in her book *A Problem from Hell: America in the Age of Genocide. New York Times* journalists, meanwhile, compete to outdo each other in imperial arrogance whenever they write on the Balkans and its chronically violent inhabitants.

These imperial and colonial attitudes still define the terms "civilized world," "international community" and "civil society." Balkan people were never too impressed by civilization. As early as 1871, the founder of the Balkan socialist movement, Svetozar Marković, ridiculed the entire "civilized world," from *Times* to the obedient Serbian press. The civilized world, he wrote, "was composed of rich Englishmen, Brussels ministers and their deputies (the representatives of the capitalists), the European rulers and their marshals, generals, and other magnates, Viennese bankers and Belgrade journalists." Marković was an anti-authoritarian socialist who believed, as do I, in pluricultural Balkan Federation organized as a decentralized, directly democratic society based on local agricultural and industrial associations. This is the kind of antinomian imagination that needs to be rediscovered: a horizontalist tradition of the barbarians who never accepted the civilized world that is now collapsing.

For readers interested in the topic of European universalism, I would recommend Edward Said's classic *Orientalism*. Another useful book is Immanuel Wallerstein's *European Universalism: The Rhetoric of Power*. Recent scholarship on Eurocentrism includes some truly groundbreaking writings building on traditions of dependency theory and world systems analysis, such as *Coloniality of Power* by Anibal Quijano, *Local Histories/Global Designs: Coloniality, Subaltern Knowledges, and Border Thinking* by Walter Mignolo, and *The Underside of Modernity: Apel, Ricoeur, Rorty, Taylor and the Philosophy of Liberation* by Enrique Dussel. Among the books devoted to Europe and the Balkans, few studies stand out: Maria Todorova's fascinating critique *Imagining the Balkans*; Vesna Goldworthy's cultural study *Inventing Ruritania: Imperialism of the Imagination*; Milica Bakić-Hayden's *Nesting Orientalisms: The Case of Former Yugoslavia*; and Božidar Jezernik's anthropological study *Wild Europe: The Balkans in the Gaze of Western Travellers*. Bogoljub Šijaković wrote the short but powerful *A Critique of Balkanist Discourse: Contribution to the Phenomenology of Balkan's "Otherness."* Outstanding work on balkanism has been done by Tamara Vukov, whose essay "Military Neo-Balkanism" is forthcoming.

Among many excellent works on Balkan history, I would single out L.S. Stavrianos' political history *The Balkans Since 1453*. The most impressive account of Balkan civilization can be found in many works of Traian Stoianovich, and especially his *Balkan Worlds: The First and Last Europe*. M. Mazower's *The Balkans* is an excellent short rebuttal of the balkanist idea that people are born into the Balkans with some special quality that makes them want to kill one another.

For those interested in the process of destruction of Yugoslavia, Ed Herman and David Peterson provide an extensive bibliography in their essay "The Dismantling of Yugoslavia: A Study in humanitarian Intervention (and a Western Liberal-Left Intellectual and Moral Collapse)." I have found particularly useful the works by Susan Woodward, *Balkan Tragedy: Chaos and Dissolution after the Cold War* and *Socialist Unemployment: The Political Economy of Yugoslavia, 1945–1990*, as well as Robert Hayden's study of the complicity of the international legal community in Yugoslav break up, *Blueprints for a House Divided: The Constitutional Logic of the Yugoslav Conflicts*. Misha Glenny authored a couple of very informative books, including *The Balkans: Nationalism, War & the Great Powers, 1804–1999*.

Among the best works on humanitarian interventionism in Kosovo are two books by Noam Chomsky, *The New Military Humanism: Lessons from Kosovo* and *A New Generation Draws the Line: Kosovo, East Timor, and the Standards of the West*. A more general work on the subject of humanitarian intervention is Jean Bricmont's *Humanitarian Imperialism: Using Human Rights to Sell War*. David Chandler gives a thoughtful and well-researched account of Bosnian humanitarian misadventure in *Bosnia: Faking Democracy After Dayton*, and extends the account further in the more recent *From Kosovo to Kabul and Beyond: Human Rights and International Intervention*. Mahmood Mamdani explains how the same civilizational complex was applied to the reality of Darfur, in *Saviors and Survivors: Darfur, Politics, and the War on Terror*. John Grow wrote a useful book on the international community during the Yugoslav war in his *The Triumph of the Lack of Will: International Diplomacy and the Yugoslav War*. William Robinson's *Promoting Polyarchy: Globalization, U.S. Intervention, and Hegemony* is still one of the few books on the topic of so-called democracy-promotion and building of civil societies in exotic places.

Should Milošević Be Tried at The Hague?

June 2002

The recent arrest of Yugoslavia's ex-president Slobodan Milošević provides a context in which to offer a brief analysis of the current Yugoslav intellectual climate.

It is most expedient, for our purposes, to begin by identifying the phenomenon hereafter referred to as "the Belgrade consensus"—a set of positions unanimously advocated by non-governmental organizations and liberal intellectuals in Belgrade on the question of Milošević's legal fate, and concerning the somewhat more complicated problem of what intellectual engagement in today's Yugoslavia entails. The Belgrade consensus is informed by three arguments: the argument about the validity of The Hague Tribunal; the argument about the political expediency of cooperating with that institution; and the argument about collective guilt. In this treatment, I will try to bring into question the legitimacy of all three of these arguments which currently exercise public opinion in Yugoslavia and which—strange as it may sound—are almost universally accepted in Belgrade's progressive circles. The intellectuals and activists who oppose this consensus have conveniently been labeled "ultra Leftists" and thereby have been successfully eliminated from the public debate.

Is The Hague Tribunal really legal and legitimate, as Belgrade's liberals contend? The supporters of Milošević's extradition most often begin with the assertion that The

Hague Tribunal is an administrative body created by the UN Security Council; they seek the legal basis for the assumed duty to cooperate in UN declarations, which require member states to accept and carry out its decisions. Furthermore, they see no legal obstacle in the Constitution of the Federal Republic of Yugoslavia, since, according to article 17, the option of extraditing a Yugoslav citizen is excluded only in cases involving another state.

And yet, an entirely different picture emerges from our own analysis. It is indeed true that UN member states have an obligation to carry out decisions of the Security Council, but only in cases in which such decisions are legally valid, i.e. when arrived at in accordance with the specific powers conferred upon it by the UN Charter.

It is well known that the Security Council has been entrusted with the "primary responsibility for the maintenance of international peace and security" which implies its right to investigate any dispute capable of endangering the fundamental values of the so-called international community, as well as the right to recommend appropriate procedures with a view to resolving a particular dispute (Chapter VI of the Charter.)

In case these recommendations prove ineffective and, as a result, there is a breach of peace, the Security Council has the right to apply coercive measures, including those of a military nature (Chapter VII of the Charter.)

Evidently, there is no provision for the Security Council's authority to establish any type of international institution, especially not one of a judicial nature. For this reason, article 29 of the Charter, which the Security Council invoked in establishing The Hague Tribunal does not constitute a legally valid basis, as it merely authorizes it to "establish such subsidiary organs as it deems necessary for the performance of its functions."

However, subsidiary organs can only be considered bodies of an expert or operative nature, such as commissions, subcommissions, committees or bodies of a similar scope.

In this respect, as representative bodies would qualify the many expert commissions attached to other UN organs (the International Law Commission which prepares the blueprints for international conventions) or committees like the well known Legal Committee. As an international court can in no case be a "subsidiary body" but only an independent institution, so too can this tribunal have no legal foundation, especially not in the above-cited article of the Charter. Consequently, the tribunal is illegal under international law, and all its decisions so far can accordingly be considered not legally binding.

Jurists are well acquainted with the tenet that the independence of the judiciary is the primary basis for its legal competence. Otherwise, courts are subject to the political dictates of another authority (usually the executive), which is an element of dictatorship.

Moreover, one of the intrinsic characteristics of the contemporary systems of capitalist democracy is precisely the strict division of power into three branches—legislative, executive and judicial—a division that, above all, assumes their mutual independence in the exercise of authority.

In the case of The Hague Tribunal, however, the principle of the independence of the judiciary has been entirely invalidated, although it is a legal and political principle that ought to be fundamental.

In addition, all previous practice in establishing international courts further refutes the claims of those who accept the authority of The Hague Tribunal: in all cases so far on record, the formal and factual shaping of any kind of international tribunal has rested exclusively on the will and interest of states, thereby securing its requisite legitimacy.

Thus, the UN Charter provided the basis for the establishment of the International Court of Justice with authority to resolve disputes between states; all the members of the Charter are ipso facto members of this court's statute.

The International Tribunal for the Law of the Sea was established in 1982 by the UN Convention on the Law of the Sea as a tribunal with a specific jurisdiction.

The European Court on Human Rights was established by the Convention for the Protection of Human Rights and Fundamental Freedoms, which was adopted by the members of the Council of Europe as long ago as 1950.

The Allied agreement of 1945 established the so-called Nuremberg trials for the purpose of prosecuting suspected Nazi leaders; their statute was adopted by the many states with an interest in these trials. The 1948 Convention on the Prevention and Punishment of the Crime of Genocide provided for the establishment of a special criminal court for this type of crime; the fact that it has not been established to this day is a direct consequence of the absence of will on the part of a number of states.

The same reason prevented the establishment of a criminal court for the prosecution of U.S. crimes in Vietnam, which resulted in the formation of the Russell Tribunal as a kind of "court of conscience."

Finally, at the international conference held in Rome under the auspices of the UN, the statute for a permanent International Criminal Court was adopted by the will of 120 states (the U.S., of course, voted against it); its taking effect was conditional upon ratification by sixty signatory states.

The examples cited above offer clear insight into the procedure for securing legitimacy for international courts. In the case of The Hague Tribunal, this procedure was patently disregarded, whereby this institution was stripped of its legitimacy and this tribunal turned into a scandalous precedent in international practice of this sort.

Such a precedent indicates the likelihood of future disrespect for international standards in this area, particularly the use of such quasi-tribunals to effect the political interest of capitalist elites.

As for the above-cited constitutional article on extradition, the estimate of it as legal grounds for the extradition of a citizen of a sovereign state is more than suspect.

As an instrument of international legal aid for criminal cases, extradition applies to citizens of a foreign state; both

SHOULD MILOŠEVIĆ BE TRIED AT THE HAGUE?

the procedure itself, as well as the conditions under which it is carried out, is subject to strict regulation by internal legislatures.

As a rule, however, domestic citizens are not liable to such measures, and a statement to such effect is usually articulated on a constitutional level.

International practice has so far shown that the question of extradition is most often regulated by bilateral or multilateral contracts or else it is executed under the principle of reciprocity.

For our purposes, the European Convention on Extradition concluded by the member states of the Council of Europe in 1957 and amended in 1975 to extend to [those who commit] war crimes and crimes against humanity may serve as an illustrative example.

A particularly interesting detail of the convention is the contractual provision by which states reserve the right to refuse the extradition of their own citizens, even those accused of severe breaches of the laws and customs governing war (article 6. paragraph 1a.)

Here again the standard negative stance on the extradition of a state's own nationals has been expressed.

For this reason, I do not see why the FRY (Federal Republic of Yugolavia) should be considered outside the established framework of such practice.

Keeping in mind these facts, which dispute the legality and legitimacy of The Hague Tribunal and indicate the common understanding regarding the option of extraditing one's own citizens, we are free to conclude that there is not a single legal basis for the FRY's duty to meet such demands from The Hague.

To be sure, this is not a position to be construed as an attempt to exempt Slobodan Milošević, or any other Yugoslav citizen, from criminal responsibility, if it has been established.

In fact, domestic internal criminal regulations require the authorized judicial organs to react in every specific case in accordance with their official line of duty.

Therefore, claims that domestic judicial organs are not competent to carry out such procedures remain unacceptable.

The FRY is duty-bound, as a signatory to the General Framework Agreement for Peace in Bosnia and Herzegovina (article 9), to "cooperate in the investigation and prosecution of those who have committed war crimes and other breaches of international humanitarian law," but, as can be seen, even this article does not provide for the hand-over of Yugoslav citizens.

The argument for the legality and legitimacy of The Hague tribunal—an argument that constitutes the first part of the Belgrade consensus—has thus been stripped of all factual support.

However, is cooperation with The Hague tribunal as useful and politically advantageous as proponents of the Belgrade consensus insist? Hardly. The handover of Slobodan Milošević to The Hague would make the Serbs the only people in memory whose president has been extradited and sentenced.

From this situation, a host of harmful implications would follow. First and foremost, it would legitimize the bombing of the FRY by countries of NATO. The few hundred Serbian and Albanian civilian casualties would be forgotten. Payments of war reparations for a completely devastated infrastructure would be avoided.

The new military humanism, by now a fully ensconced ideology, would be given its definitive stamp of approval. The burden of collective responsibility for the wars in the Balkans would be borne exclusively by the Serbs. Milošević, a politician who under no circumstances ought to enjoy our sympathy, would be idolized in Yugoslavia as a sort of socialist or nationalist martyr, depending on the interpretation.

Finally, is the extradition of Milošević our moral duty by which alone we can atone for the collective sins of our nation? In order to fully understand and evaluate this position—on which, as a matter of fact, the entire Belgrade consensus rests—it is necessary to uncover the origin of this unusual argument that enjoys so much sympathy among Yugoslavia's liberal intelligentsia.

It seems to us that the answer should be sought in the phenomenon of "balkanistic discourse"—the only discourse that from the point of view of power has the authority to speak about the Balkans.

If we were to approach the problem of "balkanistic discourse" from Levinas's perspective of "otherness" (much popular these days in liberal intellectual circles in Yugoslavia), adopting the primacy of the ethical over the ontological, we could apply the relationship I-Other to Europe and the Balkans. Forgetting that it can build its own identity only through a relationship with the Other, Europe is closing itself off in an essentialist framework and rendering the Balkans an impersonal object of knowledge, thereby annulling their Otherness.

In this sense, knowledge appears exclusively as an extension of power, since the establishment of a Balkan identity stands in the service of immediate political interests. In our view, "balkanistic discourse" is thus a colonialist discourse that deprives the Other of the right to self-determination.

The historical thesis presented here is not all that original; it assumes a centuries-old, deep European involvement in the political, ethical and confessional state of the Balkans. The famous myth of ethnic conflicts—"the Balkan powder keg"— is not an effect of inherent, genetic traits, but of a planned revision of the Balkans' ethnic-confessional image and structure, and the constant practice of transferring populations by Rome, Byzantium, the Ottoman Empire and the Hapsburgs.

Led by the old Roman strategic motto *divide et impera*, which itself incidentally arose during the Roman campaigns in Dalmatia, the great powers have always sought to prevent the territorial consolidation of the Balkans. "Balkanistic discourse" came into existence to obscure this sort of political practice. From "balkanology" to assorted "experts on the Balkans," the manufacture of knowledge has produced its own reality.

The erstwhile discipline of Austro-Hungarian balkanology provides an excellent example of the ties between academic institutions and centers of power, as well as of how an "Austro-Hungarian Balkans" came into being and acquired a referent in reality. Today, a renewed connection between knowledge and power is evident in the correspondence between the scientific and media-produced image of the Balkans, and the currently prevailing attitudes in foreign policy.

The uniform assessment of the Slavic character as primitive and the Balkans as a "repository of evil" allows us to discern an intention to indict as a reliable instrument of control/conquest. In this way, "balkanistic discourse" is characteristic of a method of projection in which one's own sins are projected onto the Other. The effective manufacture of knowledge engenders feelings of fear and guilt, and as a consequence encourages uncritical acceptance of imposed, alien values, or heterophilia ...

One aspect of the construct of a new, fictional "Balkans" is particularly important: the semantic imprisonment with which we are confronted as a result of linguistic violence, beginning with the verb "to balkanize," which most of the world's dictionaries define primarily as "to divide." Linguistic terrorism is only one part of the larger process of stigmatization that aims to establish social control and the imposition of silence upon the Balkan peoples so as to allow others to speak in their name.

Thus, everyone can speak about the Balkans but the Balkanites themselves: their right to speak has been taken away by a "balkanistic discourse" that has imposed upon them the idea of a geographically conditioned collective guilt. But can such a concept as collective guilt apply to an entire people—in this case, the Serbs?

In writing about the German people's guilt for the crimes committed during World War II, the German philosopher Karl Jaspers asserts that a people cannot be guilty, be it in a political or moral or criminal or metaphysical sense. As Dušan Kecmanović has pointed out, the citizens of a state can be held politically responsible for allowing—through voting, passivity, or conformism—the creation of a regime that will go on to perpetrate, in their names, crimes against its own citizens or those of another state.

Responsibility, however, is not the same as moral guilt. Jaspers rightly points out that moral guilt applies only to cases in which people are entirely insensitive to the suffering of other people and have unconditionally identified with their army and their state to the extent that they are unwilling to know about the misdeeds being committed by their state's army.

The very concept of a people's collective guilt is founded on two mistaken assumptions. The first is the idea that the category of "a people," as an entity, is equivalent to all those individuals who belong to it. Such a categorical, typological designation of human beings has, throughout the course of history—i.e. even when there were no nations and ethnicities, although there always have been divisions into groups— brought enormous misfortune upon human beings by turning them against each other. The other mistaken assumption treats all members of a given ethno-national group as identical from the outset, as having always shared the same values, and the same objects of love or hatred. Finally, it is worth noting that numerous and serious negative consequences come with the use of the term "collective guilt." I will point out only one. When an ethno-national group is declared morally guilty, its members inevitably perceive this sort of label as a threat, regardless of whether they believe (and they usually do not) that they have a reason to feel guilty.

The experience of threat to the group causes the group, in defense, to strengthen internal ties and to close itself off from the outside; the group becomes exclusive and homogenized. This paves the way for an ever-greater number of antagonized groups as well as increased antagonism between groups.

In the final outcome, those who are marked for collective guilt suffer as much as those who proclaimed them guilty. The only benefit here is derived by those who care to have the peoples of a given region, in this case the Balkans, continue to watch each other over the barrels of their guns even after hostilities have ceased. And that is just one, by no means unimportant, reason for which collective guilt ought not be used as either a concept or an argument.

Let us emphasize in our conclusion the need to establish a critical meta-project of "balkanology from below" that would examine the historic and institutional "manufacturing of the Balkans." This project must become the responsibility of every genuinely engaged Balkan intellectual, because what is at issue here is the falsification of knowledge—a falsification subservient to the interests of power. One of the most impressive attempts in this direction is a recent book by Bozidar Stijakovic, published in English as *A Critique of Balkanist Discourse*.

Stijakovic, in this delightful book, urges us to formulate a new idiom, which could be called "balkanology from below," as opposed to various established approaches to the Balkans. It is the *conditio sine qua non* of the struggle for the recognition of our own identity, even our own name—the name Balkans has today, surely not for the first time nor by accident, been supplanted by the formal, geographic designation of Southeastern Europe.

The principle of "the Balkans to the Balkan peoples" calls for an immanent consolidation: the realization of the need for Balkan unity, a new internationalist unification that is in the spiritual interest of Europe itself. Once seen through the prism of our interpretation, all three of the arguments that make up the Belgrade consensus have to be rejected.

Neoliberal ideology, the manufacture of acceptance and guilt, and the whole complex of ideas that the liberal mandarins and so-called non-governmental organizations are trying to market, need to be opposed by scientific arguments and by intellectual and activist engagement.

In this respect, grassroots initiatives like the Initiative for Economic Democracy offer reasons for a cautious optimism.

Who Was Djindjić?

March 2003

Serbian Prime Minister Zoran Djindjić was a longtime dissident. During his student days in the mid-1970s, he left Serbia for Germany to join other dissidents who, with the help of Western intellectuals, were escaping harassment in Titoist Yugoslavia.

After his return to Belgrade, Djindjić abandoned his anarchist ideas and in 1989 was among the founding members of the Democratic Party, one of the main anti-Milošević parties. A master tactician and a ruthless technocrat, he soon took over as its leader. Djindjić came to international prominence at the end of 1996, when he was one of three opposition leaders who inspired and coordinated nearly three months of mass street demonstrations against the attempts of the Milošević administration to annul the victories of the Zajedno (Together) coalition in municipal elections across Serbia.

The demonstrations—unprecedented in both length and intensity in recent European history—brought victory. Djindjić's prize was to become the mayor of Belgrade in 1997. During the Kosovo conflict, when NATO carried out its aggression against Yugoslavia, Djindjić took refuge in Montenegro and the West; leaving the country, and his suggestions that "Serbia should be bombed" were not received with support in Yugoslavia. After the aggression against Yugoslavia, Djindjić— probably the most unpopular of Serb politicians at the time—

stayed in the background, directing the ultimately successful campaign of another opposition leader, Vojislav Koštunica, in the race against Milošević.

Koštunica gained the largely honorary post of Yugoslav president, while Djindjić took over at the center of power as prime minister of Serbia. Djindjić transferred Milošević to The Hague Tribunal in 2001 in the face of opposition from the people and many Serb political forces, including President Koštunica. He introduced neoliberal capitalism of the worst kind. His media manipulation and his technocratic behavior made him more and more unpopular as Serbia was becoming one of the poorest countries in the region. Every day, more than fifteen thousand workers were protesting in the streets. More than nine hundred thousand people in Serbia (out of a population of about seven million) were fired, unions were aroused, and social unrest was brewing.

So-called Workers Resistance from Kragujevac, an industrial city of Serbia, was vehemently protesting against Djindjić's neoliberal policies. Coalitions and social movements, such as Another World is Possible and many others, were starting to take shape and to resist IMF-iseration of the country. A handful of intellectuals and journalists were fighting against an imposition of the false debate wherein you have to choose between neoliberal "reformists" or "ultranationalists" and there emerged a so-called Belgrade consensus—a convergence of the neoliberal and nationalistic political elite and intellectual commissars who were restoring the capacity of coercion against the people who tried to look beyond only options of nationalism and neoliberalism.

With regards to political parties, there was a power struggle between Koštunica and Djindjić for much of the past two years. Koštunica has enjoyed popularity, and Djindjić was detested because of his technocratic approach and so-called reforms of stabilization, privatization, and liberalization in the spirit of the Washington Consensus. Yet Djindjić was very successful and used his links with President Đukanović of Montenegro to establish a loosely knit union of Serbia and Montenegro.

The power struggle with Koštunica finally went Djindjić's way with the replacement of Yugoslavia by the union of Serbia and Montenegro over the past month. This left Koštunica without an office and transferred him back to the opposition. Djindjić was not able to enjoy the fruits of his almost absolute power for more than a few weeks. There are a lot of speculations about today's assassination. According to one scenario, perhaps the most probable, Djindjić was a victim of his own alliances with organized crime. Post-Yugoslavia, as every other "country in transition" (towards complete poverty) has seen the formation of a new class, a group of oligarchs who made their money under Milošević and found new protectors in Djindjić or Koštunica. A virulent element of this new class, comprised of business people and politicians, was organized crime. Another scenario is to interpret Djindjić's assassination as a political plot. There is a suggestion that he was perhaps executed by Albanian nationalists, who are gaining more and more strength in the south of Serbia.

Djindjić's circle, neoliberal technocrats, will use this situation and benefit from it. This is not good: I saw it happening with Milošević, who had become almost a martyr after his extradition to The Hague. As I am writing these lines, one of the TV stations loyal to Djindjić is broadcasting the movie *JFK*. There is also another danger—that of organized crime transforming this situation into gang warfare. After this, gangs and mafia in general, could be encouraged. And a situation of complete disorder could be introduced.

In the best scenario, neoliberals in power will use and exploit this opportunity for their own benefit and further impoverishment of the country. Nationalist forces could be encouraged as well. As for the people who are fighting for another Serbia and against neoliberalism and nationalism—for them, the situation doesn't look very promising, at least at the moment.

Post-Yugoslavia and the Exceptional State of Serbia-Montenegro

Tamara Vukov Interviews Andrej Grubačić about the Serbian State of Emergency

Translated by Tamara Vukov

April 2003

The tradition of the oppressed teaches us that the "state of emergency" in which we live is not the exception but the rule.
—*Walter Benjamin*

Tamara Vukov: On February 4 of this year, the Federal Republic of Yugoslavia was replaced by the new state of Serbia and Montenegro. Following the assassination of Prime Minister Zoran Djindjić on March 12, 2003, this new political entity has undergone the majority of its existence in a state of emergency. While the imposition of the state of emergency has largely been presented as a progressive opportunity to install true democracy and restore order to the nation, can you describe what these emergency measures look like and what is actually being done in their name?

Andrej Grubačić: The state of emergency represents the insane attempt of a small group of people to take the house in which they live and expand it into a nation-wide prison. Even stranger, this insane attempt has succeeded. The government reacted to the murder of Zoran Djindjić by introducing a state of emergency. The police were granted the right to arrest and imprison people for thirty days without the customary judicial proceedings, while the arrestee is left without any right to a lawyer. The police have acquired the right to enter homes without a warrant, the unfettered right to tap phone conversations, to follow, to spy, and to search. The minister of police can now detain whoever strikes him as suspicious. Strikes and political assemblies have been outlawed, and the right to movement had been seriously restricted. Censorship has been introduced, while any public debate about the reasons for the introduction of the state of emergency and about its eventual repeal has been outlawed. Human Rights Watch has already reacted, warning the Serbian government that such authoritarian behavior is in contravention of European Union directives, not to mention ethical ones.

The second serious aspect of this state of emergency is that no limits have been set around it. Based on the decision of the parliamentary president, the state of emergency is about the hunt for those guilty of the assassination, but also for other guilty parties of several other crimes. It was introduced for a completely unspecified and indefinite period of time. It is difficult to determine when all the parties guilty of some unspecified crime will be captured, and which crimes need to be resolved according to the government before "adequate conditions" are attained for the withdrawal of the state of emergency.

Consider the conduct of the constitutional procedure for which the national assembly was automatically convened during the implementation of the state of emergency. The gathering that was called in the house of the National Assembly was not an assembly of sitting members. No one ever tried to determine how many members were present, and according to several members, the electronic system for recording attendance was disconnected.

In short, post-Yugoslav society has had its freedom revoked without any clear indications or promises regarding when it will be returned. And whether it will be returned at all.

TV: What are some of the domestic impacts of the state of emergency politically and in terms of the police crackdown you referred to? Is it limited to the targeting of organized criminals as has been largely portrayed in the media? Or are

broader constituencies and forms of political dissent being targeted?

AG: Minister of Justice Vladan Batić has claimed that a modern Serbia requires modern prisons with a minimum of two thousand places. It seems that we have arrived! Modernization in contemporary Serbia seems to mean the construction of modern prisons.

However, I don't know if there will be enough room in these prisons for the seven thousand working people who have thus far been detained and imprisoned under the state of emergency. They include anarchists, retirees who publicly rejoiced over the murder of the premier, a few folk singers, newspaper columnists, as well as so-called direct criminals, to borrow the minister's jargon. The former are all "indirect criminals"; they are guilty of opposing the so-called Europeanization of Serbia.

TV: So if the measures being taken under the state of emergency have not been restricted to the reasons for which it was implemented, i.e. tracking down Zoran Djindjić's murderers and targeting organized crime syndicates, is there a broader political agenda at play? Is it being recuperated politically at all, and if so, in what sorts of ways?

AG: There is no question that the murder of premier Djindjić is a hideous crime. But does that justify such a broad and total seizure of freedoms of the entire society? I think the answer to this question is a resounding no. You cannot jail a whole society, yet the implementation of a state of emergency does, in effect, put the entire society in jail. The simple fact that the state of emergency has not been withdrawn after several days shows that it is being used to conduct a power-turf war between different interest groups. The interest group in power is using its own weapons—terror and violence—to eliminate another interest group.

The Serbian government is clearly attempting to criminalize all opposition, all competition, or any dissident, political option. It is employing a method of martyrization of the murdered premier, with the help of the disciplined media and intellectuals who are granting legitimacy to such an assault on human rights and logic, to maintain power even after the withdrawal of the "state of emergency," which is likely to become permanent in Serbia.

In a recent interview given to a well-known Belgrade daily, minister of justice Vladan Batić presented his own particular categorization of "evil suspects" in response to the question of who the murderers were. To begin with, the minister indirectly put the majority of citizens into question as possible suspects in the murder of the premier. He then went on to declare how "thankful the citizens are, smiling, in high spirits" and, in general, "grateful to the government for the introduction of the state of emergency which has allowed them to feel more secure." Is this really the case?

Why, for instance, have strikes been outlawed? What could the connection between a strike of discontented workers and the murder of the premier possibly be? Strikers didn't kill the premier. According to official accusations, the murder was the work of criminals who were in secret negotiations with the premier.

Furthermore, Batić expressed an intense animosity towards "journalists, analysts, and columnists." Where does such animosity come from? Batić considers them to be a third category of criminals to be fought. All critics of the reforms are likewise equated with murderers. Particularly journalists and dissidents.

An incompetent government is spreading panic in order to hide its own responsibility. Could this murder have been prevented? After the murder, no one tendered his or her resignation. No positions were shuffled. The same people are leading us through a state of emergency. One party is misusing a tragic event. The declaration of a state of emergency has squelched public debate, tied the hands of all free-thinking people while ordinary state functionaries basically lynch all non-conforming thinkers throughout the media. Is this democracy? It seems that it is.

A few days ago, the vice president of the government announced that we should not complain that there is no opposition. Now we are a democracy, so opposition is no longer necessary—we are so democratic that no opposition needs to exist. This is so-called total democracy: a situation in which democracy, in its total self-fulfillment, abolishes itself. They are so devoted to democracy that they no longer need it.

TV: In such a context of criminalization and suppression of dissent that you describe, has there been any organized reaction or overall response from so-called civil society? I'm thinking particularly of the burgeoning NGO sector often funded by Western organizations that massively expanded in post-Milošević Yugoslavia, and whose mandate it is to monitor "human rights."

AG: It is interesting to note how this suspension of elementary human rights is being viewed by the so-called non-governmental organizations (NGO), an exceptionally powerful factor in the political life of Serbia, along with a large number of so-called rent-a-dissident types.

Prior to the current situation, they knew how to vehemently protest even the smallest of incidents in which the rights of a citizen belonging to an ethnic minority were endangered, when it came to criticizing "nationalism" (which is the issue from which these organizations profit the most, since the foreign aid that sustains most of them is based on this). Now when citizens' basic freedoms and rights are denied—not for one individual, not in one community, but to the entire society—the NGOs and rent-a-dissidents are supporting it, promising complete loyalty to the Serbian government. There is a constant stream of televised exchanges between state intellectuals and "dissidents" who discuss how Djindjić's death is "international," or how "the state of emergency is finally severing the umbilical cord from the East." Or in a somewhat more morbid tone, how "Djindjić's funeral was a plebiscite for a public in need of faith and hope," or how the "political murder of the premier is a terrible thing," because "we have to pay in tears for every joy," so that we might one day attain a "catharsis, a catharsis of the ordinary citizen."

TV: Given that open media criticism of the state of emergency is forbidden and censorship is in effect, what has been the impact on wider public debate and the many questions raised by the state of emergency?
AG: The public is being bombarded by unbelievable stupidities. Ministers promise that there will be regular provision of water and electricity. Why wouldn't there be? Has war broken out? Images of maternity wards are being broadcast in the media, with promises that they will defend children's nurseries. They proclaim that water sources are not polluted. Food provisions have been normalized. Public transportation, they say, is running on time. Police curfews have not yet been introduced. Economic reforms continue full steam ahead. The vultures from international bureaucracies have also started arriving, promising accelerated entry into the European Union.

Why didn't this government arrest organized criminals immediately after the October 5th "revolution"? Who was stopping them? Journalists? Columnists? Analysts and commentators? Why didn't they confiscate the property and riches of the Milošević-era elite? Why did they allow them to get even richer and to acquire everything through accelerated privatization? Who are they financing? Why is there greater and greater poverty in an already devastated economy? Ultimately, these are all questions that the current government, gripped by a collective neurosis, will have to answer one day.

TV: I want to turn a bit to the wider context of power and rule that led up to the current state of emergency. Regarding Djindjić's assassination, Sonja Biserko of the Helsinki Committee (a vocal NGO) recently proclaimed that "the abject act marks the beginning of liberation from Milošević-era pathology" offering an unprecedented opportunity for reform. To what extent do these current measures represent

a real break from the prior regime as claimed, and what has (or hasn't) changed in the transition between the former and current political systems?

AG: In fact, in order to fully understand the current state of emergency in Serbia, it is necessary to go back for a moment to Milošević's Serbia and provide a short analysis of what we might call "Milošević's system."

Milošević's regime was authoritarian. There existed parties, elections, and a parliament, but not true democracy. The constitution and many other laws were seemingly democratic in nature, but in fact were nothing more than a screen for the rule of one person.

Milošević, however, was not a dictator. His style of rule was very particular, and could hardly be called totalitarian. He tolerated, or was forced to tolerate, some independent press and a few very influential local television stations. Likewise, Milošević did not try to create some sort of Stalinist cult of personality. It is striking how rarely he appeared on television; many mention his ascetic simplicity, the lack of a need to show off his authority.

Finally, though Yugoslavia is rightly considered to be one of the most corrupt countries in Europe, it is not at all the case that Milošević ruled solely in order to enrich himself. When NATO air-bombers dropped "smart" bombs on Belgrade, they also dropped flyers and leaflets. I still have a copy of one in particular on which they printed a photo with text explaining that Milošević had a yacht and a villa "just like these" in the picture. The inability of the CIA to acquire a photo of Milošević's possessions speaks for itself. I suggest you read Aleksa Djilas's recent insightful writing on this topic. Ultimately, Milošević is not, as is commonly claimed, primarily turned towards the East, Moscow, and orthodoxy. He speaks English fluently and does not speak any Russian. In an earlier phase of his career, he visited New York regularly, and has said that he considers it his favorite city. At one time, Milošević had the impression, not entirely unfounded, that Washington would accept him despite his authoritarianism in the same way that they accepted Tito. After broken promises to both sides, both reckless nationalism and interventionism, led to the wars in Slovenia, Croatia, Bosnia, and Kosovo, one after the other, the situation obviously took a different course.

In any case, Milošević enjoyed a certain legitimacy in Serbia, and had a certain amount of support for his political project. In time, however, that amount of political support dwindled to 20 percent of the electorate. But with that 20 percent support, Milošević was able to retain 100 percent rule. Firstly, thanks to his control over the major media, he confused and demoralized a dissatisfied and disoriented citizenry. When it would come time for elections, they would stay home, or would give their votes to the so-called fake opposition. On top of that, the existing electoral system allowed 30 percent electoral support to translate into 50 percent parliamentary representation. All that was required was a suitable coalition partner, and one would achieve stable rule. And coalition partners were never in short supply, because power and rule in Milošević's Serbia brought great riches.

That is how Milošević arrived at a parliamentary majority and domination of rule. That is why he did not need to resort to any exceptional, dictatorial measures. All political projects and decisions were carried out by formal parliamentary means. You can find a more complete analysis in essays published by Slobodan Antonic, whose views I am merely repeating below.

The foundation of Milošević's power was based in his rule of his own party. The Socialist Party of Serbia was the true seat of Milošević-controlled political rule. As the total master of the Party, he achieved control of the Parliament as well. By constant changes to electoral laws (1992–1997), he built a system in which, at any moment, the party could switch its representatives and replace them successively. Control of the legislative branch of the government in formulating laws, also gave Milošević full control of the executive branch—in other words, of the government in general (as the legislative and executive branches were not separated).

Once he gained full control over both legislative and executive power, Milošević only had to establish control over the judiciary. According to the Constitution of Serbia, judges were permanently appointed, but were elected and dismissed by parliament. Because he controlled the parliament, Milošević was also able to control the judiciary. According to a law that came into effect on July 30, 1991, all judges (2,939) and prosecutors (619) were to undergo purges through so-called re-election in parliament. These purges, however, were very selectively and sloppily carried out, so that many who were not doing their jobs according to basic principles or professionalism retained their positions simply because they were following orders and directives coming from the top of the government. This resulted in a situation in which many of the other judges opposed the judicial theft of the local elections of 1996.

From then on, Milošević proceeded with a rearrangement of the state of the judiciary. In 1997, when Milošević further consolidated his rule, he also set out to further "resolve the state of the judiciary." This effectively meant the firing of around sixty "unsuitable" judges, who were guilty only of upholding the principal of an independent judiciary.

That is how ultimately the entire political and judicial elite was put in a position of dependency on Milošević. The same was true for the police and law enforcement elite. With the passage of a 1995 law on the appointment of members of MUP-a, the Serbian police force, Milošević consolidated the exclusive right to promote police officers to military generals and appoint senior cadre in the police. Under another set of special rules, Milošević took over the direct supervision of the Department of Interior Security. This allowed him to not only become one of the main masters of the war in Bosnia and Herzegovina, but also to control the Serbian opposition.

Particularly important for the functioning of Milošević's rule was the direct political supervision of the economic elite. In Milošević's Serbia, the primary means of capital accumulation did not take place on the market. To the contrary, the major financial profits to be had were achieved via state intervention—in other words, through state monopoly, systematic privileges, monetary speculation and shady financial transactions, generalized larceny and appropriation of property, illegal imports, backroom deals, and bribes. It was a given that, in such a system, the power elite could not only easily convert their own "political capital" into real, financial gains, but also to control and influence the flow and direction of the entire economy.

That is how Milošević succeeded in constructing a tight clientalistic net around the entire national economy. It was a net that spread out to encompass anywhere that capital was being produced, starting with himself and his family, all the way down to factory workers and vendors on the street. Entry into this protected net meant guaranteed financial gain. The most powerful members of that net, the economic elite, could count on rapid accumulation of riches thanks to the market monopoly, from rigged participation in state "barter arrangements" (the import of oil and gas), to the illegal trade of cigarettes, weapons, and other goods. This was achieved via the granting of import-export permits, on the acquisition of foreign currencies based on a rigged, lowered exchange rate, in the privileged granting of land, etc. The middle members of this privileged net could count on unrestricted trading (even on a small scale), on good/full employment and high state salaries, on the right to buy state-owned apartments at an exceptionally low price, etc.

In the 1990s, a unique structure of power was installed in Serbia. I have called such a structure a kleptocracy. The dominant paradigm of the "Milošević doctrine" is what we might call, from this historical perspective, an authoritarian isolationism.

TV: So how did the context change in the post-Milošević era, with Djindjić's ascent to power? What was the legacy of this authoritarian isolationism, and what was brought in to replace it?

AG: With the *petooktobarska revolucija* (the October 5th revolution) and the overthrow of Milošević, many hoped for real, progressive change. However, instead of any meaningful step towards economic and participatory democracy, which many true Yugoslav Leftists had hoped for, a new system was installed, with a new authoritarian doctrine: that of Djindjić. Djindjić's system might be called an authoritarian modernism: neoliberalism with a local accent.

Djindjić constructed a chancellery system, to his misfortune simultaneously paralyzing the presidential system, marginalizing the parliament, and building his own subministries within the official government ministries.

One Yugoslav historian has called this "Djindjić's naïve cunning." It was also his biggest mistake. He should have sought to reduce his rule, and to increase the role of a coordinator or negotiator who would not take absolute power. Such a strategy might have held a better future. Instead of that, he accrued more and more control, combined with less and less popularity and authority. He was not respected even by the so-called elite. Had he pursued a somewhat different strategy, he might have been able to say: "I'm not popular amongst the people, but 'intelligent' people, judges, business people, the press elite, and well-known intellectuals are on my side." That is one possible form of power politics: I do not want popularity but authority. However, he had neither popularity nor authority, yet accrued greater and greater power.

Djindjić's system really showed its true colors in the *junski udar* (the June takeover), which could be considered the crucial watershed in the political life of post-Milošević Serbia. It should be noted that this takeover was very skillfully executed. Djindjić, in other words, was not Milošević, who reacted with much greater and more open brutality towards his political opponents.

The takeover was initiated when the presidency of DOS (the coalition of opposition parties that overthrew Milošević), which consisted of the presidents and key ministers of the various coalition parties, passed a motion on May 24, 2002, to revoke the mandates of thirty-six DOS members of parliament who were "most frequently absent from the regular sittings of Parliament." The parliamentary majority passed this motion on June 12.

At first glance, the motion seemed innocuous: "the aim is to establish order in the country, so that elected members of parliament actually work sufficiently to merit their pay," explained premier Djindjić. In actuality, however, such a motion was completely illegal. Among those thirty-six unseated members, the majority was from the DSS, the party of Vojislav Koštunica, the Yugoslav president and most serious political rival to Djindjić in his role as prime minister.

In fact, it was understandable that DSS members had abstained from these regular sittings of parliament, given that the DSS had decided to boycott these sessions in protest over Djindjić's political maneuvering. What was all the more humorous, the DSS wouldn't have been able to replace its thirty-six unseated parliamentary members with other DSS members even if it had wanted to, because their member's list only had thirteen remaining names on it. Because the DSS was unable to replace its revoked seats with their own members, those seats went to other parties from the DOS coalition—first and foremost to the Democratic Party of Zoran Djindjić. Outraged by this ridiculous theft of parliamentary seats, all the sitting members of the DSS, the strongest and most popular party in Serbia, resigned from parliament.

This is how Djindjić successfully employed an anti-parliamentary takeover to significantly increase his political power. For a significant period, he threw his major rival, Koštunica's DSS, out of the game and thereby seized a parliamentary majority that would neatly and efficiently control the passage of governmental laws.

So that is how the question of parliamentary quorum was effectively resolved in Djindjić's favor. Soon after, the rules were further altered to include an exceptional expansion of the parliamentary president's power. He gained the power to punish elected members for "disrupting order in Parliamentary sessions" by revoking their parliamentary seats for up to ninety days.

The third important advantage gained by premier Djindjić in the June takeover was his unchallenged rule of the remainder of the DOS coalition. From that point on, not one of the remaining parties in DOS had enough sitting members to challenge and oppose the government.

Why didn't Djindjić's political takeover arouse a serious public outcry? Firstly, because it was skillfully executed through a preplanned and complex procedure that most ordinary citizens did not fully grasp. Secondly, and more importantly, because Djindjić in the meantime succeeded in gaining control of the most influential mass media in Serbia. When the first open showdown between Djindjić and Koštunica took place in August 2001, the extent to which Djindjić had succeeded in tipping the balance to his advantage in all the media was clear. In addition to the most watched commercial television station, TV Pink, the influential TV Politika and TV Studio B, the daily newspapers *Novosti* and *Danas*, along with *Nedeljni telegraf* all clearly fell into line with his political camp. By June 2002, Djindjić had also gained control of the daily Politika, the state television (RTS), and the other large private television station (BK Telecom). So when Djindjić executed his political offensive, no one had any reason or interest in publicizing or even explaining it, let alone opposing it for the patently antidemocratic takeover it was.

Basically, by mid-2002 Djindjić had easily taken over Milošević's entire system of political control of society. He had total control of his party. With the government and parliamentary majority behind him, he easily secured control of the boards of directors of the most important businesses from the oil industry to forestry. Likewise, the majority of the middle management elite as well as a portion of the social elite harboring political-management ambitions rushed in to put themselves at his service.

That is how a new post-Milošević clientalistic network was secured by Djindjić. Moreover, economic "transition" and "privatization" became the ideal excuses for its additional expansion. Djindjić, exactly as Milošević had, succeeded in gaining control of the legislative, executive, judicial-political, economic, and even partly over the military-police elite. Milošević's system was thereby transposed into a new, neoliberal Serbia.

I have already described how the executive branch ruled the judiciary under Milošević's rule. The new regime continued that practice. A new purge organized by the loyal minister of justice, Vladan Batić, took place by precisely the rules established under the authoritarian Milošević regime, in which the minister of justice acted as the direct head of the judicial elite.

On what was Djindjić's successful expansion of his power based? His power base was never among the voters or the electorate. Like Milošević towards the end of his rule, Djindjić and his party could not count on more than 20 percent of the electorate's support. But, like Milošević, Djindjić was able to seize 100 percent rule with 20 percent of the vote.

TV: Following his assassination on March 12, much of the Western media participated in a kind of canonization of Djindjić, framing him as the only forward-looking, pro-Western politician in the region, as the only one able and committed to bringing in progressive reforms, hope, and a future for the country. You have already pointed out the extent to which such a characterization is hardly neutral, not to mention the accompanying agenda of political and economic reforms that are being vaunted as supposedly assuring the future of the country. What are the some of the implications of such a characterization and the agenda of reforms being implemented?
AG: Djindjić installed his own specific ideological monopoly on neoliberal reforms and reformism. The notion that he is a "pragmatic reformer," who is trying to "lead a dark and backward Serbia into Europe"—such ideological nonsense was quickly supported not only by Western governments, and all sorts of analysts, but also the disciplined media, and members of the local "fake" opposition: the influential non-governmental organizations. Neoliberals had been overjoyed that

"justice had been fulfilled" and that Milošević finally found himself "where he belongs" (i.e. The Hague). Furthermore, domestic liberals were sympathetic to the long line of laws and policies proposed by Djindjić's government (on privatization, work, taxes), in order to bring Serbia into the world of "strict but just market capitalism."

Such a logic of power recalls in many respects another Eastern European case, that of Slovak premier Vladimir Mecijara's (1991–1998) "pragmatic, pro-Western reform," which very quickly showed itself to be nothing more than reckless self-preservation. Mecijara took four years to achieve clientalistic control over national resources and the public media. Thanks to the already developed clientalistic system that he inherited, the Serbian chancellor hurtled down that path much more quickly. In the few months prior to his murder, Djindjić held absolute power in his hands. This absolutism cost him his life.

I have shown that there was no essential difference between Milošević's and Djindjić's system. The same outcry, from the depths of Milošević's time, continues to resound in the wasteland of transition. A similar, voracious logic of power saturated both systems.

TV: Djindjić's murder has also largely been portrayed in the Western media as the terrible price paid by someone who was valiantly trying to crack down on organized crime and political corruption. Having long ignored and overlooked it, it seems that much of the Western media have suddenly discovered "organized crime" as a political factor for which ordinary Yugoslavs have long paid a heavy price. What is the word inside Serbia and Montenegro regarding the actual circumstances surrounding Djindjić's murder?

AG: Different scenarios have been proposed to explain the murder of Djindjić. The one that seems the most realistic to me says that Djindjić made "the wrong deal with the wrong people," a deal that he himself probably broke. I believe that Djindjić really did go after and tried to liquidate some group of organized criminals, who likely had a good deal of experience in war crimes gained in the Yugoslav wars, and were linked to state security forces. But the reason for this is not because Djindjić had clean hands or that he was on a one-man crusade to rid the country of organized crime. Rather, because he effectively established absolute power, Djindjić was most likely trying to deceive some of the very people with whom he himself had collaborated to gain power, and whose names could be found on the wanted list for The Hague "tribunal." Such people do not forgive double-crossings in their agreements and dealings.

A not insignificant number of people also believe that Djindjić was the casualty of a "great chess game," in which the German chess piece—Djindjić himself, who was particularly tied to German political circles—was simply switched for a pro-American one. I consider this version to not be very likely.

TV: To what extent might we be able to connect the current state of emergency in Serbia and Montenegro to wider geopolitics and the global state of emergency we seem to be living under in the past few years with the advent of the Bush doctrine?

AG: The social control through extreme panic that the government is exploiting to keep the population under control might be familiar to North American readers. This assassination might seriously be considered a sort of local, Balkan version of the September 11th effect.

After September 11, 2001, America was introduced to one type of state of emergency, which was the starting point for a permanent global state of emergency in which the whole world lives today. It appeared in its full clarity with the military order declared by the president of the United States with the decree of November 13, 2001. That decree concerned the status of non-citizens (those without U.S. citizenship) who are suspected of terrorist activity, subject to a special court that employs indefinite detention and the turnover of suspects to military commissions. The American Patriot Act of

October 26, 2001, had already granted authority to the attorney general to arrest any "alien" suspected of posing a danger to national security. The innovation in the orders of President Bush lay in the radical erasure of the status of these individuals, and in the very production of an entity whose legal status cannot be fully classified, officially described, or named publicly.

One could argue by analogy that the state of emergency in Yugoslavia in many ways resembles the recent American clampdown. Terrorists (or in the Serbian case "organized criminals") are not the only ones to suffer, but all those who do not agree with neoliberal reforms are targeted. The Serbian government has declared a local, preventative war on all of its citizens. This war is permeated by explicit tactics of psychological denunciation: citizens are encouraged to regard one another as potentially suspicious and to inform on one another to the police. This was a post–World War II practice, a technique of social control that was brought in to Yugoslavia after the break with Stalinism in 1948, and that, in later Yugoslav social history, unfortunately had very serious consequences.

TV: What do you think the future political impact of the state of emergency will be in Serbia and Montenegro after it is lifted? A partial repeal of the state of emergency is currently being debated, yet several politicians have indicated that certain measures may be retained even after its lifting. For example, the police may retain certain powers that they did not previously have. What are the prospects for the near future politically speaking?

AG: This state of emergency cannot resolve the myriad social problems that exist in today's Serbia. Current social conditions are truly catastrophic. Poverty is deepening vastly and spreading widely. The number of unemployed is approaching one million people. Every day over fifteen thousand workers demonstrate. Seventy percent of the population declares itself to be below the poverty line. In one breath, the smell of poverty and the smell of despair are spreading throughout Serbia. The depth of citizens' discontent cannot be put down with violence.

If Milošević's system functioned under a doctrine of authoritarian isolationism, and under Djindjić we had authoritarian modernism, then this is a system of authoritarian idiocy!

One well-known journalist wrote the following lines a few months before the murder of Djindjić: "In Tito's Serbia, it was dangerous to think because you could always end up in prison. In Milošević's Serbia, it was dangerous to think because you could be declared a traitor. The danger of thought in Djindjić's Serbia is in creating extreme feelings of loneliness and isolation, to the extent that, if the coexistence of the post-Milošević extremists continues, leads one to the inevitable question: "Can I retain my sanity?""

In post-Djindjić Serbia, it is dangerous to think because you can end up in prison, you can be declared a traitor, and in any case, you will be brought to the brink of total isolation.

Post-Yugoslavia After the State of Emergency

August 2003

The Serbian government often likes to point out that the state of emergency had helped rid the country of the most lethal heritage of Milošević's regime—the legitimacy of organized crime. To some degree, this statement is most probably true. During Milošević, organized crime was integrated into the system. However, it has remained so to a great extent even after the outstanding "Serbian revolution" of October 5, 2000, financed by Western governments, articulated by politicians, and facilitated by citizens that were fed up with Milošević's authoritarian rule.

The assassinated prime minister and "the hero of democracy," Zoran Djindjić, wanted to take advantage of the old linkage between criminal and state security structures to strengthen his own position in power. In 2001 and for the most part of 2002, the mob felt very comfortable in the new political landscape. Early in 2003, it seems as though a showdown between the government and the major part of a mob with rising political appetites was imminent. The mafia killed Djindjić, its former ally, but the late prime minister's heirs to the government, who were also formerly allied to the mob, managed to survive in a clash between two antagonized power circles—one operating within the institutional framework and the other operating underground.

The power has remained in the institutions; some mafia bosses have been arrested, while others that managed to stay on good terms with the authorities are spearheading the "transition" and "honest business." The backbone of one of the most important structures in Milošević's regime has apparently been broken. There is no doubt that it will take the mafia quite a long time to recuperate under the present conditions and the fact that it has been pushed deep underground is the only positive effect of government measures during the state of emergency.

As for the negative effects of these measures, it has to be said that the state of emergency had a much more powerful impact on the opposition that it did on the mafia. This includes the opposition within political parties, but also the radical non-parliamentary opposition. During the forty-two days of the state of emergency, the government crossed the line that stands between an openly authoritarian regime and a formally democratic order.

Their confrontation with political opponents and critics was largely erratic and hysterical, however, and did not take the shape of methodical persecution. For example, at a government briefing for the media held on April 11, 2003, they said that "Operation Sabre had entered the most delicate phase: flushing out the instigators and financers of the assassination on the late Prime Minister Zoran Djindjić" and that the investigation had lead towards Vojislav Koštunica's political affiliates, who is just by chance the leader of the largest opposition party.

It seemed that it was a matter of hours before the main political players in the opposition would be labeled as criminals and their leaders brought in for interrogation. Moreover, the Minister of Culture and Media, Branislav Lečić, kept announcing a special committee that would aim to find out which mechanisms brought the media into a "dark state of mind," while the Minister of Justice, Vladan Batić, accused "a part of the independent media of having taken part in plotting the assassination." During this time, anarchists, pensioners, political opponents, and folk singers all had a unique opportunity to hang around together in prison.

The whole ordeal was not only a blatant attempt to break the back of the opposition, but also to snuff out any kind of criticism against the government's policy. But these were threats and hysterical fits of an organized absurdity called State of Emergency. However, this government has systematically weakened the institutions of the state through legal documents that were deliberately designed for this purpose during this period. First of all, the state of emergency was introduced in such a way that it violated constitutional and other laws. This was the common practice of the ruling elite even before March 12, 2003, the day Zoran Djindjić was assassinated. The explanation was always that it was "Milošević's Constitution" they were violating and kept promising a new one in the near future. Consequently, the new Serbian president was also elected in complete violation of constitutional provisions.

Serbian "reformists" offered the explanation that it was Milošević's constitution anyway. So, Nataša Mićić, who was the acting president of Serbia in violation to the constitution, was given the opportunity to declare the state of emergency, again contrary to constitutional norms. Mićić selected constitutional and other legal provisions on the state of emergency and state of war that best suited the government and fused them in what she (and the government) called the state of emergency. Mićić also received orders (as the president of Serbia!) to suspend the following human rights and liberties: the legal procedure during arrest (police custody was prolonged for thirty days without the right to a lawyer or an appeal to a relevant court); the right to the confidentiality of letters and the right to the sovereignty of one's home; the right to strike or gather (in general); the right to political and syndic action (if it compromises the state of emergency); and the right to the free flow of information that deals with the state of emergency and the reasons for its declaration.

According to the Serbian Constitution, some of these rights should not have been suspended even if a state of war had been declared—for example, the right of an individual who was put under arrest to address the court and question the legal grounds for his arrest. The principles of constitutionalism were not only violated by the suspensions of the human liberties mentioned above, but even more so by the adoption of several crucial laws in the atmosphere of the state of emergency during which the government censored information and raised suspicion that the political opposition and others who had dissenting opinions regarding their policy and actions were the "instigators and passive participants" of Djindjić's assassination.

While the public was in shock following the assassination and the opposition was in fear of persecution and independent information flow ended under censorship, the government adopted several authoritarian laws in parliament, such as the Law on Changes to the Serbian Constitution and the Law on Prosecutors; the issue of the judicial system was also resolved.

After arresting one judge because of alleged ties to the mafia, the government found an excuse to retain surveillance over the remaining 2,200 court judges in Serbia. This move rescinded a short-lived judicial autonomy that was provided by a set of laws in November 2001 and brought the judiciary once more under tight control of the authorities.

Amendments to the law on fighting organized crime and to the criminal law were also adopted. The meaning of the term "organized crime" was expanded to members of groups that do not commit crimes directly, but are still in the function of organized crime. Members of such ambiguous groups (since the term "in the function of organized crime" can have a great variety of interpretations) can be kept for ninety days in custody by the police, without access to legal representation or court protection. Potential witnesses can be held for up to thirty days.

When the Belgrade Humanitarian Law Centre protested against these amendments, claiming they were "in breach of basic European standards for protection of human rights" and that they "introduced the state of emergency on a permanent basis," the new Prime Minister Zoran Živković coolly answered that the amendments "were not among the most drastic examples of such legal provisions in the democratic world, since police custody for similar acts of crime could last up to 6 months, or even a lifetime period in the U.S.."

The Law on Public Information was also passed. This law allows the government to spread any sort of information that could "instigate violence," while journalists are now obliged to reveal the sources of practically all the information they use in their writings. When journalists protested to such measures, the government assured that, since they were a democratic authority, they would not misuse the law. A deputy prime minister in the Serbian government said that "a democratic state does not need an opposition."

The bottom line is that several systemic legal documents were brought during the state of emergency that directly violated the constitutional order and international standards on human rights. It's true that the Serbian Constitution currently in effect was brought under Milošević. However, the problem with Milošević's rule was not that the constitution was particularly bad, but that it was used as a facade for his authoritarian rule. The new government, from Djindjić to Živković, led by what I have called a paradigm of authoritarian modernism and disregarded the constitution and the laws whenever they saw fit. Frequent breaches of the constitution and the laws resulted in a state of legal uncertainty and an atmosphere of a permanent state of emergency.

At present, there are no limitations whatsoever imposed by the constitution and the legal system. There are no rules that the government has to abide by and they can resort to anything. The so-called "friendly civil society" and "advocates of human rights" have been transformed into intellectual commissars of the sitting government. All these intellectuals, analysts, and NGO activists chorused that it was our government and we just had to trust them.

These are the same "human rights campaigners" who gained their reputation and wealth "fighting" Milošević's authoritarianism and Serbian nationalism, now speak of "national interests," "danger to the system," and "salvation for the state and the people." In this kind of atmosphere, in which the majority of information sources were either under the direct control of the political elite or their intellectual commissars and the entire "friendly civil society," the new authorities upheld a system that is devoid of an independent judicial system, public criticism, parliamentary control over levers of state power, and free elections.

The same pattern of authoritarian idiotism continued after the state of emergency was formally rescinded on April 22, 2003. The fact that the Serbian oligarchy did not impose a totalitarian order is not a matter of their self-control, or the strength of democratic institutions, or the pressure of the general public. That the government managed to restrain itself just before it seemed it would cross the line and uphold totalitarian rule has been interpreted by most Belgrade analysts as a result of strong pressure coming from Western diplomats.

The ruling coalition clings to the image of "pro-European politicians" and to a Serbian state that is supported by the West. This is why the government had to restrain its authoritarian instincts. Serbia has apparently been rescued from "an iron broom" (an expression so Bolshevik in nature that it is hard to translate it into English) by U.S. and British ambassadors who simply laid down the rules of the game to our boys. And the boys obeyed. And although this is some advancement in comparison to Milošević's era, the fact that the U.S. ambassador is protecting Serbian democracy does not give it a promising future.

The political and social situation in Serbia is very difficult. Serbia is a country with the largest number of strikes in Europe, a country where more than one million unemployed workers march, and a country in which transition boils down to the property of eight million people pouring into the pockets of eight people. An atmosphere of poverty and desperation looms over Serbia. The fact that more than 50 percent of the population lives at or below the poverty line does not upset the neoliberal elite too much, as they maintain their course of technocratic reformism.

The struggle for a different Serbia is led by a handful of dissident intellectuals and a social movement in the making, called Another World is Possible (*Drugaciji svet je moguc*— DSM) and comprised of a variety of anti-authoritarian collectives. DSM initiated the Belgrade Indymedia project several days ago. The magazine called *Global* is distributed at gatherings of the unemployed or at forums against privatization.

Can this movement, as well as other similar initiatives, succeed in providing a clear progressive articulation of social unrest? It remains to be seen whether they will manage to turn today's social monologue into tomorrow's social conflict that will confront the model of a civil society of intellectual commissars and NGOs with a model of a participatory society and, by mobilizing a collective awareness and potential for subversion, approach the ideal of a politics from below. One thing is crystal clear, though: with the situation of Serbia today, we have no time or right to be pessimistic.

Between Old Yugoslavia and "New" Europe

April 2003

In the month prior to the most recent events that rocked Serbia, the question posed to me most frequently concerned the February 15 antiwar demonstrations and the small number of people in Yugoslavia who had protested against the planned bombing of Iraq. In Belgrade, unlike Zagreb where over ten thousand protestors were mobilized, only around two hundred people assembled publicly to demonstrate against the impending military action against Iraq. The Belgrade protest was organized by the non-governmental organization Women in Black.

The Yugoslav radical and anti-authoritarian coalition Another World Is Possible organized a somewhat different protest in the coalition's tradition of direct action and creative disobedience. For the Night of the Red Noses, monuments in Belgrade and Novi Sad "shed blood in a sign of solidarity with the Iraqi people" by way of washable paint, since it would appear that "monuments seem to have more feelings than people."

So how is it possible that after brutal and direct experience with the NATO bombing, after many hundreds were killed, after the destruction of the RTS Television station (in which sixteen people died), only two hundred people gathered for the protests? Is it possible that Yugoslavs do not feel solidarity with the Iraqi people, despite the fact that they themselves not so long ago underwent the military and psychological torture of bombing?

There is no doubt that Yugoslav public opinion is against the war in Iraq. Although, I have to correct myself here: in fact, it is Serbian and Montenegrin public opinion that is in question, since, on February 4 of this year, Yugoslavia ceased to exist and was replaced by the new state of Serbia and Montenegro.

If Europe today is divided amongst the "old" and the "new," its newest state has once again been left somewhere in between. "Old" Europe bombed us, while "new" Europe ardently supported them. Both the so-called old and "new" Europe's heartily participated in something that was primarily and ultimately an American war against the Serbs and Milošević. Public opinion in Serbia and Montenegro is not oblivious to the current differences between Paris, Bonn and Washington, but it instinctively rejects the notion that the current rivalry between Europe and America over Iraq is a matter of moral superiority.

Post-Yugoslav public opinion cannot view these diplomatic disagreements as a great battle between a peaceful, multilateral and refined Europe on one side, and a militant, isolationist and impudent America on the other. The opinion that prevails is that the differences between Western allies today are of an essentially strategic rather than of a moral nature.

Another type of international naiveté engenders resistance in post-Yugoslav public opinion, which is not prone to accept the line of reasoning which claims that the most sophisticated international policy towards volatile regions by well-intentioned foreigners requires the accurate demarcation of the good/innocent players from the bad/evil ones, with the sorting out of evil tyrants and dictators into an all-together separate category. Nor are they inclined to believe that somewhere in the wings awaits a better, more benevolent leader whom the grateful people will sweep to power by their own hands, as soon as the West helps them to overthrow the tyrant.

They have learned through their own very difficult experiences that things tend not to work that way, and are very distrustful towards Western neoliberal politicians and intellectuals who claim that they can save the village by burning it down. Even Belgrade's neoliberal intellectuals, that otherwise highly unsympathetic lot, are opposed to the war. Against all expectations, they have not called for the "regime change" of Saddam Hussein through bombardment. It is notable that even those neoliberals who most vociferously advocated the ground invasion, occupation and "denazification" of Serbia during the NATO bombardment today shudder and refrain from publicly prescribing the same medicine against the regime of Saddam Hussein.

People in Serbia remember all too well that they were the first upon whom the theory of collective guilt was tested and exercised. According to this doctrine, "people bear moral responsibility for the ways in which they are governed." Accordingly, the people of Serbia must bear "responsibility" (and collective punishment), firstly because they voted for Milošević, and secondly because they did not overthrow him by force, to the extent that they cannot be considered to be wholly "innocent under the bombs.'

Albanian intellectuals in Kosovo are in a rather different mood. There, we find Veton Surroi, who is considered to be an enlightened liberal intellectual among the Kosovo Albanian elite, recently proclaiming in the International Herald Tribune that the bombing of Kosovo proved false the peace slogan "Bombs cannot bring democracy." Serbian authorities have framed this unease and nonalignment with the main ruling camps in international relations as Belgrade's attempt to remain "neutral" in the conflict. Yet such a desired-for neutrality likely has as much to do with the current conflict between the two Europes and one America as with the war against Iraq.

On the other hand, Montenegro, with its already familiar lack of measure and style, tripped over itself to rush into the embrace of Washington and introduce itself to the "new" Europe. The precise content of the letter of support for U.S. policy on the Iraq crisis from Prime Minister Milo Đukanović to Bush remains unknown to the public. The purpose of this exercise also remains unclear, whether his aim was to recommend Montenegro to NATO, to distinguish its policies from that of Serbia, to obtain money, or there was some other reason. It raises all the contested questions of the political relations between Serbia and Montenegro, between Montenegro and Europe, and particularly between Montenegro's own internal divisions.

Some analysts attribute such behavior to internal political conflicts between independentists and unionists regarding whether or not Montenegro should develop an international approach and foreign policy that is independent from Serbia. In the current case, the Montenegrin government's approach is not only independent but also diametrically opposed to that of Serbia, which chose not to take sides in the conflict between America and Europe.

Thus far, the greatest amount of support to the movement for Montenegrin independence has come from the United States. In his courteous reply to Ðukanović, U.S. Secretary of State Colin Powell did not explicitly mention the possibility of Montenegro, whether with or without Serbia, moving closer to the Western military alliance (which, for most of the post-communist countries that now make up the "new" Europe, has always been the most attractive bait.) On the other side, French President Jacques Chirac has warned the ex-communist countries that they are diminishing their chances of entering into the European Union by throwing their support behind the U.S. policy towards Iraq.

The Montenegrin Minister of Foreign Affairs (since Montenegro, though belonging to a state union with Serbia, has its own Ministry for Foreign Affairs) stated that, "Montenegro has traditionally maintained good relations with Washington, and the U.S. have thus far rendered significant financial and expert aid to Montenegro. In addition, Montenegro has always been on the side of liberating, antifascist movements throughout its history, and sees its future today in Europe ..."

But I have yet to answer the question so often asked of me, the question with which I started this essay: why did so few Yugoslavs take to the streets on February 15? And why now, one month before the assassination of the neoliberal Prime Minister Zoran Djindjić that has brought the country into a state of emergency, with a systematic clampdown on political freedoms and the criminalization of any opposition.

In the domestic neoliberal press, the prevailing attitude holds that the poor response of citizens to the "antiwar" demonstrations is caused by their feelings of guilt. According to these journalists, Yugoslavs feel "suppressed guilt" for the crimes of their military in the wars of the former Yugoslavia. The journalists argue that people cannot recognize themselves in the slogan "not in my name," because they themselves allowed the killing of other peoples on their behalf. And so, according to this popular psychoanalytic argument, the answer lies in the psychology of guilt. Such is the way in which the doctrine of collective guilt developed during the NATO bombing continues to be mobilized to support a neoliberal agenda in the region.

The argument is more than shaky. Serbia and Montenegro today are going through the "nightmare of transition," i.e. the economic transition to neoliberal capitalism. Following immediately upon the nightmare of over ten years of war, the destruction of the country's industrial infrastructure, and over $30 billion in damages from the NATO bombing, over a million people in a country of eight million have recently lost their jobs under the new economic policies. More than 70 percent of the country's citizens have declared themselves to be poor, while 20 percent of the population is dying of starvation.

When we add the organized ideological attacks of neoliberal commissars targeting the total demoralization and depoliticization of the people to this picture of upheaval, dislocation and devastation, we begin to get an accurate reading of the situation—in other words, a true reply to the question posed at the outset of this essay.

Yugoslav Absurdistan

June 2003

According to articles in several influential U.S. magazines about strategic matters, the U.S. government is finalizing plans for the relocation of the entirety of its military forces stationed in Germany to new bases in the Balkans: Serbia and Montenegro, Bulgaria, and Romania. This move has deep political, strategic, and economic implications, particularly for the formalization of political discord within NATO that could either lead to the diminishment of the union's scope, or to a major change of course in its activities.

In essence, this move reflects the continued and deepening divergence between what U.S. Defense Secretary Donald Rumsfeld recently called "old" Europe (i.e. Western Europe), the United States, and what he proclaimed to be the "new" Europe, (largely composed of those central European former members of the Eastern Bloc located on the western and southwestern periphery of the Warsaw Pact). Strategically speaking, this would create a new geopolitical bloc—a new NATO of sorts—strategically reoriented towards the Middle East and the Caucasus, the East Mediterranean and Maghreb (the countries of North Africa).

Interestingly enough, Croatia has signaled its disinterest in the stationing of American bases on its territories. Far from taking a principled stance, however, it instead foresees negotiating a separate military agreement with Germany, on the basis of which it would permanently extend hospitality to German military forces for the first time since the short-lived fascist (Nazi) Independent Republic of Croatia (IRC, 1941–1945).

The Croatian government has chosen to position itself strategically and to throw its fate in with a European Union headed by Germany. Bulgaria, Serbia and Montenegro, and Romania are leaning more towards the United States, as well as a more broadly based conception of the European Union than the version proposing German leadership. The Czech Republic—which thus far has not played a role in any of the political negotiations regarding American bases—nonetheless remains one of the key pillars of American designs on Europe, and is soon likely to become the focus of American investments and diplomatic efforts.

The plan under negotiation also foresees the relocation of air and naval bases, as these are key to the transportation of land forces. Based on proposed plans emerging from the negotiations: a) the Danube will represent a key artery for the transportation of military resources from Western to Eastern Europe, and b) Bulgaria, according to recent press reports, is negotiating for the installation of an airbase in the vicinity of Varna, near the airport which the U.S. Air Force has already used for air transportation to the Middle East during the war on Iraq. Varna also houses the North Zone of the Bulgarian navy headquarters, as well as an air force station at sea. This relocation will have serious economic consequences for Germany, as well as for Serbia and Montenegro, Bulgaria and Romania.

To date, the majority of USECOM (U.S. command for Europe) military forces, sixty-five thousand soldiers in total, are stationed in Germany. It is expected that up to forty thousand soldiers could be stationed in the Balkans in the near future. This would provide a significant economic injection to ailing local economies, as well as accompanying investments in the development of infrastructure (and the additional economic spin-offs of air and navy base personnel). At the same time, the German economy itself would suffer a significant loss.

No less significantly, the stationing of American forces in the Balkans would seek to ensure a certain level of American political support and, in a sense, military protection to those countries. It would also act as a compensation of sorts for the recent shift in Turkey's relationship towards the European Union, NATO and the United States, which is a casualty of the war in Iraq. To a certain extent, the stationing of American forces further east would reduce their dependence on Turkey, and would also significantly reduce the costs of American military installations by shifting expenditures away from the higher prices of the German economy.

Belgrade, the capital of Serbia and Montenegro, remains a major historical hub of the Balkans and this part of Europe. Former Yugoslavia (Serbia and Montenegro) of today is a country with one name but two different passports, a country that has no coat of arms, no flag, and no national anthem. Those who currently hold power in this new country are called the Opposition. As of yet, it remains unclear who in the Opposition works for the government, or who is the president of this union of countries. As a result, this new state union (which came into existence on February 4 of this year) has acquired another name by which it has come to be popularly known among its people: the state of Absurdistan.

Absurdistan's heads of state have started to prepare the Serbian public for a highly unpopular move, which they plan to make in the very near future. It involves the signing of a bilateral agreement with the United States that would ensure the non-extradition of U.S. citizens to the permanent International Criminal Court. In the Balkans, such agreements have already been signed by Romania (which, in turn, became a member of NATO), Bosnia and Herzegovina (not considered a sovereign state), Macedonia, and Albania. Croatia and Slovenia are resisting such agreements for the time being.

In Absurdistan, there is no one left to offer resistance: former president Koštunica opposed while he could (prior to having his position eliminated under the new state union), public opinion is generally considered unimportant, and the present governments in Belgrade and Podgorica are apparently undivided in their intention to conclude such an agreement with Washington. Absurdistan's Minister of Foreign Affairs has already stated that this is a difficult offer to refuse, while the president of the union of the countries has offered a careful, yet suggestive formulation: the decision taken will be "realistic."

The country's leading lawyers have not challenged the judgment of those advocating an affirmative response to the American request, and the so-called human rights advocates have voiced no protests. The only public critiques issued have been made by social movement activists (such as the Another World is Possible anti-authoritarian coalition).

Thus far, thirty-four countries have signed such agreements with the Americans. According to an open warning recently issued by the American embassy in Zagreb, Croatia, stands to lose $19 million in equipment and training if it doesn't sign the contract by July 1.

It is no accident that Absurdistan is the last on the list of Balkan countries from which the United States has demanded guarantees ensuring that U.S. citizens cannot be extradited to the International Court (the jurisdiction of which America does not recognize). The United States waited as long as it possibly could before starting to exert pressure on Belgrade, aware that such a demand is particularly awkward and delicate for a country that it bombed just a few years ago—a country whose people largely believe that the United States committed war crimes during said bombing, a country that is continually expected to extradite its citizens to another International Court with a much more limited and exceptional jurisdiction, the one in The Hague.

Based on a recent statement by U.S. President George Bush concerning the sale of American weapons to Belgrade, it might be concluded that Belgrade has been definitively removed from the list of countries that would jeopardize

American national interests, and that there no longer exists any obstacle to military cooperation between the two countries. Yet, immediately following this statement, it turns out that one remaining obstacle exists in the form of the International Criminal Court.

So where is the problem with the signing of such a bilateral agreement? First, it is in the dissatisfaction it will cause in the European Union, i.e. in the "old" Europe to which Absurdistan has deep down always counted itself to be strategically tied. All of the EU countries have recently made public appeals to all of the West Balkan countries to, "if at all possible," not sign these bilateral agreements with the United States regarding the status of American citizens in the International Criminal Court of Law (at risk of imperiling their potential accession to the European Union).

Is there a more general guiding principle to this dilemma behind which Belgrade could be said to stand firm? As far as human rights and war crimes are concerned, it is very difficult to answer such a question conclusively. Absurdistan was bombed in the name of a post-Westphalian principle that renounced the absolute value of state sovereignty for the sake of human rights. America is now asking Absurdistan to confirm in writing that American sovereignty is the supreme principle, while that of Absurdistan is considered by them to be exactly the opposite.

What moves are Absurdistan's statesmen likely to make in the coming month? Negotiations with the Americans continue, with strong prospects for the conclusion of a final agreement in the affirmative. Absurdistan's diplomatic calculations will become clearer pending the outcome of several key dates. First, June 15 is the deadline for the White House and State Department to inform Congress whether or not we have fulfilled their demands for continuance of American financial aid and depending on the answer, many things will become clearer. Second, it will become clear by June 21 at the European Union meeting in Thessaloniki whether or not Absurdistan stands a chance of joining the European Union at an accelerated pace, perhaps as early as 2007. After that, little time will be left to put the finishing touches on the latest of the U.S.-Balkan bilateral agreements before the July 1 deadline.

A "New Phase" in the Balkans

December 2005

The scandal which erupted after Noam Chomsky's recent *Guardian* interview (that "exercise in defamation that is a model of the genre," according to Chomsky himself) is not, at least at first glance, completely unexpected: the Balkans, we can say with some pride, are back in style. Once again, we can partake of journalists' uninformed inanities about Kosovo, Bosnia, Serbia and other "permanent focalpoints of crisis" (*Frankfurter Allgemeine Zeitung*)—areas in which, over in the distance, on the edges of Europe, on a "doorstep of Europe" (Tony Blair), "in the black hole of our own Middle East" (*Il Manifesto*), "insanity giggles" (Milan Kundera) and where, in the autumn of European nationalism, peoples "imprisoned by history" (*Times*) still await their "debalkanization" (*La Republika*).

The influential Italian political magazine *Limes*, deprived of the gentle auto-irony that sometimes follows imperialist jargon, posed a key question: "Who will debalkanize the Balkans?" Maybe, just maybe, are the peoples of the Balkans themselves capable of this Herculean task? Or does their historical slumber not permit them to do so? After Paddy Ashdown, that postcolonial Harry Potter, abandons this dark "region marked by unseen evils" (*Berlin Zeitung*), who will protect the Balkan peoples from the black magic of ethnic hatred? Is it perhaps smarter that this peninsula, like

Saramago's stone raft, be simply cut off from the Europe to which it doesn't, in any case, belong? To the sorrow and misfortune of the Balkan peoples, Western politicians, journalists and "Balkan experts" have still not given up on their civilizing mission in this exotic locale.

In his last address to the U.S. Congress, Nicholas Burns brought out the past and future of U.S. politics on the Balkans. He spoke mainly of Bosnia, which must immediately be given "greater stability," and Kosovo, which may, perhaps, "be ready for some form of conditional independence." In any case, it is absolutely necessary, according to Burns, to create a "new image of the Balkans." The new historical image of the Balkans originated in the aftermath of the Yugoslav wars in which the "international community" participated from the very beginning by bankrolling "democratic" opposition parties (that were in fact rabidly nationalistic, thereby lending legitimacy to violent secessionist movements), and by arming the ethno-nationalist paramilitaries that would eventually come to constitute new armed forces. What does the Balkans look like today? It is a patchwork of nation-state remnants, such as Slovenia; the vassals of the international community, like Croatia and Serbia and Montenegro; and the three protectorates under military watch—Bosnia and Herzegovina, Kosovo, and Macedonia (the latter facing the serious risk of a new civil war, potentially even more brutal than the one that ended in 2002). When it comes to the protectorates, the "international community" has, to date, had two paradoxical solutions: in Bosnia and Herzegovina, the imposition of a "multiethnic at any cost" approach; and in Kosovo, the preparation for a "monoethnic independence," at least partially due to the year-long post-occupation ethnic cleansing in the opposite direction (of which we hear almost nothing in the Western press) during which nearly all the non-Albanian inhabitants were exiled and over 150 monasteries were destroyed.

But how do we explain the newly photogenic Bosnia and Kosovo? Perhaps it's best to start with Bosnia, which one Russian journalist (correctly, it seems to me), calls the "model for Kosovo." In the Balkans, "success is a real rarity," writes Jonathan Steel, apparently relieved of the burden of the concerned European. Especially in Bosnia, which is more a "patchwork than a real state" (*Politika Daily*). Two so-called entities—the Muslim-Croatian federation and Republika Srpska—have remained practically "irreconcilable enemies." This "Balkan colony of the international community" is made up of 10 cantons, 14 parliaments, and 145 ministries. Sounds complicated? The peoples of Bosnia themselves remain perplexed, more than ten years after they were forced to accept this somewhat bizarre arrangement. Government administration accounts for 70 percent of the national budget. Social services and pensions must be paid out of the remaining funds even as the official unemployment rate in Bosnia hovers above 40 percent. What follows from this state of affairs? Empty government coffers and corruption so widespread that it is not "part of the system but is the system." An American diplomat with enviable cultural sensitivity, partial to invoking picturesque historical parallels, has said that, "Bosnia looks like the Wild West of our movies." He's right. To date, more than two billion euros of international "donations" and "development aid" have vanished in Bosnia. Bosnia is an epicenter for arms and drug smuggling and trafficking in women, where local and especially international politicians collaborate with local criminals. Organized crime is the sole remaining domain of a multiethnic Bosnia. Bosnia has been transformed into a protectorate-laboratory in which the "international community" observes how to transform "failed states" such as Kosovo and Iraq into stable and obedient ones. Paddy Ashdown remains at the head of "Dayton's Bosnia." In January, however, Ashdown will be replaced as colonial governor, or to put it more formally, as the High Representative for Bosnia, by former German telecommunications minister Christian Schwarz-Schilling with nine years of experience as a samurai-diplomat of the international community. He announced himself with racist, anti-Serb statements. According to the *Berlin Zeitung*, Ashdown, "a former member of the British Royal Navy accustomed to battling in close quarters, is leaving because he was unable to win substantial support during his mandate." He has been "criticized by Serbs, Croats and Muslims as an arrogant colonial ruler."

A shift change at the beginning of the year holds more than symbolic meaning: in 2006, the whole country is due for reorganization at the behest of the NATO leadership and according to the plans set by their "Balkan experts." The Muslim-Croatian federation and Republika Srpska are to be fused into one central state. This step is obviously tied into independence for Kosovo, which is explained as the wish of the "overwhelming majority of the Albanian population of Kosovo to form an independent state." The idea is very simple: if the Serbian part of Bosnia, as an entity with state-like characteristics, is dissolved, then Kosovo can be granted independence without fear that Republika Srpska will do what the "overwhelming majority of its population" wants, which is to join Serbia and Montenegro. Before we go on to Kosovo, however, it would be useful to briefly pause on the question of the Bosnian Constitution. This document, at first glance, reflects a desire for the establishment of what in conventional political theory is sometimes called a "normal state" (the medical equivalent would be a "normal cancer"). But, just as in the case of the famous Dayton constitution, the new text at issue was not only launched but also written outside of Bosnia.

As British historian David Chandler correctly argues,

> Bosnia requires a state, government and constitution
> which are the product of the Bosnian people's
> engagement, interest and determination and I am
> not certain that this American suggested highest legal
> acts is the best solution. I think that the Americans
> are solving their own problems, not Bosnia's, because
> the Americans and all the others involved in the work
> of the office of the High Representative for Bosnia
> try to avoid responsibility and blame for the state of
> affairs in Bosnia, for the terrible economic situation,

and especially for the desire of the youth to leave the
country and their alienation from the political process.

In other words, according to the diagnoses of Balkan experts,
the people of Bosnia lack the requisite political capacity necessary to be credible on the question of their own constitution. Moreover, the design of the new constitution presupposes a situation in which, at a basic level, decisions are
made in Washington and Brussels and carried out according
to the political will of Brussels and the "high representative
of the international community" who has the responsibility
to instruct the Balkan tribes in the political culture. The truth
is that "it is time to rethink the way in which Bosnia is organized." Equally truly, this project requires the abolishment of
the insulting colonial institution of the high representative
and his dictatorial authority, and the granting of decision-
making power over the constitution, number of entities and
the cantons along with the entire political process to those
who actually live in Bosnia. I've already mentioned that the
development of the new Bosnian constitutional Frankenstein
is linked to the "new phase" now beginning in Kosovo. The
"new phase" is a phrase used by Kofi Annan, warning of the
"necessity of beginning a new phase in the Kosovo political
process." Kosovo, usually mentioned in the Western press
only when some newsworthy violence erupts, is again a topic
of diplomatic concern. The so-called status talks begin this
month with an announcement first made by Washington's
undersecretary of state in a task that fell to the United States
after a series of unusual coincidences. The UN has nominated
a special negotiator, as has the European Union.

Does that mean that one phase has already ended? As
a reminder, the first phase of the "democratic project in
Kosovo" encompassed no more and no less than the "development of democracy," "economic prosperity" and "recognition of the rights of minorities." Moreover, under the oversight of the NATO council and the UN, the current situation
(already one of permanent post-conflict, especially in the

aftermath of the attacks on the non-Albanian residents last March) has become increasingly unlivable. The disputes can be summarized formulaically: as long as what Belgrade offers to Kosovo Albanians is "some more than autonomy but less than independence" while Kosovo politicians insist on "more than autonomy, not less than independence," the "international community's" "compromise solution" for this "immature political ambience" is preparation for "independence without autonomy." Annan has nominated the diplomat and former Finnish president Martti Ahtisaari as special envoy during the Kosovo negotiations. This nomination comes as no surprise. Few players on the international political scene have such a frighteningly efficient reputation as this former diplomat. Namibia, Yugoslavia, Northern Ireland, Eritrea, and finally Aceh: Ahtisaari has always stuck his fingers into peaceful initiatives. Now it's Kosovo's turn. By founding the Crisis Management Institute in Helsinki, Ahtisaari sought to create a monopoly on peaceful conflict resolution: where the "international community" lights a fire, Ahtisaari arrives to extinguish it. All you need to do is call him. This Finnish fireman's greatest success was the peaceful settlement in Aceh. If a "lasting compromise" in Kosovo is reached next year, the Nobel Peace Prize will certainly not evade his humanitarian grasp, especially as he was already this year's frontrunner candidate.

Ahtisaari's deputy is Austrian diplomat Albert Roan, also an expert in "Balkan stabilization." In an interview with Austrian magazine *Die Presse*, Roan gave an overview of his mission to "Europe's stone raft": "We have to admit that the Europe of the 1990s betrayed the Balkans. We were unable to prevent war or extinguish crises. Europe did not exactly distinguish itself, but now we have a singular opportunity to once and for all stabilize the Balkans and the entire region, bringing the Balkans closer to the European Union. Different obstacles stand in our way—Kosovo, the relationship between Serbia and Montenegro, the Bosnian situation. Its imperative that its protectorate regime be transformed into a normal governing state." In Kosovo, we have the opposite interests. We have to try to include the interests of the majority Albanian population in Kosovo, the Serbian population of Kosovo and Belgrade, and the interest of the international community in stability in the Balkans. The solution must not cause conflict. The problem arises if one side insists absolutely on its wishes. Then it will be difficult. One must be compromising. The solution must be lasting. It must be a guarantee of stability."

Undersecretary Burns is also visibly worried about stability. Speaking to the U.S. Senate, he opined that NATO will use force if any of the parties to the Kosovo status negotiations employ the threat of violence as a political tactic. In Burns's thinking, the talks may well "bring about independence." The Kosovo Albanians shouldn't rush to begin independence day celebrations just yet though, explained the undersecretary and Balkan expert with a schoolteacher's concern: "they need to prove that they are worthy."

However, when we compare Burns to his colleague, former U.S. special envoy for the Balkans Richard Holbrooke, the cowboy-undersecretary begins to look like a poster-boy for political correctness. Holbrooke, famous for his declaration that the "Serbs are shit people," on the occasion of the same Senate outing, said, with now celebrated candor, that Belgrade will have to find a way to let go of Kosovo. To that he added that the province's independence would inevitably lead to the dissolution of Serbia and Montenegro's linkage. Among other things, both Burns and Holbrooke have supported a referendum on independence for Montenegro.

In exchange for Kosovo (a territory to which the people of this "primitive country" are somehow inexplicably "historically tied") they have offered to Serbia an institutional promise: the magical delight of membership in European-Atlantic alliances. That is to say, as Burns emphasized, nations that contain within a "great territorial conflict" cannot be participants in this kind of integration. This practice is well known in the Balkans: in the 1990s, local criminals promised security to storeowners in exchange for a cut of the profits. The Kosovo negotiations, carried out by Serbian and Albanian political "elites" and unfolding under strong pressure from the "international community," may well conclude with the termination of 1999's UN Resolution 1244 under which Kosovo must remain a part of Yugoslavia. This means that for the first time since the end of the Yugoslav wars, a new Balkan border will be drawn along ethnic lines. We will have to wait and see what sort of an explosive charge this latest gambit by the "international community" holds. It may be quick and it will be fiery, in which case Annan may, in some fatal sense, turn out to be right: a "new phase" in the Balkans is indeed beginning.

The Departure of the Balkan Clouseau

February 2006

In ancient times and during the Middle Ages, enlightened people spoke *de mortuis nihil nisi bene*—nothing ill of the dead. This polite habit can be explained by the fact that the Middle Ages saw nothing of the Ibrahim Rugova phenomenon. Reporter Gojko Beric, of the Sarajevo paper *Oslobodjenje*, himself prone to historical reflection, conjures up somewhat different historical categories. There are, he writes, politicians whom "only death transforms into national legends." "His death," according to Beric, "brings us back to the eternal enigma of personalities who changed history only to find that in the end, history would determine their fate."

While my humble education as a historian prevents me from fully understanding the metaphysical meaning of the "eternal enigma" which confuses the Sarajevo reporter, I agree that the historical significance of Rugova is a mystery. I remember one my attempts as a student, writing in one of those deathly boring academic journals that intellectuals pretend to study religiously, to compose "a history of the ordinary person." I attempted to reconstruct the life of one entirely ordinary French peasant whose everyday existence illuminated and, to some extent, explained, the reality of that distant age. When it comes to Ibrahim Rugova, however, the intellectual instinct, which presents itself to a historian, is entirely different. How to write the history of an entirely insignificant man? A man who, like Sellers's brave Inspector Clouseau, is internationally recognized as a genius despite his tragic-comedic antics?

No, let's stop here for a minute. Just who was this Ibrahim Rugova? According to the mainstream Western press, he was a poet, a writer, and a man of peace, nonviolence, and tolerance. According to *Kathimerini (Athens)*, he was Don Quixote and a visionary. In the "international community," as represented by *Globe and Mail*, he is most commonly referred to as the Balkan Gandhi. Some have also called him the Balkan Roland Barthes, after the celebrated French literary theorist, who (according to Rugova's friends) once greeted him in a university hallway during a stay at the Sorbonne.

Rugova was also a president. Not of a state, really, at least not a real state, but he was president of Kosovo, one of the lower rung Balkan international protectorates exercising a dubious sovereignty. Rugova founded the Democratic League of Kosovo, and he was, according to the Independent Bangladesh, a leading intellectual in formerly communist Yugoslavia. Kosovo Premier Berisa called him, not intending anything negative, the father of the "Kosovo-Albanian nation." UN Special Representative Søren Jensen-Petersen wrote somewhere that Rugova left "a legacy of determination, curiosity and dialogue." An article in the Luxembourg magazine *Tageblat* argued that Rugova's Kosovo showed "genuine progress on the road to democracy, the rule of law and a market economy." They probably didn't give much thought to the persecution of tens of thousands of Kosovo Serbs and Roma. Or perhaps ethnic cleansing, when performed by our friends, can be considered democratic?

The Paris magazine *Le Figaro* sketches the career of the "Balkan Gandhi." When Rugova won the leadership of the Democratic League of Kosovo in December of 1989, our Gandhi undertook a whole series of initiatives: a declaration of independence (July 1990); the adoption of a constitution for the self-proclaimed republic of Kosovo (September 1990); a referendum on the independence of the region (September

1991); and a victory in parliamentary elections (2000). In 1998, the European parliament awarded him the Andrej Saharov prize for contributions to democracy and the protection of human rights. A reporter for the *Independent*, Vesna Zimonjic, describes Rugova's "accomplishments": the Kosovar politician adopted a Western value system (I'm not entirely certain whether this is meant as a compliment); laid the cornerstone for an independent Kosovo (in other words, defined Kosovo's ethno-nationalist politics); and shaped Kosovo's "national question" at the same time as he planned to erase Kosovo's national divisions (just to be clear: the reporter offers us no argument in support of this thesis).

Zimonjic claims in the same article that in comparison with other international statesmen, Serbian officials in Belgrade expressed much cynicism at Rugova's death and showed little sympathy. This sort of behavior does, of course, warrant every condemnation, especially if it actually happened: yet when Boris Tadić, the president of Serbia, of which Kosovo is still a part, announced that he would attend the funeral, nationalist Albanian leaders forbade his attendance. Zimonjic also writes that Rugova "began his political career at a time when the country was sickened by Milošević's regime, and now leaves it completely healed. He took the illness with him." This rather unusual metaphor hides the fact that the real "illness" suffered by Kosovo's politicians is ethno-nationalism. And, unfortunately, Rugova did not take that illness with him.

What was Rugova really like? I will try and offer a somewhat different picture. This "man with the silk scarf" was some "type of a monument to himself" (*Frankfurter Allgemeine Zeitung*): a caricature of an intellectual, famous for his silk scarves (that were apparently popular in Paris at the time when Pristina's existentialist ran into Roland Barthes), for his photogenic cigarette, and for his strange habit of presenting guests with rocks (at the end of a meeting with Pristina's humble Sartre, each visitor would receive a map of the "Republic of Kosovo" and "a piece of independent Kosovo," a gift-wrapped sparkling rock.) Many did not hide their delight at the "Yugoslavian Havel." One American diplomat confessed to Belgrade journalist Zoran Cirjakovic that "I do not understand how he succeeded, with that fake smile and those empty words, to lead on so many diplomats."

The newspaper *Der Tagesspiegel* writes that Rugova was an authoritarian party leader: party congresses were rare, decisions were made in secret, and critics were expelled from the party and attacked in the party newspaper, *Boti Sot*. These allegations are confirmed by loyalist Baton Hadziu when he says of Rugova that he was, "more than a leader, [he was] a political symbol who functioned more in keeping with monarchist principles." Burdened by a mania for glory, he would often humiliate his colleagues in the presence of foreign diplomats in the typical manner of a provincial intellectual. A group of his fellow party members warned the International Crisis Group (ICG) of Rugova's "dictatorial inclinations." The ICG pointed out Rugova's utilization of communist party organization principles and lack of democratic instinct, describing him as an "inactive and authoritarian like a sphinx." "Homeland Security," the party's secret police, announced in its second communiqué that its goal was to enforce correct behavior on the part of party members. Rugova's son Ulke is one of the party's key members, but also one of the most privileged and wealthy businessmen in Kosovo. Nepotism, a lack of democracy, and absolute loyalty were the primary principles of Rugova's political behavior. Much more dangerous than his political style (and much less entertaining than his provincial intellectualism), however, was his ethno-nationalist politics which we can call the Rugova Doctrine.

Rugova was an intolerant extremist who for years uncompromisingly insisted on nationalist goals. He is most responsible for the fact that Kosovo—despite the miners' strike and street demonstrations; notwithstanding the existence of an international solidarity perspective; and in spite of social struggle, labor resistance, and the work of social movements—wound up with the cruel nationalism of the KLA. Kosovo's nationalists, together with their Western mentors, played a well-organized game in which they were assisted by the unintelligent inert bureaucracy of Slobodan Milošević's regime. Serbian nationalist Milošević is represented in the West as the "Balkan butcher," while the Kosovo nationalist is celebrated as the "Balkan Gandhi." Rugova, as president of nothing, imagined hospitals, schools, parallel universities and a tax system, putting in place a nationalist auto-apartheid. The West, meanwhile, in conflict with Milošević, needed a Kosovo symbiosis of Gandhi, Havel, and Solzhenitsyn. This false picture was maintained for years. The "Balkan Gandhi" pretended that he had nothing to do with the nationalist terrorism of the KLA, even suggesting that it was a "provocation of the Serbian secret service."

Opposite of this "man of peace and understanding," a sharper political line was taken by another nationalist politician, the KLA's political representative Adem Demaçi, dubbed the "Balkan Mandela" by the Western media. A writer for the Italian newspaper *Il Manifesto*, Ennio Remedino, relates an interesting anecdote. When two Serbian civil servants, workers at the state radio station, were disappeared, their spouses came to the paper to ask for assistance. Remedino, who was then in Kosovo, immediately spoke with Rugova. The supremely uninterested "Gandhi" sent him to Demaçi, but "Mandela" simply shook his head and said, "one more widow." After NATO's aggression—that seventy-eight day terror against civilians during which NATO served as the KLA's air force—Rugova conjured, this time as a "near statesman" of an international protectorate, a theory of contra-apartheid: ethnic enclaves for the small number of stubborn Serbs and Roma who refused to leave Kosovo. The catastrophic result of the fifteen year long reign of this nationalist politician is the creation of a political climate in which freedom from Serbia became synonymous with freedom from Serbs and Roma. It was this sort of logic that incited the murderous ethnic cleansing of Serbs and Roma in March of 2004.

What awaits Kosovo in what Standard-Vienna has called "post-Rugova era"? The big question is: who could succeed him as president and as the head of Kosovo's delegation to talks with Belgrade on the future status of the region? George Vukadinovic, editor of *Nove Srpske Politicke Misli*, argues that in recent times Rugova "did not play an important political role. But his death could have a large impact on the negotiations in Vienna. Albanian negotiators will now probably be even more extreme ... In these sorts of situations, and especially in Kosovo, the question is who will be the new "godfather," not only who will be leader."

According to *Rossijskaja Gazeta*, suggested candidates for the new "godfather" include former leader of the KLA Hashim Thaçi, Kosovar media magnate Veton Surroi, and Kosovo parliamentary leader Nedzat Daci. *Le Monde* has also put forward the name of Ramush Haradinaj, the former KLA commander currently enjoying temporary freedom while awaiting trial in The Hague. He has, according to the French paper, managed to unite "young pacifist intellectuals, guerilla veterans and Western diplomats." Certainly an unusual mix! Also making an appearance on Kosovo's political scene is a true gentleman, Behgjet Pacolli: owner of the Mabetex Group who (according to a court in Lugano) helped former Russian president Boris Yeltsin open an account in a Swiss bank, and (according to a court in Trent) laundered several million dollars used to buy and sell military aircraft that was later sold to a Latin American state with the assistance of the current Russian secret service. According to Italian newspaper *Il Manifesto*, Pacolli was involved in transferring mafia money from Russia through various Western banks and offshore companies. His friend Ibrahim Rugova, our "Gandhi," often said that it was time for him to settle down. Nonetheless, Pacolli is now entering politics. He has stepped forward to build the new American university in Pristina. The cost? Spare change: approximately $20 million. The university will be built with Russian taxpayers' money so that in addition to the world's largest military base (Camp Bondsteel, where the CIA interrogates secret and unlawful detainees) the United States can (at no cost) also get its own university in order to build and theorize the future of Kosovo. According to *Financial Times*, this dynamic businessman is also the founder of the Alliance for a New Kosovo, a Washington lobby group that counts among its sponsors former Secretary of Defense Frank Carlucci, also Chairman of the Carlyle Group.

Kosovo's nationalist leaders transformed Rugova's funeral into a staging of the founding of a Kosovar state. What sort of a state will it be? N. Gvozdev, editor of the American magazine *National Interest*, offers one answer: "I'm afraid that the West, as in Iraq, will be disappointed by the democratic paradox, because the Albanian politicians are not prone to multiethnicity or divisions of power in the manner which the West would like." He feels that there is no real difference between "conditional" and "true" independence. This is to say that in Washington, "the prevailing feeling is that a united Bosnia and an independent Kosovo suit American strategic interests. The Serbs are on the losing side, seen as just punishment for Milošević's crimes during the 1990s." Does that apply to the Serbian and Roma civilians imprisoned within besieged ethnic enclaves? What will happen to them when the international forces withdraw from this protectorate born of bombing?

Kosovo's independence is clearly only a matter of time. Washington has "already made the call" (*Kurier*), and only the creation of a timeline remains. The negotiations over its status, postponed by Rugova's death but likely to begin next month, are largely a matter of political theatre. There is no chance that UN standards will be fulfilled. As reported by *Neues Deutschland*, promises about the protection and return of Serbian and Roma refugees were false, as were idealistic pronouncements of a multiethnic and multicultural Kosovo. Independence means the beginning of the Albanization of Kosovo, the ultimate triumph of the logic of borders, ethnic conflict, and nationalism. That is the true legacy of Ibrahim Rugova.

Between Balkan Primitivism and European Future

If you read the mainstream press last week, there is a probability that you have read that, in Serbia, that "pivotal Balkan State," people went to the polls for a "crucial election," the most important one since the fall of "deceased strongman" Slobodan Milošević's regime in 2000. This is an election, according to mainstream international news sources, that could return Serbia "to the nationalist instability or open up better prospects of integration with the EU and the West."

Both Western and Eastern European leaders, "from Slovenia to Slovakia," urged the Serbs to "reject the nationalists." Michael Polt, the U.S. ambassador to Serbia, advised the people to ditch an orientation and "retrograde vision of extremists who would be happy to turn Serbia into an isolated island blinded by nationalism." These extremists are, presumably, the "ultra-nationalist" Serbian Radical Party led by Vojislav Šešelj, "a former warlord on trial for crimes against humanity."

The choice, according to the free press, was simple enough: to go back to the "unhappy past," or to "march into a bright, European future." This "Euro-Atlantic agenda" would have to encompass removing "the immediate hurdle on Belgrade's way to Brussels": arrest and extradition of the remaining suspects wanted by the International Yugoslav War Crimes Tribunal, accepting the independence of Kosovo, "a tiny war-torn territory on the way to full independence," and the continuation of a wholesale privatization in accordance with "European standards."

The international community suggested, as the best choice, "a highly regarded young former finance minister Božidar Djelić," who is a candidate of the "pro-European" Democratic Party, and one of the "most capable and level headed politicians in the Balkans." The Serbian people (ungrateful as always) have awarded him, for his previous ministerial efforts, the nickname Boza Derikoza ("Takes the skin of your back").

The other right choice would be Čedomir Jovanović, the former Serbian government's vice president and the chosen candidate of the American Embassy on Kneza Miloša Street, who is "a leading reformist politician" (also known, among the same ungrateful subjects, as "Čeda cocaine").

The alternative agenda would be to simply surrender to the macabre forces of Balkan primitivism, campaigning on the platform to "end the corruption and keep Kosovo within Serbia." Interestingly and perhaps not surprisingly, the voters (perhaps blinded by the effects of the "good war" in 1999, which left a few thousand dead, while simultaneously heralding a "new era of freedom and democracy") have chosen to disobey the advice of the international community. The "extreme nationalists romped to a comfortable victory," taking as much as 29 percent of the vote, a point up from the last election in 2003, but, as BBC reports, still failed to gain an absolute majority. As the attempt to divert "xenophobic instincts of Serbian masses" have failed, Serbia now "faces weeks of political horse-trading and coalition building."

What has really happened in the Serbian elections? Actually, nothing much. Despite the sound and fury of the recent elections; despite the apparent struggle between the "traditional" and the "transitional," and despite whatever might be the final electoral outcome, in contemporary Serbia nothing depends on the local political parties. As a "modern" Algerian politician proclaims from the pages of the recent book by novelist Mohamed Moulessehoul, "ever since the world has existed, the society has obeyed a threefold dynamic of those with an upper hand: those who govern, those who crush, and those who supervise."

Translated into the context of contemporary Serbia, those who govern are the so-called reformers: Democratic Party, Democratic Party of Serbia, and G17 (a political party of neoliberal experts). The Democratic Party won sixty-five members in parliament, the Democratic Party of Serbia won forty-seven, and G17 won nineteen. The most probable coalition, according to the convincing majority of Serbian political commentators, is the one made of the aforementioned parties with "Euro-Atlantic aspirations."

Those who "crush" are two extremist political formations, the neoliberal and aggressive Liberal Democratic Party (of the "Čeda cocaine" and supported by both the American embassy and so-called civil society), who won a surprising fifteen seats, and the Serbian Radical Party (a right-wing populist organization of the familiar sort that mushrooms all over transitional Europe), with a remarkable but insufficient number of eighty-one seats. The Serbian Socialists have, perhaps unexpectedly, won sixteen seats. Those who "supervise" are, of course, members of the "international community."

How can we explain the success of the nationalist-populist Radical Party, a monster that excites the Western press so much? Is there perhaps a place for an alternative explanation to the diagnosis of xenophobic instincts deeply ingrained in Balkan body politics?

According to the so-called international definition of unemployment, there were 475,000 unemployed in Serbia in 2000. In 2005, after five years of democratic life and neoliberal transitional miracles, the number of unemployed went as high as 720,000. The rate of unemployment was 21.8 percent in October of 2005.

The conclusion of the local neoliberal experts? The best transition always assumes temporary growth of unemployment. "Transition," according to one of my favorite local experts, always fond of poetry, "might be defined, at the same time, as a process of destruction and a process of creating good jobs." But not all the jobs are good, admits our expert. The sector of the self-employed, created after the privatization (the destruction) of public companies, employs five hundred thousand people, which is 20 percent of the national employment. We should bear in mind that Serbia has some eight million inhabitants, and that the informal economy "employs" several hundred thousand people.

The same expert offers an obvious but still ingenious solution: Serbia has to stop being a "traumatic society" and finally join the club of "post-traumatic societies." The only way to do it, in case you had any doubts, is to continue with the traumatic processes of privatization, transition, and European integration. This sophisticated solution was less obvious to the traumatized people voting for the anticorruption program of the Serbian Radical Party.

The fate of Kosovo, formally part of Serbia (but since the "good war" of 1999 an International Community protectorate with a colonial viceroy) is in the hands of Western powers; more precisely, it is in the hands of Contact Group—an organization formed during the Bosnian wars in 1994, comprised of the states "most interested in the Balkan affairs": United States, Russia, England, France, Germany, and Italy. The very same type of international organization was established for Somalia and, at the recent NATO summit in Riga, for Afghanistan.

According to the *Guardian*, UN mediator on Kosovo Marti Ahtisaari, has delayed revealing his solution for Kosovo until after the election, "for fear of handing the victory to extreme nationalists who vow never to give up the province." According to Reuters, his plan, which is still kept in secrecy, entails taking Kosovo from the sovereignty of Serbia, and setting it on the path towards independence, with "significant autonomy" for the 114,000 Serbs and Roma.

Kosovo would have the right to apply for membership in international organizations such as the World Bank, IMF, and United Nations. NATO would train a civil defense force that would eventually become Kosovo's national army. In all other areas, Kosovo will continue to be a colonial subject to the "international community." The European Union is setting up a police force of more than a thousand officers to monitor judges (and prison guards). Nobody can tell what's going to happen to the Serbs and the Roma, "the most sensitive part of the plan," once they are left completely unprotected.

If this information is true, Serbia will most likely (and quite regardless of the future local constellation of power) try to reject the plan in hopes that Russia will use its veto power over the proposal in the UN. Agim Çeku, the prime minister of Kosovo and a war criminal of Kosovo Liberation Army fame, has declared that the Albanian Kosovars will not be "entirely satisfied."

There seem to be two perspectives at play here: one that might be called a "dangerous precedent," favored by the Russians and based on the expectation that the example of Kosovo might provoke other people in the same situation to try and realize their "separatist ambitions"; and another that might be called "constructive flexibility," favored by the United States and European Union, that would like to see Kosovo as a "transitional laboratory," a "blank site" inside the system of international law and a colonial playground for practicing geo-strategic state-building and the extraction of lucrative raw materials.

Predictably enough, what nobody talks about is the nightmarish situation of Albanian, Serbian, and Roma people, living in a state of perpetual transitional chaos of utmost poverty and despair, manipulated by local governments, and being left only with the troubling solace of ethnic belonging and national antagonism.

In the Serbian province of Vojvodina, a group of rebellious workers have occupied a factory. This once famous pharmaceutical company has been stolen from the workers according to the illegal structure of local privatization (and what privatization is legal?). After a few long months of occupation, and after some of the most amazing examples of courage I have ever witnessed in my life, the workers have forced the private armies of the new owners, and transitional privatization officials, to back off.

A few days ago, after the blockade of the Business Register Agency by some eighty workers of the Jugoremedija factory, this respectable agency overturned the illegal recapitalization and brought the ownership structure to where it should be, with workers, as shareholders owning 58 percent of the workplace.

A comrade of mine, intimately involved in this struggle, sent me an email, saying that the name of the person who signed the document is Maglov ("foggy"). The last name of the director of this surreal Agency is Okolisanov ("to beat around the bush"). The last name of the director of a related Agency is Stimac ("the fraudster"). And the last name of the director of Central Depository Agency, yet another Buñuelesque institution of Serbian transitional system, is Uzelac ("robber"). If we were to make a cartoon about this struggle, we wouldn't have to change the names, continued my comrade. The problem is that the name of the cartoon is Serbian reality. And this reality is being decided in petty global rivalries between New York, Moscow, and the European Union.

And what about the local politicians after the local elections? Together with local oligarchs they have made a wise choice. In the words of Mohamed Moulessehoul's Algerian reformer,

> The world transforms itself at the whim of its appetites.
> From now onward nationalism is only to be evaluated
> as a function of interests. We got off to a bad start.
> Our revolution proved as a fiasco. To progress from a
> caricature of a socialist system to the opening up of
> the market, we must pay a customs duty. It is a duty
> we have to pay as not to be excluded from the new
> world order. That's what we are doing at the moment.

Eisenhower's Mistake:
A Tale of an Astonishing Letter to
the Former German Chancellor

February 2007

The first time I heard of Willy Wimmer was during the NATO "freedom through bombs" campaign in Serbia in 1999. "Never before so few lied so thoroughly to so many, as in connection with the Kosovo war," he famously observed. "People died for this." Wimmer, then a member of the Christian Democratic Union party in the German Bundestag, was referring to the organized media's attempt to convince the population of Germany that there was indeed a humanitarian catastrophe in Kosovo, one that would necessitate a humanitarian intervention.

The attempt was, as we know, all too successful. NATO spokesman Jamie Shea said at the time that, "The political leaders played the decisive role with regard to public opinion." He was referring to German politicians, those "democratically elected representatives," who "knew which news was important for public opinion in their country. Rudolf Scharping did a really good job. It's not easy, particularly in Germany, whose population for fifty years had known only military defense, meaning the protection of their own country, to send German soldiers hundreds of miles away."

Explaining the difficulties that the new definition of security policy entailed, Shea commended "not only Minister Scharping, but also Chancellor Schríder and Minister Fischer" all of whom provided "an outstanding example of political leaders who don't just run behind public opinion, but know how to shape it."

Shea was probably at his cynical best when he described the reasons behind his optimism: "It makes me optimistic to see that the Germans have understood that. And despite the very unpleasant side effects, the collateral damage, and the long duration of the air raids, they stayed on course. If we had lost public support in Germany, we would have lost it throughout the alliance."

As readers of ZNet probably remember, among the many news items, which "were important for public opinion" in Germany, was information provided by Minister Scharping in April of 1999 that the Serbs have installed a Nazi-style concentration camp for few thousand Kosovo Albanians in the football stadium of Pristina, the capital of Kosovo. In his efforts to persuade the nation to "stay on course," comrade Minister Joschka Fischer, the ex-radical German Foreign Minister, compared the Serbs to the Nazis, calling for military intervention with a crusader fervor: "There must never be another Auschwitz!" I remember how, sitting in shelters and trying to ignore the buzz of humanitarian tomahawks around us, we were joking that in order for Germans to prevent the return of "Nazism" in a region that built its identity on the fight against German Nazis in World War II, Fisher and Schroder had resort to a Nazi propaganda not seen since 1945.

A few days ago I was reminded of Wimmer, one of the few conservative German politicians arguing against the war in Kosovo (and predictably criticized by *Frankfurter Allgemeine Zeitung* as a "conspiracy theorist"). A well-informed Serbian conservative weekly published a translation of the letter from Wimmer to the German Chancellor Schroder. The letter is a report from a conference held in the Slovakian capital of Bratislava, organized by the State Department and the American Enterprise Institute. The subject of this conference, attended by numerous prime ministers "from Baltic to Macedonia," was the Balkans and expansion of NATO.

Wimmer had heard many interesting things in Bratislava. For instance, that Operation Horseshoe—the plan allegedly conceived by the Serbs to drive the Albanian population out of Kosovo in 1999—was a propaganda invention and that the purpose behind the Kosovo war was to enable the United States to correct an oversight of General Eisenhower's in World War II and to establish a U.S. military presence in the Balkans with a view to controlling the strategically important peninsula. He heard a high-ranking American official saying that the American aim was to draw a geopolitical line from the Baltic Sea to Anatolia and to control this area as the Romans had once controlled it. One would suppose that the American *mare nostrum*, or "our sea," is not the Mediterranean but the Atlantic. Wimmer had a distinct impression that everyone agreed (and could have cared less) about the fact that NATO humanitarian attacks were illegal under international law and were done very deliberately, in order to establish the precedent for future "humanitarian" actions without a UN mandate.

One of the many interesting things about this letter is that Wimmer is by no means a Leftist activist, or a Left-leaning critic of "American imperialism." He was, at the time of writing the document, not only a defense policy spokesman of the conservative Christian Democratic Union (CDU), but also a vice president of the Parliamentary Assembly of the Organization for Cooperation in Europe. After reading the published translation of the letter in the Yugoslav language, I have tried (not without some difficulties) to dig out the original. I have discovered that the document was published in the government journal *Blätter für deutsche und internationale Politik* (pages 1059–1060). The translation below, however, is of the text that I found on the website of University of Kassel.

Readers interested in the nature of U.S. politics in the Balkans, especially in the light of the recent Ahtisaari plan for independent-but-not-autonomous Kosovo, as well as those more generally interested in the nature of U.S. foreign politics, could benefit from this rough translation (for the quality of which I duly apologize).

Berlin, 02. 05. 2000

Highly Esteemed Mister Chancellor,

Last week, I had the opportunity to attend a conference in Bratislava, the capital of Slovakia, organized by the American State Department and American Enterprise Institute (Foreign Policy Institute of the Republican Party). The main subject of the meeting was the Balkans and the process of NATO enlargement.

The conference was attended by high political officials, as indicated by the presence of numerous regional Prime Ministers, as well as ministers of foreign politics and defense. Among the many important topics discussed, a few deserve special emphasis:

1. The organizers of the Conference (U.S. State Department and American Enterprise Institute) demanded a speedy recognition of Kosovo, according to international law.

2. It was explained by the organizers that the Federal Republic of Yugoslavia must be kept out of every rule-of-law organ, and especially out of the Helsinki accords.

3. European rule of law is a hindrance to NATO. The American system of law is therefore more suitable for Europe.

4. The war against Yugoslavia was fought to rectify an incorrect decision of General Eisenhower during World War II. In this manner, because of the strategic reasons demanding the stationing of U.S. soldiers in this region, the faulty determination has been corrected.

5. The European allies took part in the war against Yugoslavia in order to de facto overcome the

dilemma which presented itself after the acceptance of the "new strategic concept" of the Alliance in the April of 1999, and to overcome the inclination of the Europeans to secure a previous mandate of the UN or the Organization for European Security and Cooperation.

6. European allies may legally reason that this war against Yugoslavia, which was outside the treaty's domain, was an exception. However, it is clear that this is a precedent, upon which they can and will call at any moment.

7. NATO should now fill the area between the Baltic and Anatolia as Roman forces filled it during the height of the Roman Empire.

8. In addition, Poland must be surrounded from the north and the south by democratic neighbor states; Bulgaria and Romania should provide the territorial connection to Turkey; and in the long run, Serbia must be kept out of European development (probably to further the safety of the American military presence).

9. North of Poland, it is important to establish complete control of all access routes from St. Petersburg to the Baltic Sea.

10. In each process, the right for people's self determination should be given priority before all other regulations or rules of the international law.

11. The statement that NATO's war against Yugoslavia was a violation of all relevant regulations and rules of international law did not encounter any opposition.

After this conference, where the discussion was very open and candid, we cannot avoid the long-lasting importance of the conference conclusions, especially taking into account the professional rank and competence of its participants and organizers.

The American side seems to be conscious of the fact that in order to pursue its interests, it needs to undermine the rule of law developed as a result of the two World Wars. Power must be above justice. Where international law stands in the way, it must be removed. When a similar development was embraced by the League of Nations, the Second World War was not far away. A way of thinking that puts self-interest in such an absolute position cannot be called anything but totalitarian.

With friendly regards,
Willy Wimmer

The Balkans: The Independence Will Be Supervised

March 2007

I was reading an EU journal today, I think it was the *Frankfurter Rundschau*, when a curious article attracted my attention. European defense ministers are meeting in the German town of Wiesbaden to discuss "State-Building in the Western Balkans." Javier Solana is going to be there, as well as His Excellency the General Secretary of NATO. The central problem these European gentlemen are going to confront is the set of "challenges to state-building in the Western Balkans." Although the so called negotiations over Kosovo's independence are still going on—the real ones between Europe, the United States, and Russia, and the formal ones between the colonial elites of Serbia and Kosovo—one of the points for discussion is how to organize the independent Kosovo. Here, we encounter a new definition of what negotiations mean in civilized Europe: the purpose of negotiations among the "small nations" is to negotiate until you reach the decision that has already been made by the important Euro-nations. It also seems like there are going to be 2,500 soldiers in Bosnia instead of 6,500. That's good. But the article ended with a rather grim prediction of difficult times ahead for state-building in the Western Balkans.

I think that I understand the part about new geography. The label "Western Balkans" is the latest in a line of attempts to deflect the subversive anticolonial connotations of this misbehaving peninsula. Renaming the Balkans has a long and fascinating history. From Austro-Hungarian balkanologists to State Department experts of today, from Southeast Europe to the Western Balkans, the idea was always the same: to debalkanize the Balkans, for which purpose a more neutral language is useful. U.S. President Clinton was very clear about the fact that "Europe has no other option but to bring the entire area of Southeast Europe into the European family … and debalkanize the Balkans once and for all," even if this takes "bomb[ing] the fuckers" (Richard Holbrooke).

One could ask why is this attention so necessary. Experts seem to be in agreement that it is because of the savage and barbarian ways of the people in the Balkans, ways that need to be tamed and civilized. However, they disagree about the source of this "innate savagery." According to Robert Kaplan, author of *Balkan Ghosts*, it is the absence of light: "[The Balkans] was a time-capsule world: a dim stage upon which people raged, spilled blood, experienced visions and ecstasies. Yet their expressions remained fixed and distant, like dusty statuary."

Others, like one famous British journalist, blame table manners:

> The ferocity of the Balkan peoples has at times been so primitive that anthropologists have likened them to the Amazon's Yanamamo, one of the world's most savage and primitive tribes. Up until the turn of the present century, when the rest of Europe was concerned as much with social etiquette as with social reform, there were still reports from the Balkans of decapitated enemy heads presented as trophies on silver plates at victory dinners. Nor was it unknown for the winners to eat the loser's heart and liver … The history books show it as a land of murder and revenge before the Turks arrived and long after they departed.

Vesna Goldsworthy, author of the wonderful book *Inventing Ruritania*, calls this line of argument "racism of nuance." I agree with the racism part, but have to say that I don't see a nuance. Goldsworthy cites one former UN representative in Kosovo who wrote in the *Guardian* that governing Kosovo is like "dressing a child: you give it the trousers of economy, the shirt of education, the jacket of democracy, etc. And all the while, the child wants to run out and play outside in its underpants. If we let it, it could hurt itself." Could underpants be at the root of the Balkan problem?

Simon Winchester would disagree. He thinks it is something to do with the mountains: "Just what was it that had marked out this particular peninsula, this particular gyre of mountains and plains, caves and streams, and made it a byword, quite literally, for hostility and hate? What forces were really at work here? ... The two [mountain] chains smashed into one another to create a geological fracture zone that became a template for the fractured behavior of those who would later live upon it." And just like "these strange and feral Balkans" are outlandish and unlike the rest of Europe, its inhabitants, "the wild and refractory peoples of the Balkans," are fundamentally (and anthropologically) different: "One might say that anyone who inhabited such a place for a long period would probably evolve into something that varied substantially, for good or for ill, from whatever is the human norm." Sounds convincing.

Although all these opinions of illustrious experts are very illuminating, it is George Kennan who in my opinion came closest to the truth. Kennan was a key figure in the U.S. policy of containment, and one of the first and foremost U.S. Balkan experts. He had recognized history as a crucial difficulty that civilized Europeans and Americans are up against:

> What we are up against is the sad fact that
> developments of those earlier ages, not only those
> of the Turkish domination but of earlier ones as well,
> had the effect of thrusting into the southeastern
> reaches of the European continent a salient of non-
> European civilization that has continued to the

present day to preserve many of its non-European characteristics, including some that fit even less with the world of today than they did with the world of eighty years ago.

Kennan is quite right to point out two factors: one is the ethnic and cultural mix of the Balkan peoples—a "Macedonian salad," a peninsula always much more diverse and tolerant of diversity then the (rest of) Europe. The other factor is its stubborn refusal of what is forced upon us as "Europe" and "civilization." If we are to try to identify some of the most important aspects of the history of the Balkans, we cannot but point out the persistent vision of a surprisingly consistent utopia, of a decentralized communal society, in perpetual struggle against centralization, colonization, and cultural norms imposed by its civilized Western "Other." Debalkanization of the Balkans assumes the attempt to eradicate the history of this upside down world, a decentralized and fragmented world of anticolonial struggles; heretics (*bogumili*); maritime and land pirates (*hajduci and uskoci*); rebels and revolutionaries; anti-authoritarians; Romanis; self-governed communities; socialist federations; partisans; and antifascists. Balkanization is indeed all about fragmentation, but it is not (only) ethnic fragmentation: balkanization implies resistance and a decentralized and federated alternative to the violent centralization of states and empires. This is why balkanization needs to be arrested and why the Balkans need to be renamed and "debalkanized."

But what is "state-building"? It appears, to me at least, to be a new concept. In yet another article, in yet another EU journal, I have discovered that the art of state-building is inseparable from "good governance": It involves "good governance based on the rule of law, human rights, and civil liberties; a free-market economy; pluralistic democracy; and above all, socio-cultural changes and acceptance of new values and responsibilities across the board." According to the article, the essence of state-building is "the concept of good governance and good society." The essence of good society is "free market and pluralistic democracy." The vehicle to a good society is civil society. The civil society is everyone who agrees to listen to the international community. The civil society must be educated by the international community. The international community includes "governments, international organizations, non-governmental organizations, development and aid projects, etc." and "is facing the challenge of transforming itself in accordance with the requirements of different countries" transformation processes." For these processes to work we need a strong state: "a strong state is essential to the success of the liberal-democratic project in the developing world," as Francis Fukuyama notes in his *State-Building: Governance and World Order in the 21st Century*. The author of the mentioned article, state-architect Pajic, who served as a senior legal adviser to the International Crisis Group's Bosnia office, is a fan of Tolstoy: "the opening sentence of *Anna Karenina* may apply to Bosnia: 'All happy families are alike, but an unhappy family is unhappy after its own fashion.'" He proceeds to ask: "What makes Bosnia different and unhappy?" A naïve native would think that it has something to do with the presence of occupying forces in his country. But this is too simple of an explanation. You might end up being called a conspiracy theorist by the *Guardian*.

According to Ian Williams from the *Guardian*, the solution for Bosnia is integration, Dostoevsky-style: "Perhaps even more responsibility rests with those at Dayton who rewarded the ethnic cleansers with control of half of Bosnia, including Srebrenica. Even though the Republika Srpska is rushing to apologize for the massacre, its very existence in the state of Bosnia and Herzegovina enshrines the apartheid principles of the ethnic cleansers. It is well past time to revisit the whole ramshackle arrangement, and integrate the country."

If the state-building project for Bosnia is integration, it is a supervised independence project for Kosovo. Kosovo, which according to Timothy Garton Ash is not under occupation but in limbo, needs to be independent, not because this is just or legal, but (according to state-architect Paddy Ashdown on

BBC) for ethical reasons, as "Serbia has lost it's moral rights to rule Kosovo." According to Garton Ash, the best way is to accept the Ahtisaari plan—the one that both the Serbs and Albanians reject and about which Kosovo's Roma are never asked:

> Martti Ahtisaari, the UN secretary general's special envoy for the future of Kosovo, has come up with an impressive set of proposals for moving out of limbo. His plan may not actually use the word independence, but everyone understands that it would give Kosovo independence. However, this independence would be supervised and constrained by a so-called International Civilian Representative, and backed up by an international military presence.

Revolution will be televised, independence supervised, and everything will be advertised (in the *Guardian*!).

One of the reasons for concern and widespread attention in the mainstream media for my troubled region is the recent ruling of the International Court on Justice (ICJ) that Serbia (those savages again!) is not responsible for the 1995 massacre in Srebrenica. This "unbelievable ruling" caused quite a bit of consternation among latte-sipping Western humanists. This is from a recent *Chicago Tribune* editorial: "under the international court's ruling, Serbia has escaped the stigma of genocide and been relieved of financial obligation for the killings. The court pointedly did not absolve Serbia of political and moral responsibility, but it's ruling is a disappointment. Many Serbs are, and will remain, in denial about the atrocities committed on their doorstep." According to state-architect Antonio Cassese (former president of the International Crime Tribunal for former Yugoslavia), in his article for Italian *La Republica*, this is a legal genocide. Let's hear from state-architect Ian Williams again:

> Judging from the behavior of Serb nationalist politicians and those who vote for them, there is only

a slender likelihood of acknowledgement, let alone contrition, from a disturbingly large proportion of the population ... The ICJ judgment on Serbia's role in the Bosnian genocide was, as the diverse comments on this site have shown, confusing. Its demand for proof of clear instructions from Belgrade to the perpetrators of "acts of genocide," would have exonerated Adolf Hitler from the Holocaust—the event that inspired the genocide convention.

Let's bomb the fuckers again. It is interesting that Walter J. Rockler, a prosecutor at the Nuremburg war crimes trials, takes a very different position from the EU-humanitarians and state-architects:

The [1999] attack on Yugoslavia constitutes the most brazen act of international aggression since the Nazis attacked Poland to prevent "Polish atrocities" against Germans. The United States has discarded pretensions to international legality and decency. And embarked on a course of raw imperialism run amok ... In reality, when we the self-appointed rulers of the planet, issue an ultimatum to another country it is "surrender or die." To maintain our "credibility" we must crush any resemblance of resistance to our dictate, to that country.

In other words, what needs to be done is to prevent the spread of "balkanization." In the conclusion of his *Guardian* musings on desirability of Kosovo's independence, state-architect Garton Ash, between a few sips of latte, expresses an exciting viewpoint:

Kosovo is many things to many people ... Tell me your Kosovo and I will tell you who you are ... Whatever else it is or was, Kosovo is today a small but vital challenge to the international community in general and the EU in particular ... The EU now needs to be clear, united, forceful and strategic—four things it

usually fails to be beyond its own borders ... If ever
there was an issue which brings together European
values ... The way forward for Kosovo is not nation
building or even state-building, but member-state-
building ... Because only then will peace be secured
in the Balkans and Europe be whole and free. As it
approaches its 50th birthday this March, the European
economic community that became a union has an
extraordinary story to tell about the spread of peace,
freedom and the rule of law.

If this is your Kosovo, then you are a serious EU-intellectual.

European values are so complicated. I have just learned
what state-building is, and now I have to grasp the concepts
of nation-building and member-state-building. But, unlike
Garton Ash, I don't believe that the solution is to get "the
Balkans into Europe." Quite on the contrary, I think that we
need to get Europe into the Balkans. As soon as possible.
Together with the Yugoslav avant-garde artist Ljubomir Mićić,
I believe in the need of the "Balkanization of Europe." Mićić,
the editor and critic around whom the expressionist movement of "Zenitism" coalesced in the 1920s, created a concept
of "Barbaro-Genius Decivilizer," which proposed the Balkans
as a point of origin for a new kind of civilization. The mission
of the Balkan "barbaro-genius" is to oppose and overcome, to
"balkanize" its decadent Western other:

> European culture is cruel and cannibalistic. That is
> why Zenitists work on the balkanisation of Europe
> and want to expand ... to all the continents in the
> name of the new barbarism, in the name of new
> people and new continents, in the name of a terrible
> struggle: East vs. West! The Balkan peninsula is a
> cradle of pure barbarism, which preaches a new
> brotherhood of men. That is the idea of our new
> culture and new civilization, which will come of a
> final clash between two old giants, the East and the
> West, whose urge to fight each other is in their blood.

It is an ingenious and typically Balkan-cosmopolitan attempt to destroy what probably is the oldest dichotomy inherent to European universalism—the one between civilizers and savages—and to offer an alternative as old as the Balkans itself to nationalism, colonialism, and capitalism. In this idea, Balkan people need to find the strength and orientation for a new politics for another Balkans. It should be a politics of a Balkan Federation: a participatory society built from the bottom up through struggles for the creation of an inclusive democratic awareness, participatory social experiments, and an emancipatory practice that would win the political imagination of all people in the region. It is a politics that says unequivocally to the European Union and its state-architects in Bosnia and Kosovo: get the hell out of here!

The Americans Are Coming!

December 2007

On the eve of Condoleezza Rice's visit to Romania, the foreign minister of that country was in a great emotional state, almost in tears, as he emphasized the global and historical significance of the visit in lyrical terms: "That which our grandparents and parents have been waiting for sixty years, and which hundreds of prisoners hoped for back in the time of communism, is now happening: the Americans are coming!"

And they have indeed arrived.

It looked like an imitation of Guantanamo, recalls Alvaro Gil Robles, the human rights commissioner for the Council of Europe. In the largest military base in the Balkans and in Europe, camp Bondsteel in Kosovo, Robles saw between fifteen and twenty prisoners. All of them were dressed in orange suits. An American soldier who was on the base told him that the prisoners had been sent from Guantanamo to Kosovo. The visit of the Human Rights Commissioner Robles to Bondsteel, that "little Guantanamo," as he called it in his report, took place three years ago. The report, however, remained almost unnoticed until a few weeks ago, when the CIA's secret prisons in Eastern Europe became international news. Since then, there has been talk in the mainstream European press not only of Bondsteel but also of Tuzla and other places in Bosnia-Herzegovina. The spokesman of the American forces in Kosovo rebuffed such charges, saying, "We have no secret prisons here." Robles does not deny this. Because, as he says, the prison was public. In an interview given to the magazine *Der Spiegel*, he says, "There was no attempt to hide anything or hush anything up. Everyone knew what was going on in Camp Bondsteel." Nice.

This has been confirmed by the Red Cross. This year, the Red Cross has made only one inspection of the prison at Bondsteel. Over the course of 2002, however, the organization had made all of fourteen visits to Bondsteel. The Red Cross did not publish the results of the prison inspections. But, as the spokesman of the Red Cross has said, "We can start with the fact that our team saw what Robles saw at Bondsteel."

What, exactly, did Robles see? In the interview cited above, he says that he really did see prisoners over there who were in a situation

> which you would absolutely recognize from
> photographs of Guantanamo … prisoners were
> housed in little wooden huts, some individually, some
> in pairs or threes. Each hut was surrounded by barbed
> wire. Guards were patrolling between them. Around
> all of this was a high wall with watchtowers … At the
> time of my visit there were fifteen prisoners. Most of
> them were Kosovo Albanians or Serbs, and there were
> four or five North Africans. Some of them wore beards
> and read the Koran … Because these people had been
> arrested by the army they had not had any recourse
> to the judicial system. They had no lawyers … I wrote
> in my report: this is no longer acceptable. We must
> introduce democratic standards, based on the rule of
> law.

Courageous. But where is this Bondsteel? Camp Bondsteel is situated in the Balkans, according to *The Economist*, that "most savage and least stable corner of Europe," close to the small Kosovo town of Urosevac. Let's be reminded that Kosovo was liberated by NATO troops in a humanitarian operation which according to *Financial Times* "forced the Serbs to reject a regime of genocide and domination," and which caused 1,800 civilian casualties along the way. The liberators" first humanitarian gift to the local population was the construction of a base that is considered the largest U.S. military base built on foreign soil since the Vietnam War. It covers over 320 hectares of land. About four thousand American soldiers live there; they enjoy the use of a library, news kiosk, a beauty salon, a Burger King, and a few churches. On November 29, a darts tournament was held there.

This military base is a symbol of American humanitarian interests in the Balkans, what The Economist has called "Europe's last dirty backyard." It is situated directly over the future oil and gas lines which, according to plan, ought to lead from the Bulgarian port Burgas—now an American base where, it is suspected, "terrorist interrogations" of the not-so-legal variety have also taken place—through Macedonia and Kosovo, all the way to Valona on the Albanian Adriatic coastline. The study for this plan was made by the company Halliburton (formerly run by American Vice President Dick Cheney), which—surprise, surprise!—also built Camp Bondsteel.

So it is here in liberated Kosovo (on whose independence the U.S. government insists for unknown reasons) that, according to Robles and other witnesses, one of the "illegal" prisons can be found—in point of fact, a CIA prison for "humanitarian interrogations."

It is very likely that camp Bondsteel isn't the only site for torture ("humanitarian interrogation") in the former Yugoslavia. According to the magazine *Neues Deutschland*, soon after the NATO humanitarian troops liberated Bosnia-Herzegovina from its own citizens, rumors began to circulate that American soldiers were interrogating prisoners from "Arab states" (those who, with American aid, had come to Bosnia to fight on the side of the Bosnian Muslims), imprisoning them and, if needs be, allowing them to disappear. The sources of the German paper warn of the significance of the American camp next to the town of Tuzla, which provided a sort of model for the construction of Bondsteel in Kosovo. The camp in Tuzla is logistically better connected than the one in Kosovo, for it is here that American Boeing 737 aircraft, which the CIA uses to transport prisoners, can make a landing. It is not certain whether some of the American "Hercules" planes or the C-17 transporters that fly into and out of Bosnia on a daily basis also carry within them the prisoners of the new global democracy.

It's worth recalling that during the 1990s, a decision was made within American intelligence circles to form a special national intelligence team (NIST). In addition to CIA members, it contains specialists of the Pentagon's secret service DIA, NSA and NIMA. NIST is in Saudi Arabia, Somalia, Kenya, Israel, Zaire, as well as in different regions of the Balkans that are under American control. Thus, in Tuzla, there exists a unique bureau for cooperation of the American services. In Tuzla, there is also a rather long runway that offers all the conveniences that long runways usually offer to large aircraft; it also allows members of the secret services to act within a legal framework, in humanitarian fashion, and in the interest of the Bosnian citizenry when "unloading the disappeared," and instruct them in the ways of the new global democracy without breaking U.S. law.

As part of "friendly cooperation" U.S. services have constructed special centers for the fight against terrorism in more than twenty states. The model for these centers, known in abbreviated form as CTICs, were the bases which had been formed over the past few decades in South American state-protectorates as part of the U.S. war on drugs. In true cosmopolitan fashion, use was made of the experience of French torture squads that had offered lessons in democracy in Algiers. It is suspected that more than three thousand people have been "handed over" to CTICs, as the deputy CIA director for "operations abroad" recently hinted. The prisoners, who have been declared terrorists, are brought in by extralegal means.

All this, however, did not sway the democratic fervor of the Romanian minister with which I began my commentary. Upon the arrival of Rice in Romania, a member of "the coalition of the willing," the elated foreign minister signed a treaty (of course a bilateral one) on the regulation of a "permanent American military presence" on Romanian soil. Romanian dissidents and social movements were also "very excited," though for other reasons: this treaty allows the U.S. government to build and maintain military strongholds on the shores of the Black Sea. Relations between the states of Romania and America have been characterized as a "strategic partnership; Until now "no other state of the former Warsaw Pact has made such a treaty with the U.S.." A historic achievement indeed.

The withdrawal of the Romanian contingent (which numbers about a thousand) from Iraq and Afghanistan is not a topic discussed in Bucharest. It remains unclear whether the hospitable Romanian hosts have asked Condoleezza Rice for an explanation regarding "the unauthorized prison detentions of those suspected of Al-Qaeda membership" on the Mihail Kogălniceanu base near Konstanca. Ten days ago, the Council of Europe requested an investigation from Romania with regard to these charges and, according to *Neue Zürcher Zeitung*, threatened "serious consequences in the event that the allegations should prove true." Rice and the Romanian president didn't appear too perturbed. After the signing of the agreement, they offered no less than an exciting redefinition of the concept of democracy: the essence of the democratic process, at the time of "our" war against the invisible and ubiquitous terror, is reflected in the cooperation of secret services.

Even so, the Romanian president denies the existence of secret prisons perhaps because, as in the case of Kosovo, they are in fact public. At the same time, he indirectly confirmed that the landings of American planes (planes that perhaps have been used for the transport of prisoners) had taken place. Such landings will continue in the future, stressed the Romanian president with a glimmer of pride.

One gets the impression that the Bulgarian government—yet another member of the club of what Rice has called "young democracies"—is jealous of its Romanian neighbor's democratic success (not to mention of Poland's, whom the U.S. president has called "our biggest friend in Europe.") The military cooperation of the U.S. and the "young Bulgarian democracy" is no secret. During its operations in Iraq and Afghanistan, the American military has used the bases in Sarafov and in the vicinity of Burgas, the second biggest port on the Black Sea. When it comes to the stationing of American soldiers in this young democracy, two locations are most frequently mentioned: the military base Novo Selo in the east of the country and the Besmer airport. More and more often, there is mention of the strategically highly important port of Burgas. The U.S. financial "support" of Bulgarian-American "friendship" is very profitable, for both the military and civilian sectors. After this summer's floods, the Bulgarian government received American aid in the amount of a million dollars. And although the Bulgarian government announced a planned withdrawal from Iraq at the beginning of next year, it simultaneously announced a planned enlargement of its forces in Afghanistan. As Vienna's *Die Presse* reports, accounts of alleged secret CIA prisons in Bulgaria have led the Bulgarian president to confess that an investigation into such activity is indeed under way, as is the one about "possible fly-overs" by CIA planes over Bulgaria.

Rice also managed to find time for a visit to Germany. There, she made the acquaintance of Chancellor Angela Merkel, that "highly intelligent woman ... who is so committed to a Europe that is whole and free and at peace." Although we can agree with Rice that Europe is not free, this statement nevertheless comes as something of a surprise. It is evident that Rice is talking about a new political concept of "the new democracy": the global form of power in which the cooperation between states" secret services holds the most important place.

In her statements to ARD and *Deutsche Welle*, Rice maintains that speculations about secret CIA prisons in Poland, Bulgaria, and Romania (she did not mention Bosnia and

Kosovo) are only a "product of a misunderstanding." "The U.S.," said Rice, "is only fulfilling the first and most basic obligation of any state—to protect its own citizens." Apparently, from themselves. For when asked who the adversary is, Rice responded: "I would hope to remind everyone that we are partners together in this very difficult war on terror, a war in which the terrorists live among us and which they clearly are determined to kill innocent civilians. Now, that was a wedding party in Amman. It was a railway stop, a traffic stop in London and in Madrid. They go to hotels and blow up innocent people. So we're dealing with a different kind of war ..." For which, evidently, we need a different type of democracy, too.

Rice then offered an anthropological appreciation of terrorism that, in addition to her legal and philosophical talents, revealed the touch of a poet within her: "The terrorists have no regard for innocent life. The terrorists live in a lawless and law-free society. They live in a world that crosses these boundaries in shadowy ways. They're stateless in a sense." Truly, is there anything sadder than a "person without a state," unaware of "the many challenges that we face in these quite historic times"?

As Rice said: "We don't condone torture. We are determined to do everything that we can to protect our citizens but within a lawful framework." This, also, is the essence of democracy: "And so when these difficult issues come up, I would hope that we all go back to the fact that we share common values in our struggle. We are always willing to engage in the discussion and debate within democratic societies. It's only healthy that we do." Of course.

And so, the war against terrorism opens up a new global/historical panorama in which so-called democratic societies are in conflict with so-called undemocratic societies, or "failed states." Legal obligations that prevail in democratic societies do not prevail in the failed ones. Somewhere in between those two definitions, in the Balkans and in Eastern Europe, there exist "young democracies" and "states in construction." In these regions, international law applies only to a certain extent. Yet even in democratic states, given that "the nature of war has changed" and "terrorists now live among us" (in the old Eastern Europe, this used to be called informing on your neighbor), there is a tension which requires that the legal framework be periodically shrunk whenever a "state reason" demands, so that the state can protect "its own citizens"—if needs be, against their will—from themselves.

With a crusader's sigh, Rice says: "we are fighting an enemy that is ruthless, that if we don't use intelligence before the fact, if we don't get intelligence ... the sad fact is that the terrorists have the upper hand ... In order to stop them, we need good intelligence, we need good intelligence cooperation."

This, then, is the definition of a new global democracy. Intelligence cooperation. The torture of prisoners arrested in the "black sites" of Eastern Europe. Torture in the name of democracy. Occupation in the name of freedom. Bombing in the name of humanitarian intervention. Protectorates in the name of state-building. Wars of terror in the name of a war on terror. Is this really what "those hundreds of prisoners hoped for back in the time of communism?"

Kosovo: A New War in the Balkans? From Supervised Independence to Unsupervised Violence

December 2007

I have been receiving a lot of emails recently, asking if there is going to be another war in Kosovo. This commentary is an attempt to respond to these inquires. What are the latest developments regarding the future of Kosovo? According to the BBC, mediators in talks between Kosovo and Serbia have concluded that no agreement can be reached on Kosovo's final status ahead of a UN deadline of December 10. Who are these mediators? The mainstream media call them the "troika': European Union, United States, and Russia. After 120 days of deciding the fate of the Serbian, Albanian and Roma people who live in Kosovo, the "troika" was "unable to break a deal" and solve the "looming Kosovo crisis." Kosovo, to remind readers, is still a Serbian province, at least under international law. It was "liberated" in 1999, in the course of "NATO's first war," a humanitarian intervention whose aim was to promote democracy in this semi-barbaric part of the world, sometimes referred to as "Wild Europe" by its civilized Western European neighbors. The newly established democracy is a colonial protectorate hosting American military basis and Guantanamo-like prisons used for interrogation purposes in the "War of Terror." The remaining Serbs and Roma are being periodically "cleansed," and pushed to remote enclaves. Roma, for the most part, live in camps built on contaminated ground. The colonial government removed the Roma from three refugee camps built on toxic wasteland only to relocate them to a camp in north Mitrovica, abandoned by the French because of the lead poisoning. They live in fear, waiting for the next move of the Albanian government.

The newly elected Albanian government of Hashim Thaçi (war criminal of UCK/KLA fame, and one of the leading members of the Kosovo criminal cartel) has threatened to declare independence unilaterally after the UN deadline. Thaçi's threats are supported by the statements of the governments of the United States, Britain, Germany, France, and Italy, insisting that the international community (and this community is truly international, as it embodies international people outside of Kosovo who are deciding the lives of people of Kosovo) "must honor its responsibilities to Kosovo." Russian Foreign Minister Sergey Lavrov has accused his negotiation partners of impatience: "Regrettably, our Western partners are blocking such [talks] by saying that Kosovo's independence is unavoidable." NATO spokesman James Appathurai is tired of talking: "the NATO point of view is ... that the process should now move—that there needs to be movement towards resolution." Lt. Col. Dave Grossman of Kosovo Force (KFOR) says that "NATO will stay here as long as it is needed, and as long as the international community sees it as a proper means to put out this conflict." NATO as a proper means of putting out the conflict? In his reaction to these "proper means," Aleksandar Simić, an advisor to Serbia's Prime Minister Vojislav Koštunica "told the Belgrade media that Serbia had the legal right to use war as a means of defending its territory if Kosovo declares independence." This made His Excellency Wolfgang Ischinger, the European member of the "troika," very angry and upset. How dare Simić! His Excellency told the reporters that he believes that, "it is inadmissible and intolerable that even before the troika report is out one of the parties expresses himself in this way." Interestingly enough, he did not find it "inadmissible and intolerable" for the envoys of the international community and NATO to say, even before the "troika" report is out, that the independence of Kosovo is "imminent."

Nor did he mention Thaçi, who has assured the European Union and Washington that he, impulsive as he is, changed his mind and that he will wait and declare independence after some more meetings of the international community, but not later then early in the new year.

Kosovo's Albanian President Fatmir Sejdiu also said that independence for Kosovo "will happen very quickly" but refused to give an exact date. Colonial governor of Kosovo Joachim Rücker is certain that "the people of Kosovo have enough maturity to let international mechanisms work." By these international mechanisms, he probably means the forth-coming European Union summit in Brussels on December 14, expected to send a signal of support to Kosovo from a majority of the EU states. It is also probable that Serbia will be offered a "carrot': a promise that, one day, it will be permitted to join the European Union. It is also safe to say that as soon as this declaration is issued, Serbs and Roma from the "Serbian north" of Kosovo, as well as enclaves in the center and south of the region, are going to be attacked. A new circle of ethnic vio-lence will ensue, and Kosovo, "the crucible of Europe's most divisive conflict in recent memory," will explode into a full-blown regional conflict. In a recent report, the International Crisis Group, which is strongly in favor of Kosovo's independ-ence, expressed concern over possible "unsupervised, possi-bly violent, independence process." It is important to note that the independence being promised to Kosovo's Albanians is a supervised independence, meaning that this independ-ence given to the Albanians would be supervised and con-strained by a so-called International Civilian Representative, and backed by a strong international military presence (this was, in more honest times, called occupation).

And so, the only answer I can give to the question whether or not there is going to be another war between NATO and Serbia, and between Kosovo's Albanians and Kosovo's minor-ities, is yes. There will be another war. If the "international community," with its army and its colonial apparatus, does not leave Albanians, Serbs and Roma to decide their future for themselves, the war (or, in the least, "localized" and internationally supervised violence and another wave of ethnic cleansing of Serbs and Roma) will be inevitable. The only chance for peace in the Balkans is the end of the occupation of the Balkans, in Kosovo as well as in Bosnia. European and American gentlemen, international "humanitarian" NGOs, dear concerned members of the international community, please leave. And don't forget to take the BBC journalists with you.

Kosovo's Unworthy Victims:
An Interview with Paul Polansky

May 1, 2007

In its rush to proclaim a supervised independence for the "embattled and violent" region of Kosovo, the international capitalist community is ignoring and covering up a tragedy of Roma people in this colonized region, a tragedy for which the community in itself is responsible. If there is one point where Albanian nationalists ("independence and mono-ethnic self-determination"), Serbian nationalists ("autonomy without independence") and Euro-colonialists ("supervised independence without an autonomy") are in any kind of an agreement, it is the systematic disregard for the Roma or Gypsy population in Kosovo. We can read all kinds of concerns about "human rights" in Kosovo, as exemplified in the recent statement of the under secretary Nicholas Burns before the House Committee on Foreign Affairs, but absolutely nothing about the horrific fact that in three camps built by the UN High Commission for Refugees, where some sixty Gypsy children under the age of six have been exposed to such high levels of lead that they are highly likely to die soon or to suffer irreversible brain damage. This number represents every child born in the camps since they were built five and a half years ago. This continues to be non-news, the same way Roma continue to be the so-called unworthy victims of Kosovo's colonial nightmare. It is for this reason that the Freedom Fight collective from Serbia has prepared a short interview-commentary with Paul Polansky. Paul is one of the most important contemporary writers and activists concerning the hidden and suppressed history and reality of the Eastern European Roma. He is the head of mission of Kosovo Roma Refugee Foundation. In his poetry collections *Living Through It Twice, The River Killed My Brother*, and *Not a Refugee*, Polansky delineates a painful history of the atrocities of Czechs, Slovaks, Albanians, NATO, and the UN against the Roma. His books on Kosovo's Roma include *Blackbirds of Kosovo, UN-Leaded Blood* as well as forthcoming oral history of Yugoslav Gypsy survivors of Nazi German and Nazi Croatian concentration camps.

AG: Roma people are Europe's most marginalized and oppressed citizens. Could you tell us: is there any significant differences in life circumstances between Kosovo's Roma and Roma people in other European countries in which have you lived, for example, in Czechoslovakia? How were Roma treated in Europe during crises like World War II, for example? What is the main reason for persistent anti-Gypsyism?
PP: This is a long question (many questions in fact) and I could easily write a book about each one. Probably most of these questions will be answered in depth by the Roma themselves when I published my collection of oral histories of World War II Yugoslav Gypsy survivors. I've filmed 152 interviews from all over the former Yugoslavia. In their own words, the Gypsies suffered a great deal during the war but basically weren't targeted like the Jews. The Gypsies were murdered in several camps such as Jasenovac and in Belgrade but not all were killed and in most places they survived although able-bodied Roma were taken to work camps and many Romani women were raped. But in most places like Niš, the Romani population survived intact while the Jewish population was totally liquidated. The same thing happened to Roma throughout Europe. In some places such as Bohemia and Moravia, the Roma were decimated, but in other places such as Slovakia, 90 percent of the Romani pop-

ulation survived. Regarding differences in their lives, the further west you go the better off Roma are, having integrated more [there] than in Eastern Europe. That integration, of course, has caused some setbacks. Most Roma in Czech republic no longer speak Romanes [sic] and have forgotten most of their traditions.

AG: According to the last official statistics, Roma people comprised 2.3 percent of the population of Kosovo. Is there any data as to how many of them have been killed, how many have disappeared and how many of them have run away? How many Roma now live in Kosovo? Has anything in last eight years really been done for the return of the Kosovo Roma to their houses? In what circumstances do those Roma who remained in Kosovo live?

PP: I have lived in Kosovo since July 1999. From July to November 1999, I did the only survey ever made of all the Gypsy communities in Kosovo including Roma, Ashkali, and Egyptian Gypsies. I found that before the 1999 NATO bombing, there were 298 Gypsy communities (*mahalas*), with about 17,500 homes and a population of about 120,000 Gypsies. By the time I finished my survey, I counted a population of only 30,000 Gypsies (10,000 Roma and 20,000 Ashkali/Egyptians) still in Kosovo. About 14,500 homes had been destroyed by the returning Albanians after NATO troops had arrived. Since then, the Gypsy population has probably dropped to about 20,000 (6,000 Roma and 14,000 Ashkali/ Egyptian). Very few of the 14,500 destroyed homes have been rebuilt, probably less than 300. Not many Roma were killed, probably fewer than 1,000. Most ran away: the majority to German and Italy, and some to Serbia, Montenegro, and Macedonia. Those who remain are continually harassed by the local Albanians. No Roma were allowed to return to the jobs they had before the war. I predict that when there is independence in Kosovo, most Roma will flee to Serbia or Germany if they can afford to pay a smuggler. Ashkali and Egyptians will try to live with the Albanians but in time, they too will have to leave, as will most minorities except the Turks. Despite what their politicians say, most Albanians don't like the minorities and their long-term goal is to have a pure ethnic Albanian state.

AG: How are they treated by international aid agencies? In your book *UN-Leaded Blood*, you have stated that the UN built refugee camps on toxic wasteland. Who is responsible for that? Are those camps still there? Does anybody care?
PP: The international aid agencies in Kosovo are mainly in the hands of the Albanians. The few internationals still there are very pro-Albanian, because of course they are influenced by their Albanian staff. An example is the Swiss government office in Pristina. For eight years, the Swiss office has not hired any minority staff because the [members of] its Albanian staff have stated they will not work with any minority. UNMIK [United Nations Interim Administration Mission in Kosovo] removed the Gypsies from the three refugee camps built on toxic wasteland but relocated them to a former French camp in north Mitrovica abandoned by the French because of the lead poisoning. The French military doctors told all soldiers serving there not to father a child for nine months after leaving the camp. The Gypsies of course have not been given this warning; their wives are still aborting and those Gypsy kids born in the camp have irreversible brain damage. I took a family of eight to Germany for medical treatment. All had irreversible brain damage and organ damage. One seven-year-old kid had the liver of a fifty-year-old alcoholic. The German doctors told me these kids wouldn't live beyond twenty-five or thirty years. UNMIK was warned in 2000 by the World Health Organization to evacuate these Gypsy refugee camps. They didn't and now we have lost an entire generation of Gypsy kids.

AG: What do you say to the fact that the exodus of the non-Albanians and Roma people continued now to a greater degree then when international peacekeepers arrived? Who

made Roma people escape from Kosovo? Serbs, Albanians, NATO, or all of them?

PP: As stated above, the Gypsies were forced to leave by returning Albanians. NATO troops just stood by and watched saying they were not a police force, that they were there to protect the Albanians, no one else. I had many disagreements with KFOR forces in the summer of 1999 as I tried to get them to stop arsonists. British KFOR even detained me for protesting about Gypsy and Serb homes being burned down in front of their eyes.

AG: What is the future of the relations between Albanians and Serbs with Roma people in Kosovo? What is the future of the Roma culture of peace and tolerance in violent surroundings?

PP: In my opinion, there is no future in Kosovo for any minority except the Turks. Most Roma have already left. Their new country is Germany. About thirty-five thousand Kosovo Roma live today in Germany. If they are not deported, that will be their new country. If they are deported, they will have a very hard time surviving anywhere else.

AG: What would be better for Roma people, an independent Kosovo or not?

PP: Roma will not stay in an independent Kosovo. They don't want their kids to go to Albanian schools or serve in an Albanian army. They can't get jobs in Albanian companies, so of course they will leave.

AG: Why did you choose to live in Knez Selo, near Niš? Is there something special about that village?

PP: Yes, the air, the wonderful countryside. It's like Tuscany a hundred years ago. The village people are also very friendly. It's a nice quiet place to write and when I am not writing, I have a wonderful garden to look after.

AG: Tell us something about the new books you are writing.

PP: My next book is called *Gypsy Taxi*. [It's] poems about the origins, the traditions and the plight of the Kosovo Roma. It is 226 pages with illustrations and is bilingual in English and Serbian. It should be out in the next month. Then, this year, I also hope to publish my collection of oral histories of World War II Yugoslav Gypsies; their stories tell about their lives before, during and after World War II. Each interview was about an hour long and filmed. It will probably be published in four volumes since as a single book it is already up to 1,200 pages and I haven't finished it yet.

AG: Günter Grass gave you the Reward for Human Rights in Weimar in 2003. How would you comment on his recent testimony that he was a part of SS troops when he was seventeen?
PP: He was very frank about his past. He is a wonderful man and should be judged on what he does for other people. He has long fought for minority rights in Germany, especially for Roma. We all make mistakes in life, but not everyone confronts his mistakes. Grass did and he should be congratulated on drawing attention to his past.

AG: What have you learned from contact with Roma people? What do you think about their culture and life habits?
PP: I've spent fifteen years living with Roma and collecting their oral histories, and observing their customs, traditions and researching their origins. In the beginning, I thought that not many of their traditions from old India survived, but each day I find [them], especially when I visit the outcast tribes in India and discover the same traditions that many Roma especially in the Balkans still practice. The European Roma basically come from the Dom tribe in India and their sub-castes were Lohar, Sansi, Kikan, and Kanjar. But they did not come as one people or at one time. Today, people (even scholars) have lumped all Roma, all Gypsies, into one basket calling them all Roma. They came as many different groups from India with many different traditions and customs. They had different dialects, even different languages, and most did not intermarry and still don't. We must see them as part of the Indian Diaspora that covered several centuries. One tribe, the

Kikans even had their origins in Kurdistan before going to India in the 10th century. There in Punjab, they mixed with the Sansis before going back to Turkey in the 13th century. I have many DNA samples showing these tribal affiliations. Tribal DNA now shows where many people started from and where they went. The origin of our European Gypsies is no longer in dispute. Even the DNA on Balkan Egyptians shows they came from India; they have no Egyptian DNA.

Caligula's Horse: U.S., "New" Europe, and Kosovo
With Ziga Vodovnik

February 2008

Ancient historian Suetonius, in his *The Lives of Twelve Caesars*, writes about the attempt of the infamous Roman emperor Caligula to make his favorite horse, Incitatus, ("Speedy") a consul. American Empire has advanced this animal-friendly project by appointing not one horse but a whole stable. The name of this stable is "new" Europe. As in the case of the third emperor of the Roman Empire, the reason for lavishing horses with consular honor has more to do with imperial arrogance then insanity. Just like Caligula's treatment of Incitatus was a way of angering the Senate, "new" Europe is a way of ridiculing the European Union. This essay is devoted to one particular horse in the stable of "new" Europe, the state of Slovenia, and to the recent "Slovenian diplomatic scandal" which, as we contend, is not so much a scandal as it is a model. This essay has a twofold purpose. First, we intend to alert the international Left to the nature of American and European colonial politics in the light of the construction of, and manipulation with, the political project of "new" Europe. Second, we wish to invite the Balkan Left to define a politics of balkanization, a politics that would challenge both the imperialist and nationalist scenario for the Balkans.

Let us start with the "Slovenian scandal," which we recognize as a new colonial model. In one of our previous articles, we suggested a possible explanation of the nature of

American interests in the Balkans. We believe that our conclusions are further confirmed by the events in Slovenia,
which, to remind our readers, today holds presidency of the
European Union. European leaders woke up to an unpleasant surprise the other day, a leak of an internal document of
Slovenian Ministry of Foreign Affairs (MZZ). This document,
published in the Slovenian daily *Dnevnik* and the Serbian daily
Politika, reveals content of a meeting between representatives
of MZZ and representatives of the U.S. State Department and
National Security Agency (NSA) that took place on December
24, 2007, in Washington D.C. Slovenia's willful following of
various exotic orders coming not from Brussels (the Senate)
but from across the Atlantic (the emperor), is already a well-
known fact in the diplomatic hallways of Europe. But recent
developments directly connected with orders and promises
that were revealed in this leaked document, can mean the
final transfer of our horse to the stable of "new" Europe," a
group of states whose foreign policy is dictated by servile obedience to the United States. This, of course, also means the
official end to all illusions about the credibility and importance of the Slovenian presidency in the European Union.

Stubborn pursuit of U.S. interests, or those of the political and economic integration of which it is a part, is already
a constant of Slovenian foreign policy, or, rather its foreign minister, who personalizes and usurps it to a point
that exceeds levels of good taste, not to mention old fash-
ioned democratic standards. We remember his—and hence,
Slovenian—support of the Vilnius Declaration, which meant
"new" Europe's full support for U.S. intervention in Iraq. His
recent moves, of which we are going to mentioned only a few,
are in the same vein: public statements about the need for
immediate and unconditional independence of the Serbian
province of Kosovo; full support of Kosovo's Prime Minister
Hashim Thaçi, war criminal of repute and former leader of
the Kosovo Liberation Army (with a colorful *nom de guerre*,
Gjarpni, the Snake); recent lobbying at the International
Criminal Court for former Yugoslavia, to abandon its pressure

on officials in Belgrade to gain their full-cooperation in locating Radovan Karadžić and Ratko Mladić. All those actions, for which Slovenian Minister of Foreign Affairs does not have a mandate, gained a very clear context with the document that leaked from the Slovenian administration a few days ago—as an attempt to follow and realize the U.S. political interests in the Balkans.

The document, with the official markings VWA070767, reveals that the main topic of the meeting between high officials from Slovenian administration, the State Department, and NSA, has been Slovenia's role during its presidency of the European Union in organizing support for international recognition of Kosovo's unilateral declaration of independence. But the document also reveals other very important and interesting facts about the U.S. involvement in, and planned actions concerned with, the future status of Kosovo. The document that in recent days circulated also on the internet reveals, *inter alia*, that:

• The United States suggests that the session of Kosovo's parliament, when they would declare independence of the province, should be held on a Sunday, so the Russian Federation would not be able to call an emergency session of the U.N. Security Council;

• The United States proposes the European Union ignore any complaints and proposals from Serbia and the Russian Federation; the U.S. estimates that the independence of Kosovo will not gain full support of the European Union (only fifteen of twenty-seven countries). Therefore the support of Slovenia as the Presiding country over the European Union is crucial;

• The United States plans to avoid giving public statements about the future status of Kosovo in the coming days, but will be among the first to officially recognize Kosovo's independence;

• The United States estimates that it is of utmost importance to convince as many states as possible to officially recognize an independent Kosovo in the first few days after the declaration of its independence, and for this reason, the United States is intensively lobbying Japan, Turkey, and the Arab states, who have already shown willingness to support Kosovo without hesitation;

• The United States is currently helping the Kosovo Albanians draft their new constitution;

For understandable reasons, this document is in itself a serious international scandal. The reactions from the mainstream press and EU officials are unanimous in calling it a spectacular blunder. It clarifies, to the point of truism, the intended role of the "new" Europe in American imperial design. It provides us with irrefutable evidence of American meddling in the affairs of the EU. More importantly, it discloses the true nature of U.S. politics of humanitarian intervention (which we propose calling humanitarian imperialism). The document casts a very humiliating picture of the role of Slovenia, as well as other "new" European Balkan states, in the new colonial system.

We would like to point to another, local dimension of this embarrassment. This is a dimension that concerns the province of Kosovo. There appears to be a curious agreement between the U.S.-backed "new" Europe and "old" Europe, an agreement that is uncritically or unreflectively accepted by the international Left, about the acceptance, tacit or explicit, of the legitimacy of the Albanian Kosovo leadership; about the support for the independence of Kosovo; about legitimization of the form of colonial rule we term Thaçism; and, finally, about the very framework of solving the Kosovo problem on the level of great power negotiations of the so-called "troika"—i.e. European Union, United States and the Russian Federation.

We ask: is it possible to achieve the democratization of the region by supporting the Democratic Party of Kosovo (PDK), a political organization of the Kosovo Liberation Army (KLA)? Is it possible to achieve democratization of Kosovo by supporting the former KLA leader, and now prime minister, Hashim Thaçi? Are we not then supporting, instead of democratization, the continuation of the nationalist logic and a process of further ethnic cleansing of Kosovo? These are not academic questions. In March 2000, former UN special investigator for the former Yugoslavia Jiři Dienstbier reported to the UN Commission on Human Rights that "330,000 Serbs, Roma, Montenegrins, Slavic Muslims, pro-Serb Albanians and Turks had been displaced in Kosovo—double the earlier estimates. What that means is most of Kosovo's minorities no longer are in their original homes." In this respect, things have only deteriorated since Dienstbier's report was submitted. You will forgive our skepticism that Thaçi, a principal protagonist of Kosovo's flourishing industry of arms, drugs, and sex trafficking, will prevent the inevitable ethnic violence, or that he will strive for the restoration of democracy, multiculturalism, and the rule of law in the independent Kosovo.

And whose independent Kosovo is it going to be? Let us try to explain the Western fascination with Thaçism. Former special representative to the secretary general of the UN in Kosovo, Sérgio Vieira de Mello, was often quoted to complain: "Madeleine Albright is in love with Thaçi. Jamie Rubin is his best friend. It's not helpful. Thaçi arrived here with the impression that he has the full weight of the American government behind him. He believes he has earned the right to rule." In the past few years Thaçism was somewhat modified so as to answer to a different reality, but only on the superficial level of rhetoric, with more or less successful distancing from ideas of a great Kosovo and/or Albania. Meanwhile, in practice, it stayed more or less the same, with the usual mix of murders, kidnappings, and violent attempts to crackdown political opponents. But we should not overestimate Thaçi, who, as his nickname suggests, is a reptile of minor importance. Thaçi is important only as a metaphor of Thaçism, a form of colonial rule by way of support of local warlords whose job it is to destroy any inkling of anticolonial protest.

We had written about the problem of Kosovo before, and at some length. Our position, let us summarize it briefly, is that the international Left should not support the nationalist option (Serbian or Albanian), even when it is temptingly served in the guise of self-determination, and should most resolutely refuse to accept the imperialist option imposed, in a confused fashion, as evidenced in the above document, by the United States and the European Union. The whole tragic history of the Balkans is one of colonialism and resistance to Western colonialism. The so-called "troika," international community, great powers, or however they choose to call themselves, have no business in the Balkans. The form of colonialism that we have proposed to call Thaçism is indigenous to the Balkans the same way that Thatcherism was the politics of the British workers. It should not enjoy support from the international Left. More importantly, the Balkan Left has to step up to the challenge, and define a coherent and regional anticolonial politics that is in keeping with its rebellious, heretical history. The resistance is well under way. Factories in Serbia are being occupied by the workers struggling against privatization and for new definitions of the "transition." The "erased" of Slovenia are pointing ways to resistance formulated not in the name of nationality but of dignity. The Roma, persecuted, as always, are organizing against the imposed monoethnicity of Kosovo. This is our Balkans. We need a new Balkans, built from below, and we need a "new" Europe, built from below. We need to go back to the historical project of the Balkans without nations, to the project of Balkan Federation. We believe that the Kosovo question can only be answered in a regional framework, and we believe that the Balkans can provide a model for another Europe, a balkanized Europe of regions, as an alternative to both transnational European super-state and nation-states. The future of the Balkans is not in Europe. But the future of Europe is in the Balkans.

If the local political elites are happy being horses, ridden by European senators or American emperors, we should indulge them, but we need to get them another stable.

II. BALKANIZATION FROM BELOW

Introduction

According to the Romanian historian Nicolas Iorga, there is, in the Balkans, "a certain unity which is basic intimate and profound and which the superficial phenomena of discord, unfriendliness and conflict, must not hide from us."

These lines capture well the spirit of this section. We might describe balkanization from below as a tradition and narrative that affirms social and cultural affinities, as well as on customs in common resulting from interethnic mutual aid and solidarity, and resulting in what can be termed an interethnic self-activity, one that was severed through the Euro-colonial intervention. I maintain that in the Balkans this pluricultural reality finds its political expression in the anti-authoritarian politics of local self-government, communal use of the land, and various movements for Balkan Federation. The latter project included, in its most expansive and most inspiring proposal, all countries of former Yugoslavia, Albania, Bulgaria, Romania, Greece, and Turkey.

Essays collected in this section reflect the possibilities and limits of this process today, and specifically in the Serbian part of former Yugoslavia. I wish I could say that there is an abundance of revolutionary projects and multitude of exciting, utopian moments ready to capture the imagination of American militants. I am afraid that readers won't find Argentine-style horizontalists or Mexican-influenced Zapatistas in fragmented postwar Yugoslavia. What they will encounter, instead, is a sociopolitical landscape of desperation, destitution, and collective disappointment. They will meet hungry workers who lost their factories; angry students unable to afford privatized education; refugees still living in "temporary" camps; Kosovo Roma deported from Germany and other countries of the civilized world, and simply dropped in the middle of transitional poverty. An American activist who recently visited Kosovo told me that she had never been to such a place. She stood on every barricade from Oaxaca to Genoa, and in every war from Iraq to Lebanon. But she never experienced anything quite like Kosovo. This is a country of an absolute defeat, she told me. The words are well chosen. However, we cannot lose hope entirely. In the midst of this rather discouraging social scenery, one can see hazy contours of new "balkanotopian" projects and new possibilities of resistance. In the Serbian part of ex-Yugoslavia, as in the rest of the Balkans, with the remarkable exception of insurrectionary Greece, we can discern a very slow but promising awakening of resistance to the post-state socialist regimes. These scattered islands of unrest and self-activity have explicit or implicit anarchist sensibility. I find the words of Staughton Lynd, taken from our book *Wobblies and Zapatistas*, to be a very accurate observation of this development:

> Anarchist theorists write about networks of mutual aid that exist alongside the elections and the wars that seek to represent themselves as the whole of meaningful political activity. One thinks of forest ecology. Peel back the surface scatter of leaves or pine needles, and there will often be revealed dense tangles of interconnected roots from which new growth will eventually emerge. Even in societies subjected to the greatest violence—Guatemala in *la violencia* of the early 1980s or southeastern Europe in the 1990s—small projects present themselves in time, like bright green shoots emerging from a burned-over, blackened forest floor.

For such a brutalized and dismembered society, Lynd says, "an approach loosely described as anarchism may be singularly appropriate. For a time, anything beyond the small-scale is impractical and likewise, the need to begin again, even if on a small scale, is overwhelming."

I believe that this well explains the experiments the reader will encounter in the following section. The short-lived, anarchist-inspired Southeastern European Social Forum was an interesting, if failed attempt to benefit from the global social forum process, as are many similar feminist and anarchist groups and projects. These groups are undoubtedly schools and laboratories of new political thought regarding the future. Much more significant, and in many ways quite unique, is the political work of Jugoremedija factory workers and the Freedom Fight (Pokret za Sobodu) collective described here in series of conversations, and in the commentary on the return of self-management to Serbia. This is, I hope, a story that could be of possible use to American readers.

A few activists, students from Belgrade University and the core of what was to become the Freedom Fight collective, recognized that the only organized resistance to the encroaching tide of privatization and neoliberalism was coming from a group of workers in the Serbian countryside. They decided to go to northern Serbia, to a city called Zrenjanin, and approach the workers from Jugoremedija factory. These workers were very different from the activists. Some of them had fought in the recent Yugoslav wars. Most of them were very conservative, patriarchal, and traditional. The students went there and offered their skills. They had a few. They spoke foreign languages. They had internet access and know-how in a country where only 2 percent of the people used this service. They had connections with workers and movements outside Serbia. Some of them were good writers. A few had legal expertise. Workers were grateful but understandably quite skeptical, as were the activists. Soon, however, something like a friendship emerged. They started working together and learning from each other. In the process of struggle against the boss, the private armies he sent to the factory, and the state authorities, they started to trust each other. They both changed—workers and students. Today, after ten years of accompaniment, the same group of activists from the Freedom Fight collective plays an important role in the Coordinating Committee for Workers Protests in Serbia, where five Strike Committees represent workers from three cities and five branches of industry.

It was only later, as a result of my political collaboration with Staughton and Alice Lynd, that I recognized the similarity between this form of political relationship between revolutionaries and workers and the model of organic, radical community organizing they called "accompaniment."

I included in this selection my conversations with Michael Albert, American theorist of participatory economics. I am very fond of participatory economics, for several reasons. First, because of my active interest in the process of Yugoslav self-management. I believe that Yugoslav socialists' self-management, which should, perhaps, be called co-management, still awaits a careful libertarian examination. It was, in many ways, a typical Balkan medley: an encounter of local institutions and traditions with a number of libertarian forms, stretching from guild socialism to anarcho-syndicalism, in the overall context of Leninist centralism. Second, because participatory economics affirms Svetozar Marković's insight, for his time quite remarkable, that bureaucracy is an independent socio-economic class. Third, because I agree with those anarchists like Errico Malatesta and Gaston Leval who believed that we need to think seriously about the future libertarian social organization of society. They never understood, and neither do I, that peculiar Marxist disdain towards utopian thinking and "kitchens of the future." I do not see myself as a pareconist, however. On the contrary, I believe that we need as many utopian proposals as we can come up with. Fragmentation of knowledge, or—why not?—balkanization of knowledge, can help us discover many parts and building blocks for new revolutionary synthesis. We must find ways to translate those fragments, to make them porous, to combine different elements of utopian possibility. It is necessary, today more than ever, to see a lively debate between utopian proposals that dream of the libertarian organization of the society, always in thoughtful dialogue with local institutions and traditions. As a disciple of Svetozar Marković, our Balkan Mariátegui, I am convinced that every such proposal must blend with the local conditions and particular local institutions, such as, for instance, (modernized) Serbian family and village communes. According to Svetozar Marković, who lived in 19th century, local conditions will determine the nature of new society that the working class will establish in each country. Peasants and workers associations would everywhere be the basic social unit, but their exact nature would depend on economic and historical conditions in each country. The problem of bread, he wrote, is a problem of direct democracy. It is hard not to see the similarity between Marković's eclectic, ethical socialism—which he defined not as a new economic system, but a new way of life—and proposals arriving from contemporary peasant movements gathered around Via Campesina. This anti-authoritarian eclecticism, itself a most precious feature of Balkan societies and their revolutionary tradition, ability to connect local and global, subaltern and modern, is what I advocate under the name of balkanization of politics.

It is in this light that I would like readers to approach my dialogue with Dragan Plavsic. The book includes only a part of our conversation; the rest can be read in ZNet online archives. The text "The Kosovo Question: Some Radical Perspectives" authored by Plavsic, is a response to my commentary "Multiethnic Dream of Kosovo," followed by my response in "No State, No Nation: Balkan Federation." Both Plavsic and I are advocates of Balkan Federation. Where we part ways is in the nature of the project: where Plavsic believes in a federation of socialist states, I believe in a stateless socialist federation based on local institutions of self-government. It is here again that I return to the ideas of Svetozar Marković, who, in his opposition to dominant institutions of capitalist modernity, believed that freedom is based on the traditional social and political institutions of the *zadruga* (family commune) and *opstina* (village commune). In a dialogue with Marxism, he sought a balkanized socialism based upon communal institutions and instincts rather then upon inexorable historical laws. He argued for socialist movements that are not only anticolonial with respect to the West, but also revolutionary with respect to the Balkan past. His balkanized socialism was ethical and visionary, eclectic and humane, and on all accounts unacceptable to his state socialist critics who dismissed him as "utopian socialist." The essence of the Marković idea was democratization and decentralization of Balkan societies through the agrarian worker communes, to which he would transfer all political and economic power. His aim, he wrote in 1874, was internal social reorganization on the basis of sovereignty and communal self-government, and federation in the Balkan Peninsula. Herein, in his federalist plans, lies what is perhaps his greatest contribution: his feverish attempt to subdue the separate nationalisms of the Balkan peoples in favor of all inclusive, directly democratic federalism.

Svetozar Marković died at the age of twenty-eight. His death was a result of years spent in exile and prisons of the Serbian state. One of his last acts before his death was to help found the first school for women in Serbia. He was buried on March 16, 1875, in the presence of thousands of peasants, some of who shouted at the police assigned to maintain order to remove their hats in the presence of the saint.

Many decades after the death of Svetozar Marković, on July 15, 1924, a new publication, *La Federation Balkanique*, appeared. This was a fortnightly periodical published in Vienna in all the Balkan languages as well as in German and French. In a spirited editorial the program of this publication was defined as follows:

> The principal task of our publication as its title has
> already shown, is to propagate the idea of liberation

> and the right of self-determination of the Balkan
> people as well as that of federalization ... We wish
> that they may cease to be the common pray of
> European imperialism and Balkan chauvinism: that
> they may cease to be the arena where the latter settle
> their disastrous internal quarrels ... The working
> masses will finally be eager to unite its forces into
> single Balkan front directed against chauvinism
> and conquering Imperialism from whatever quarter
> they may come. We want liberty and peace for our
> countries and our peoples! We know also that this
> liberty and this peace are not graciously granted but
> must be conquered by a desperate struggle! And we
> are beginning this struggle!

This is the struggle and the principle that a new generation of Balkan revolutionaries must begin anew, with the same passion, but in a contemporary context, with new forms, new political sensibility, and new language. Balkan Federation: with no state, and beyond all nations.

For those unfortunate enough not to be able to read Balkan languages, you will be disappointed to know that the most interesting books about Balkan Federation movements, and early Balkan revolutionary history in general, are found only in Balkan languages. Interested American readers could find a useful overview in Stavrianos's *Balkan Federation, A History of the Movement Toward Balkan Unity in Modern Times*. This excellent book, written in the final years of World War II, was dedicated to "The Peoples of the Balkans who in fighting fascism today make possible their federation tomorrow." A wonderful overview of documents and ideas pertaining to the socialist and communist ideas of Balkan Federation are presented in a collection edited by Dragan Plavsic and Andreja Zivkovic, and published under a title *The Balkan Socialist Tradition: Balkan Socialism and the Balkan Federation, 1871–*

1915. Woodford D. McClellan, a conservative historian, wrote a Cold War classic about *Svetozar Marković and the Origins of Balkan Socialism*. Attempts to create a pan-Balkan sensibility were not restricted to the academy or factory: the Yugoslav avant-garde art and philosophical movement Zenitism is a personal favorite. Working before World War II, Zenitism's spiritual mentors, Ljubomir Micić and Branko Ve Poljanski were as good political theorists as they were artists.

Aleksa Djilas's *The Contested Country: Yugoslav Unity and Communist Revolution, 1919–1953* is a superb account of the formative days of socialist Yugoslavia. Louis Adamic, the famed author of *Dynamite: A History of Class Violence in America*, was a Yugoslav immigrant who described the plight for democratic Balkans in his *Return of the Natives* and *My Native Land: Yugoslavia 1933–1943*. The Yugoslav war, viewed from a Titoist-socialist perspective, is a topic of many books of Vlado Dedijer. The only interesting essay about anarchism in former Yugoslavia was penned by Serbian anarchist Trivo Inđić and published online as "Anarchism in Yugoslavia." Socialist self-management has been more fully addressed both by Balkan authors and beyond. Among Yugoslavs who were architects of the market socialist system I should single out late socialist economist Branko Horvat and his definitive *The Yugoslav Economic System: The First Labor-Managed Economy in the Making*. In English translation, the following books by Horvat are now available: *Self-Governing Socialism: A Reader* (two volumes), *Political Economy of Socialism: A Marxist View*, and *An Essay on Yugoslav Society*. Yugoslav self-management is also well known in the United States, where American Left economists demonstrated considerable fascination with a possible "alternative path to socialism." One such author is Jaroslav Vanek, author of *Participatory Economy: An Evolutionary Hypothesis and Strategy for Development*, a book first recommended to me by Tony Budak, a retired truck driver and organizer from Youngstown, Ohio. An early and important critique of Yugoslav socialist society, particularly its bureaucracy, comes from Milovan Djilas, in his work *The*

New Class. The foundations of Participatory Economics are laid down in many works by Michael Albert, Chris Spannos, Robin Hahnel, and Tom Wetzel. Spannos edited the collection *Real Utopia: Participatory Society for the 21st Century*, which is, without doubt, the best introduction into the utopian world of "parecon."

Anti-privatization struggles in postwar Serbia have not given rise to much work in English, a few lonely examples, however, are Ivana Momcilovic's short essay "It's Great That We Are Everywhere, We Thought That We Are Quite Alone: A Letter From Post-Yugoslavia," in the book *We Are Everywhere: The Irresistible Rise of Global Capitalism*; the forthcoming film by Tamara Vukov titled *Transition*; the book *Transition From Below: Oral Histories of Workers, Refugees and Roma in Postwar Serbia*, edited by Irina Ceric, Andrej Grubačić, and Tamara Vukov, forthcoming from PM Press; and my essay "Anti-Privatization Struggles in Serbia" in the *International Encyclopedia of Revolution and Protest*. The struggle of Jugoremedija factory is told in the book-film project *Paths through Utopia*. Meanwhile, the website http://www.globalbalkans.org/ gives updates on anti-privatization struggles in post-Yugoslav and Balkan regions. The organization Voice of Roma (http://www.voiceof-roma.com.) is a wonderful effort and resource with respect to Roma in Kosovo.

Other discussions of alternatives to capitalist imperial globality, mostly coming from the Global South, are collected in three books published by Verso and edited by Boaventura de Sousa Santos: *Another Knowledge is Possible: Beyond Northern Epistemologies*; *Democratizing Democracy: Beyond the Liberal Canon*; and *Another Production Is Possible: Beyond the Capitalist Canon*. I find the work of the so-called modernity/coloniality group exceptionally valuable. Among these scholars, a few analysts of subaltern resistance stand out: Anibal Quijano, Boaventura de Sousa Santos, Arturo Escobar, Walter Mignolo, and Enrique Dussel.

A Different Balkans is Possible

February 2002

When I went to Porto Alegre, to attend the second World Social Forum, I was in a rather good mood. Namely, I had received news about a creation of a Balkan based network committed to homogenization of the fight for alternative globalization. The name of the paper in my hands was Southeastern Europe Social Forum.

The idea was to establish the coordination of the Balkan initiatives, groups and individuals concerned with the critique of corporate globalization and neoliberal ideological program. The best way to realize this coordination—rather, the best structure in which this coordination would be efficacious—is the creation of a meta-network or forum structured along libertarian principles that wouldn't restrict the individuality of groups and persons gathered around this idea. The term social forum wasn't chosen casually: in Europe, the new social movement is organized through social forums, which are assembled on geographical principles. Despite the diversity of groups who participate in these forums, there often exist great ideological tensions caused by aspirations of certain ideological groups or sometimes the very structure of the forum, which commonly isn't sufficiently democratic. These forums have presidents, vice presidents, secretaries, and spokespersons. If realized as it was conceived in Kraljevo, a small town in Serbia, this forum would be somewhat different: it would have no presidents, vice presidents, secretaries and spokespersons. It would be an attempt to practice internal democracy through various mechanisms of cooperation. It would not insist on libertarian ideology, but rather on the libertarian principles of operating. It would try to devise systems that would prevent developments that occurred with similar attempts in Slovenia, Yugoslavia, and Croatia. The advantage of the existence of the South East Europe Social Forum is very significant: this forum would take part in the international movement, it would avoid unnecessary sectarianism, and it would stop with the practice of individual tourist activism. The libertarian structure and pluralism in organization and activities would avoid the danger of bureaucracy. People engaged would have the opportunity to organize direct actions or they would formulate intelligent critique. It would organize activist-academic anticapitalist universities, schools, seminars, and conferences. The forum would, therefore, be a kind of a "stock market" of ideas and a way for various groups to network without losing their identity, so that they can operate more easily and concretely in the Balkans and Europe.

The most important aspect of the idea of leaving behind the nuances of ideological and tactical differences is definitely practical: what's the best way to organize relations between initiatives that would operate within the forum? What's the best way to solve the issue of democratic coordination of the forum? What's the best way to secure finances for such an ambitious project? But it is a project worth mentioning and working on. It is about time for the groups from Balkans to finally take their place in the global movement.

Civil Society or Participatory Society: A Conversation with Michael Albert

August 2003

Michael Albert: To start, can you tell us something about the context of organizing in the Balkans?

Andrej Grubačić: There is a term flooding the progressive press all around the Balkans, lurking like a phantom over the editor's desk. It is present in all "critical analyses" and has become unavoidable in the discourse of the so-called non-government organizations. The term is "civil society." It refers to non-governmental elements presumably working on behalf of the social good. It seems that the term has gone beyond civility and become royalty in political journalism in the Balkans. In the West, too, it is virtually impossible to get away from this term. You encounter it even where you least expect. "Why wouldn't we ally Davos and Porto Alegre?" asked Philip Watts, chairman of Shell, in a serious tone of voice at the gathering of the World Economic Forum in New York. The very fact that at last year's Porto Alegre Forum there were three French candidates for president, eight government members with French Prime Minister Lionel Jospin, two hundred mayors of major world cities, speaks of the fact that global resistance to neoliberalism has become a planetary reality. However, it also warns of the greatest possible challenge so far posed to the subversiveness of the movement itself: in the name of the "civil society."

But you ask about the Balkans. Here the comedy of "listening and repenting," of civil society's rhetoric and practice, are at full swing. What is it all about?

The capitalist discourse is changing its bullying approach (denying it out loud), in a metamorphosis that leaves one breathless. The rhetorical fireworks include the phrases "mutual agreement," "transparency," "ethics," and—my favorite—"closeness." In order to have the current system appear in the new velvety outfit, it requires partners—those denying it. Therein begins the comedy of civil society, the noise and the well-tempered rage, the new mythology of the "citizen-mate," which in the strategy of the authorities has the aim of simply integrating the deniers.

MA: Can you give some examples?
AG: Such "partnership for social peace," in the Balkans, stands in the service of maintaining the "social monologue." Are you criticizing the neoliberal economic model of Serbian ministers? You will be asked to state your point of view. Are you surprised at the fact of Romania signing of the neocolonial agreement with the United States? The minister of the defense will welcome you and listen to you carefully. Are you worried because of the poverty in Croatia? Come to the conference on "reduction of poverty" organized by the government.

Renewing the system by criticizing it, readiness to co-opt those denying it, paternalism in the guise of participation—all these aspects of social control are as old as the system itself. According to the writing of Luc Boltanski, the sociologist, the denial that capitalism faced in the seventies has brought about the creation of a "new spirit of capitalism aimed at appeasing critique by acknowledging its appropriateness, or to simply avoid it by not even responding to it." Social control by way of civil society offers an interaction of different modes of domination. Authorities can direct fictitious conflicts in which they let the artificial opponents of their own choice specify social difficulties that they then together, through "dialogues," partly solve but at no serious loss for the capitalist system. When the capitalist system is in question, of course, the elites oppose the opposition and advocate change only in a limited manner that will not endanger the system. From this stems the leaning of "civil society" towards different variants of reformist thought that tolerates the denial of some of the aspects of the system, but does not tolerate denying the principle of the system's existence. In other words, "civil society" strives to change the rules of the game a bit here and there, but due to its being integrated, keeps participating in the game submissively.

MA: So you are implying that going beyond civil society and reformist organizing that assumes system maintenance is one thing that needs to happen. What do you have in mind for that?

AG: The concept of civil society ought to be abandoned for the sake of the vision of another society that does not rest on class, religious, or ethnic discrimination. We need a participatory society committed to authentic politics from below. In order to get closer to such a society, it is necessary to step out of the game, abandon the system, renounce abstract social-schmertz and opt for social conflict, for breaking up with traditional social-political communication and organization. Such a "conflict" would imply getting beyond endless reliance on typical political parties, hierarchical trade unions, bureaucratized non-governmental organizations, and following a path towards new models of association. It is time, here in the Balkans, for a horizontal social dialogue. Every vertical social dialogue that history has shown us has turned into a monologue in which workers first stay without a say, and then without a pay. In contrast, we need to seek a horizontal social dialogue conducted among all participants in the social-economic processes—all workers, including those who are going to lose their jobs and unemployed workers who have already lost them; refugees and "displaced persons" who have nothing to lose; Roma who have never had anything; students who cannot afford to go to the university; farmers; social movement activists; women; and many more.

MA: Where does this horizontal dialogue go?

AG: It could immediately encompass the minimum common plan, a social right that would include: request for minimum income; refutation of privatization as a model; and developing strategies subordinating profits to preserving nonrenewable resources and the real environment. But it could also seek longer-term goals for a whole new economy. Instead of advocating a productivistic cult of privatization, a horizontal dialogue would likely lead toward advocating solidarity and participatory economic relations, including a different transition which emphasizes collective initiative and real democracy, and which, in its calculations, takes into account the price of the suffering and dignity and everything else more precious than profits.

MA: You say you seek democracy, real democracy. What do you have in mind?

AG: I think that for the Balkans it is the perfect time for social movements to try to reinvent—even beyond democracy—self-management, or participatory management, as I prefer to call it. The "Yugoslav experience" shouldn't be a discouragement here. In Yugoslavia there was no private ownership of productive assets, true, but there was a market system which dramatically limited economic options and a corporate division of labor that put a ruling coordinator class above workers in power and income. Those were the roots of our economic evil. So, we haven't had, in actual reality—in so-called socialist Yugoslavia—real self-management, but only a rhetorical reference to it. We had a phenomenon that Milovan Djilas had called a "New Class" in the polity, which is true enough for the state, but to get beyond Djilas who was identifying only to a political bureaucracy, we need to see that we also had a ruling coordinator class arising from our economy's structure. There cannot be participatory management in a situation where the economy uses markets and corporate divisions of labor, whatever the state may look like, bureaucratic or not.

MA: Do you think putting forward an economic vision that advocates participatory planning to replace markets, and balanced job complexes to replace the corporate division of labor, and that favors what I guess you might call participatory management to replace authoritarian decision making, could be beneficial in the Balkans?

AG: The prospect for that kind of model, the one we call participatory economics, in today's Balkans is great. An anti-authoritarian, Left-libertarian economic system that accomplishes economic activity to meet needs and fulfill potentials while propelling solidarity, diversity, equity, and participatory management, with positive implications as well for other parts of life and society's key domains such as polity and kinship and culture, gives us a promise of a true classlessness and a powerful alternative both to the neoliberal models now favored in the Balkans, and to the authoritarian systems I like to call coordinator economies that previously existed in this part of Eastern Europe, including in my own Yugoslavia.

You are right that I would not use the term self-management in the Balkans. This is because I think that a fight over labels is a waste of time. We have to be more tactical than to cloud our meaning by misleading labels. If I speak about socialism and self-management in post-Yugoslavia, people will look at me like I am a supporter of Tito or a member of Milošević's "socialist" party. They won't hear anything beyond that wrong association. I don't think that we have time for that kind of confusion. It hurts communication, as much as if I were to try to speak to folks in Belgrade in Japanese. In fact, it is worse.

The Balkans, or the greatest part of this region, in any event, is far and away the poorest part of Europe. The most frequent word here is strike. And I don't think that we have a right to waste time in endless confused discussions about what class is a real revolutionary agent, or about what socialism really stands for. I am happy saying I am for participatory management, meaning just what you mean by self-management, to communicate my commitments in a way that can be heard without bias. And I am happy saying I am for parecon rather than for socialism, for the same reason. Being for socialism here means to people that you are for oppression. It would not open the door to horizontal dialogue. But saying you are for a new type of economy, and describing its features, may help open that door.

MA: But would people in the Balkans relate to the claim that market socialism was really market coordinatorism and that for that reason it doesn't demonstrate that there is no better future beyond capitalism?

AG: I don't think that there is widespread insight of this sort, at least not yet. But there is no impediment that prevents it. And at least some activists, and activist scholars, are trying to convey this claim. I would like to mention one network in particular, called DSM, based in my country, which is a coalition of anti-authoritarian collectives, and which is trying to figure out a good way to incorporate the idea of balanced job complexes inside of the nascent social movements here, and to find a good way of politically communicating—using "new language" that doesn't confuse people—and exploring the new ways of doing politics. There is, also, a very good initiative coming from Slovenia, where activist scholars from the entire Balkans are trying to establish an Institute for the Research of the Global Movement. I think that this project is indeed very important.

MA: Do you think people would find the idea of balanced job complexes a corrective to what they have known in workplaces—or would they see it as an ultra-Left excess that would have horrible implications?

AG: I spend a lot of time talking to workers, inside and outside of the state controlled unions. My strong impression is that they are very much in favor of this participatory model, as soon as they hear about it, and often really implicitly on their own. The same holds for grassroots activists. And, as far as my discussions about parecon as a new model of economic organization, people seem very enthusiastic. Of course, there are also people who see this as an "ultra-Left excess" or just the old ways in disguise. For example, I have been involved in a public debate recently with one of the authors of the neoliberal reforms in my country. The guy was screaming "Neocommunism! Neocommunism!" all the way through this debate. That is what he is being paid to do. But I don't think that this new class of intellectual commissars in the Balkan countries should be our audience, and in contrast working people are very receptive.

Balanced job complexes, as far as I understand the idea, means a situation where each job is a mix of tasks and responsibilities, such that the overall quality of life and especially the overall empowerment effects of the work are comparable for all. It is, in my opinion, very hard to disagree with a vision of society that gets rid of a hierarchy between managers and workers, lawyers, and assembly line workers. How can one oppose keeping the functions, but having them fairly shared?

Among working people and activists working for social justice, I encounter overwhelmingly positive reactions. A vision of participatory society where each person's mix of tasks and responsibilities accords with their abilities and also conveys a fair share of rote and tedious and interesting and empowering conditions and responsibilities, seems to people precisely in tune with their hopes. And so does participatory management—people having a proportionate say in the decisions that affect their lives.

MA: What about remunerating effort and sacrifice only? Do you think people would fear that doing this would reduce their prospects for riches or disrupt production, or do you think they would anticipate that remunerating only effort and sacrifice would enhance justice and their incomes as well?
AG: The feedback I have gotten has been very interesting. Yes, for many Leftist economists—I remember my debate with one very fine old man, and great economist, Branko Horvat—rewarding only the effort and sacrifice that people expend

in their work is very controversial. But I fail to see, I have to admit, why is it so difficult for some anticapitalists, even if they have suffered the harmful socialization of becoming famous economists, to recognize the inherent injustice in getting more income by virtue of being more productive due to having better skills or greater inborn talent, or due to having better tools, not to mention due to having more power or owning more property.

Being entitled to more consumption only by virtue of giving more effort and enduring more sacrifice is morally appropriate and it also—it seems to me—provides proper incentives due to rewarding only what we can affect, and not what we can't. It seems that people to whom I have been talking about these issues in my country—workers, peasants, movement activists—are far more receptive to this idea then my colleagues who teach and even then "anticapitalist" intellectuals in general. But I guess that is no surprise.

MA: Being from the United States, we don't encounter some of the trends of thought that exist in Europe. You are advocating participatory economics and related approaches for politics, gender, etc., for the Balkans. But I am wondering if other Left approaches are finding more response there, even among the audiences you are working with—say, for example, ideas coming out of the work of Hardt and Negri and the people advocating such focuses as "Empire" and the "multitude." Are these views gaining support in the Balkans? Do you think they are making a positive contribution? Do you see a relation to the pareconish ideas, or are the two viewpoints contrary?

AG: Yes, Hardt and Negri's book, which is very interesting, so the people who have understood it are telling me, is a popular read among Lefty intellectuals. I am not sure if it is really gaining any support. It is very hard to communicate what they are trying to say: they cultivate a style that excludes the vast majority of potential readers, leaving most of even the highly educated in a state of confusion. Reading a book which is describing something called "Empire" which has supposedly superseded nation states, in a country occupied by U.S. military forces is, I suppose, a strange experience for most of the readers. But I don't want to say that this book is not useful. I think it is of value to Marxist intellectuals in a country where "Marxism" was an official state ideology. For them, I suppose, it is challenging. But I doubt that it will have any significant influence in this part of Europe. I could be wrong, of course.

Traditional Marxist analyses of capitalist societies centered on the polarization between two classes and two alone: the capitalist class and the proletariat. Both pareconish analysis, and the one of Hardt and Negri, present a very different model, one which is meant to describe the class dynamic specific to modern times. Hardt and Negri are recognizing the central dynamic in the emergence of an entity called "the multitude." I am not sure anyone really knows what this means, but, broadly, the idea seems to be that the working class has lost its privileged position as the revolutionary agent and, instead, now there is something called the multitude, which includes housewives, farmers, students, and so on. I am not sure what is new in that, but something that does seem different is to minimize differences among constituencies. We are all just going to be in the multitude. Differences between men and women, gays and straights, different types of workers and also workers and managers, and so on, all fade into the background and get much less attention than before, it seems.

Pareconish analyses present a model, at least regarding the economy, of a three-way polarization, between the capitalist class, the working class, and the coordinator class. They also put into sharp focus differences having to do with gender, sexuality, race, etc., identifying institutions that lead to these different positions and trying to understand different needs, agendas, etc. Pareconish efforts also seek, like Hardt's and Negri's, to have people become revolutionaries—and I guess pareconish activists could call those who arrive at such commitments a multitude, once it is that large in size, but they wouldn't ignore that how different people become committed depends on their position in society, nor would they minimize that some folks are on average less likely to move left-ward than others, and may even have contrary interests. I would argue that the later analysis is more useful.

In fact, keying on the class part, with any Leftist analyses which fails to comprehend the coordinator class as an actor that can take the lead in defining a new economy, there is a good chance of it leading to a dictatorship not of the proletar-iat but of the coordinator class (of technocrats, government and party bureaucrats, professional ideologues, managers)— just as happened in Yugoslavia or the USSR.

The antagonisms which exist between the coordinator class seeking its own agenda and the working class seeking its own agenda cannot be wished away in the name of the "multitude." To get rid of the conflict one must have a move-ment that self-consciously forges new structures that elim-inate class divisions rather than putting the more educated and powerful class from our society into a ruling position in the movement and then in tomorrow's society. To be able to forge an alliance between those in the coordinator class who want real justice and the working class—to be able to build a strong movement for real classlessness—we need to recog-nize the antagonisms, not make believe they aren't there. I think the pareconish view can help with that, both by iden-tifying the problems, and by the classless vision and meth-ods it offers. The approach based on the idea of the multitude, seems instead to move back in the old directions.

MA: Finally, what about anarchist trends in the Balkans? Are they moving toward economic aims and goals like those we have been discussing, or do they have other aims in mind? Do they have a political vision for the region and more broadly? Do you think the Balkan's anarchist trends should find pareconish commitments positive, or that they should have strong criti-cisms of them?

AG: Anarchism, as a political philosophy, is going through a veritable explosion in the Balkans in recent years. Anarchist, or anarchist-inspired collectives are growing everywhere;

anarchist principles—autonomy, voluntary association, self-organization, mutual aid, direct democracy—have become the basis for organizing within a good number of the collectives in the Balkans.

But I would be very cautious with regards to the "political vision" offered by anarchists in the Balkans. Serious reflection on vision remains a "blind spot" of anarchism around here as, I guess, pretty much everywhere else. Hopefully that will change. And that is one of the reasons why I think that anarchist trends in the Balkans should recognize participatory economics as an anarchist economic vision which generates participation, classlessness and participatory management: the hallmark goals of anarchism. Parecon is in accord with all the most important themes of traditional anarchism (freedom, justice, solidarity, participation, equity), but contributes even more to what I like to refer to as "modern anarchism," through its provision of specific positive economic institutions not advocated by traditional anarchists, such is balanced job complexes and participatory planning. What we anarchists need to do is add a political vision to go with it.

The Multiethnic Dream of Kosovo

June 2004

Admiral Gregory Johnson, the NATO commander in charge of Kosovo, as recently as a week ago has linked the violent Albanian struggle for independence to "ethnic cleansing" and expressed that the recent attacks against Serbs and Romas were "orchestrated." Derek Chappell, a spokesman for the UN mission, echoed this sentiment by saying that these attacks were planned well in advance. Another UN official has been quoted as saying that Kristallnacht is under way in Kosovo. In spite of all this, the "international community" continues to try to impose a "multiethnic" solution from above.

This idea goes back many decades, and can be traced to the cultural-imperialist fixation with "Balkanism." Defined by George Kennan, one of the founders of the American Slavic Studies, he warned as early as the 1920s that the problems in the area have "deep historical roots which feed on the characteristic traits of the Balkan peoples that are obviously inherited from the distant tribal past." According to Kennan, the "aggressive nationalism" in the Balkans is an issue to which the West must pay special attention; namely, it is necessary to occupy militarily these "agitated peoples," until such time that they "calm down and grasp their problems in a right way." Therefore, it is the small Balkan peoples who, because of "their bloody wars," represent a "major problem" for civilization, and not the imperialist violence and colonialist practices perpetrated by Europe or the USA. This problem can only be cured through military occupation.

It is interesting to draw attention to the similarity between Kennan's ideological perception and the current Balkan policies of the Western powers, above all that of the United States.

The Balkans, the "Wild East of Europe," where the "enlightened states" have still not completed their "mission civilisatrice," is still the "powder keg," an "immature society" imbued with ethno-nationalist animosities that can be explained only by the barbarian history of the region, etched, in an unusual manner, in the mental outlook of a barbarian world in the "heart of Europe" (Madeleine Albright). The direct consequence of this cultural-imperialist view is the ideological desire by the benevolent international community to impose "multiethnicity from above."

Serbian "civil society," a diverse (but class-homogenous) group of rent-an-intellectuals and NGOs, fully supports the concept of "multiethnicity from above" as a solution for Kosovo. Thus, a distinguished professor, in an interview given to a Belgrade weekly, described the state of our "immature society":

> Serbia must sever its umbilical cord with the Orient, and must become Europeanized ... I had great respect for Zoran Djindjić [the Serbian "reformist" prime minister, the author of the neoliberal program who was killed because of his links with organized crime], because ... he was like a space shuttle. He was too fast for our slow Serbia. What remains is a late Byzantine synthesis of disintegration, moaning and tears. Enough of those ... Muslim tunes....
> However, viewed from our perspective, globalization is something positive. It brings to immature societies like ours a wind that is anti-provincial and does not allow insularity. All societies similar to ours face a constant threat of insularity.

We are, however, according to this professor, to be freed of this specific civilizational claustrophobia by God's intervention:

> It is as if God had looked down on this wretched Serbian people and said: if I do not help them and do not send them some generations that will be unfettered, they will simply be doomed ... They are my students ... Those kids have grown up into a non-provincial generation, they are very good in foreign languages, the Internet, I admire them and believe that they are the generation that will take a Copernican turn that is so indispensable.

The international community and local civil society seem to share the same kind of repugnance for the "mass" of unenlightened "Balkans," both Serbs and Albanians, who need to be somehow tamed; generosity calls for a "multiethnic solution" for Kosovo: they must learn how to live together and they must do so by force.

The Serbian government, a fragile alliance of neoliberals and nationalists, wavers between two solutions: imposing a model of a "cultural and personal autonomy" or a collective prayer (the prime minister had for days, at the peak of the Kosovo unrest, led people in daily prayers in Orthodox churches, while the less pious torched mosques in Serbia—a spree that they interrupted to senselessly attack Romanis, themselves refugees from Kosovo.)

In his report to Parliament, Prime Minister Vojislav Koštunica proposed "substantive autonomy for the Serbian community in Kosovo, partitioning into entities, that is to say, a cantonization of Kosovo and Metohija, as well as cultural and personal autonomy." That would be a heavy defeat for the Albanian political elite, as they are now the masters of the situation on the ground because of the bombings. They are presently positioned to fulfill their "national plan" of eliminating the other nations in Kosovo, and Serbia and the International community could soon be faced with a completely new situation. The latest campaign of violence has most likely been a sign of impatience to carry out that "national plan" as soon as possible.

Cantonization, as observed by a renowned Belgrade journalist (himself prone to the fatalism of "immature society"), "was invented by the Swiss, because they needed that kind of association in order to unite. In the Balkans we do just the opposite and reach out for the Swiss scheme to more easily divide and protect ourselves against one another." But is that truly the reality? Could there possibly be a solution that would not unavoidably imply "ethnic division" or "multiethnicity imposed from above"?

Moreover, could there be a Left-libertarian solution founded on the sheer undermining of such concepts, going from a mutual struggle to mutual aid, through putting together a mosaic of mutually linked alternative approaches in a new kind of politics? A solution not based on the ridiculous idea of bringing together so-called ethnic groups reproducing the logic of ethnicity but developing a plan that is centered around solving essential social problems such as poverty, education, housing and resisting privatization.

Ethno-nationalism in Kosovo must be surmounted, true enough, but not through a violent imposition of a multiethnic society or by defining new ethnic border lines, but instead through the alchemy of restructuring society by doing away with borders and differences through mobilizing the energies of the social movements. Can ethno-nationalism and imposed multiethnicity retreat when confronted with the organic solidarity that could possibly be achieved in the conditions of a "participatory society" along Bill Tampler's line of thinking about Palestine? I am talking about a project of a gradual transformation founded on the idea of a "policy from below"—altering politics from the bottom up, shaping society from below, seeking to overcome statecraft—a top-down system of pseudo-representative governments ultimately based on the state monopoly of violence—and one that would be reflected in a struggle for the creation of an inclusive democratic awareness, through different models of alternatives, participatory social experiments, and a transformation practice that would win the practical imagination of all peoples in the region.

That alternative differs from the one that is proposed by the Yugoslav "old Left": Trotskyists, Stalinists, and anarcho-syndicalists, who mostly talk about a project of a "socialist federation," which had been an important locus in the progressive history of the region. The organized "old Left" in Serbia, exemplified in small activist groups and parties, opposes the "border solution" in any form. Some of them seem to envision a resurrected Soviet-style socialist world, while others, without questioning the State, as a container of political life, talk about a "socialist Balkans."

The alternative approach that I have offered here accentuates the primary importance of grassroots practices. This utopian program of transformation would accomplish surmounting and leaving behind for good the separation of the Albanian and non-Albanian populations, together with the very logic of borders and ethnic conflict. Some efforts towards this goal are already in evidence.

Self-Management Returns To Serbia?

July 2006

Listservs and inboxes all over the world have been filled with the following plea for global solidarity with the workers of the Serbian factory Jugoremedija, a factory that is resisting privatization and whose workers are organizing to run the workplace themselves. The plea reads as follows:

> Dear friends,
>
> We, the workers of Jugoremedija, a worker-owned and run factory in Serbia, urgently need your help.
>
> We have been in an ongoing struggle to run our workplace ourselves.
>
> Similar to some of the struggles in Argentina to recuperate workplaces, our desire is to work, make decisions collectively that effect our work and livelihoods, and run our own lives.
>
> For over two years we have fought the privatization of our work place, we have been fired after striking and occupying the factory, and now, finally, we are on the edge of a victory. We are partial legal owners of the factory, and want to begin to work in our democratically run factory under worker control. The other part owner, and person attempting to buy the whole factory, is now trying to reorganize the factory so that we will not be able to have a work place any longer.

He wants to divide it into pieces and have the work done elsewhere.

This will take away our workplace and work. Please sign the letter to help support our struggle. For more background and information please see our attached history, or for Serbian go to http://www.jugoremedija2.com.

The Serbian pharmaceutical factory Jugoremedija, from the town of Zrenjanin, was privatized in 2000, in such a way that 58 percent of the shares were given to the workers, and the state took 42 percent. In 2002, the state sold its shares to Jovica Stefanovic, an infamous local capitalist, who made his fortune smuggling cigarettes, and who was wanted by Interpol at the time he bought the shares of Jugoremedija. As with all the other buyers in Serbian privatization, Stefanovic was not even investigated for money laundering, because the Serbian government's position at that time was (and still is), that it's better to have dirty money in privatization, than to let workers manage the company, because that will "bring us back to the dark days of self-management."

According to the PR of the company, the new owners "have been facing obstruction since the very first day by shareholders and workers who had obstructed the previous management as well, as some senior workers put it." "These are remnants of the communist self-management system in which workers were allowed to meddle in everything" corporation PR said. The first attack on Yugoslav self-management and "meddlesome workers" happened before the break up of socialist Yugoslavia. The first organized attempt to dismantle the system of self-management in Serbia dates back to the times of Slobodan Milošević. But the real full-blown process of privatization and curtailment of workers rights happen after Milošević was sent to The Hague Tribunal. In this context in transitional Serbia of the 21st century, with the transition to capitalism and parliamentary democracy, everything became allowed in the fight against what the new neoliberal government saw as the "ideological monster of self-manage-ment"—even if it means the government and the court break laws.

Breaking all the rules, the state allowed the new co-owner of Jugoremedija, Stefanovic to become the dominant owner of the factory. Through various illegal maneuvers the own-ership structure was changed: Stefanovic was given 68 per-cent of the shares and the workers portion was reduced to 32 percent. In December 2003, the workers began a strike and factory occupation, as well as a lawsuit against the recapital-ization. This was the first workplace occupation in the post-socialist Yugoslavia!

In May 2004, the state, pressed by the workers, investi-gated privatization of Jugoremedija and found that Stefanovic's investment was in violation of the contract.

The state did nothing to enforce the violation of the contract. In response, the workers, mainly women, came to the capital, Belgrade, and occupied the state's Privatization Agency for one whole day. Only after this occupation did the state begin to take the violation seriously. Meanwhile the fac-tory occupation continued. The PR agents called it "a rebellion, a state of anarchy and a taking of the factory by force, which warrants intervention, which is why professional security has been brought in, to guard it in the future as well."

The "personal security" inflicted severe injuries on a number of strikers. They even used trained dogs. One woman was badly injured, two women had dislocated arms and one worker received a blow to the head. In an incredible scene, women workers lay down in front of the security vans, and defended their factory.

Throughout the summer of 2004, Stefanovic's private army tried several times to take over the factory, but the work-ers, with breathtaking courage, kicked them out. Sometimes using their bodies to block the military vehicles. This kept the boss out . . . but he returned.

In September 2004, the private army was joined by the Serbian police who had the order to evict the workers from

Jugoremedija. Police and the private army forced their way into the factory, resulting in the hospitalization of many workers and the arrest of four of the leaders of the strike. The workers were then charged with disturbing the peace. Criminal proceedings are still taking place. Now that he physically emptied the factory he illegally fired the two hundred workers.

After participating in a Peoples Global Action conference in Belgrade in August of 2004, workers from Jugoremedija joined with workers from other factories to form the Union of Workers and Shareholders of Serbia. At first, the Union's mission was limited to fighting against corruption in privatization, but after experiencing different aspects of Serbian privatization, the Union came out with another demand—the call for a constituent assembly. They believe that the people should make the decisions that effect their lives and work places, and a new constitution can help make this happen. Graffiti appeared on the walls of Belgrade asking, "Who owns our factories?" Although without jobs for two years, the workers of Jugoremedija refused to quit. Their militancy and creative direct actions made them a symbol of resistance to neoliberal capitalism in Serbia.

Finally, as a response to a series of direct and legal actions, in May 2006 the Serbian Supreme Court reached the decision that recapitalization was in violation of the contract, and ordered Zrenjanin Economic Court to reopen the case. Last Friday, Zrenjanin Economic Court brought ownership structure back to 58 percent – 42 percent.

According to Serbian law, workers-shareholders need three weeks to call for an assembly of all shareholders, in order to appoint their management. Stefanovic needs to be prevented from dividing up the company, and a court injunction would allow the workers to democratically decide who manages their factory, and how.

Anarchy in the Balkans: Andrej Grubačić in Conversation with Freedom Fight

February 2007

Andrej Grubačić: If you could first introduce Freedom Fight to ZNet readers, and then give us something of the socio-political background of contemporary Serbia. I have just been reading the latest UNICEF report, according to which there are over three hundred thousand children today who are living in poverty or are at risk of poverty. These kinds of things were unimaginable fifteen years ago. They were, dare I say it, unimaginable not only in the times of Yugoslav state-socialism, but also in the times of Slobodan Milošević's kleptocratic regime. It seems that neoliberal, modern and European Serbia demonstrates certain atavistic social traits. Serbia is now considered to be "the last Balkan state." Balkan is still considered to be a permanent and natural powder keg of Europe, pacified by the international capitalist community, a region [whose history] is, as Richard Holbrooke pointed out, "too complicated (or trivial) for outsiders to master." How does an anarchist feel living and fighting in this "strange and feral Balkans" (Simon Winchester)?

Freedom Fight: Freedom Fight is an anarchist, alter-globalist movement created in Serbia in 2003. Beside work on alternative web-based media project at www.freedomfight.net, Freedom Fight movement promotes necessity of opposing neoliberal ideology. But that's not all, we are not just reaction to the unjust system, we also try to seek for proper alternatives for the life after capitalism. I don't believe in the so-called "end of the history," that better world is not possible. Their plan is, of course, to convince us in that, but "end of the history" is going to happen only if we let them destroy the planet—then for sure there would not be any history anymore.

The first step is to fight neoliberal ideology whose imposing here is being financed with large quantities of money. Except unmasking of promises of better life that we'll deserve by obeying orders that comes from some places far away from here, from IMF and World Bank, we have to promote alternatives which would capture people's imagination and took them away from transitional apathy and depression. We have to show people that there is better future beyond capitalism. Of course, any alternative to the neoliberal models must be also an alternative to the authoritarian systems.

Balkans is a place for geostrategic experiments of powerful states. They also want, by using force, to convince us that they are bosses and that we have to obey orders. During NATO bombing of Yugoslavia in 1999, which could be avoided if negotiations haven't been sabotaged with unacceptable ultimatums, the result was escalation of the atrocities. I can't believe that so many intellectuals abroad supported bombing as a "humanitarian intervention"! What about other places where ethnic cleansing was military aided from U.S. administration? Was that also their "humanitarian intervention"? Now, that criminal politics took the form of an economic type of oppression.

According to official records of unemployment, the rate of unemployment in Serbia is approximately 30 percent. Transitional Balkans is not a very nice place to live in. People get fired, public property is being sold for nothing, and there is extremely big gap between rich and poor. Many people that call themselves "experts" are trying to convince us that we need to make some transitional sacrifices so in the future we could live like the "whole normal world." In fact, they are just well paid exponents of neoliberal ideology. They are imposing their politics, which I often call "IMF copy/paste politics," because IMF is dictating always the same economic measures on no matter what transitional country. Slovenia was not in crises as long as it managed to avoid those measures that have disastrous effects on ordinary people's lives. Due to the neoliberal reforms, Slovenia's social security system was cut back, public utilities were privatized, and living standards for most of the population declined significantly. Serbia is also forced to conduct policies that were designed to fulfill the requirements for entry into the European Union. Elections in Serbia are often presented as most important thing for Balkan stability by international community, which is always suggesting to us who to vote for. In fact, nothing depends on the final electoral outcome. No matter what political party seizes state power, the processes of privatization, transition and European integration are going to continue. Most of the despaired people who are against these processes are voting for Serbian Radical Party, which in recent elections took 29 percent of the vote, but, in fact, that party is just a nationalist, pro-capitalist organization with fake populism.

AG: What is the role of intellectuals in Serbia today? Does an independent, critical intellectual exist? Do they take an active part in the social movements? Or do you see only "integrated intellectuals," as the late Pierre Bourdieu used to call them?
FF: Well, I'm not sure what the term "intellectual" actually means … Yes, there are people who are well educated and who possess certain knowledge, but I don't see them often raising their voice for the benefit of the underclass people. I think that at this moment, Belgrade University is a neoliberal stronghold in Serbia. Most of the professors are trying to convince us that this kind of society is inevitable. They say for themselves that they are "realistic" and that students have to pay tuition fees although all of them, during their studies, had free education. If you mean Sartre's distinction between intellectual and specialist, where an intellectual is the one who criticizes system and who is involved in fight for social justice, and a specialist is the one who is expert for certain

aspect of knowledge, then we have many specialists but outside of world of activism, I don't see any intellectuals.

AG: Now a difficult question. You are anarchists and anti/alter-globalists. You are against both the international community and the communitarian logic of Serbian nationalism. What is your position on The Hague Tribunal? According to the well- meaning, good hearted European liberals, The Hague is the last option to tame "the wild and refractory" people of Balkans. Is this Tribunal legal? Does that matter at all? Do you feel tamed and more civilized? Should anarchist support the civilizing efforts of the international community, in order for the people to achieve "reconciliation" and "collective catharsis," so they can stop being "not-yet" or "never-quite" European?

FF: The Tribunal in The Hague is an ideological institution with disputable validity. It was created by the UN Security Council resolutions 808/93 and 827/93, but Security Council is only a UN executive organ and as such it may not establish judicial organs, nor it has right to perform any judicial function.

Besides that, the other problem is the so-called "selective justice." The Tribunal in The Hague prosecutes only crimes committed in a particular space, but war crimes were committed and are being committed in so many areas of the world. This selective justice also contravenes the UN Charter principle of sovereign equality of states. The Tribunal regulates its own functioning and appears both as a legislative and as a judicial body. There are many violations of civil rights committed by this court, particularly a detention pending trial too long and the fact that there is no right to compensation of damage in case of unlawful detention.

This Tribunal has a mission to hide hands of powerful states covered with blood. Milošević should have been tried on the territory of the former Yugoslavia. Instead, he passed away in a prison cell under unknown conditions. Bigger war criminals—Clinton, Blair, Bush—are not persecuted.

AG: Could you tell us a bit more about the "politics from below"? Yugoslavia, old state-socialist Yugoslavia, was the only nation-state with a system of self-management that has existed. Does the memory of self-managed work, grassroots democracy at the level of production, and social security still exist among the people? Who are the new protagonists of the politics from below? Is it the old Left in its various—and dull!—manifestations? The workers? The students? The peasants? Anarchists and feminists?

FF: I met few activists abroad who had very positive opinions about self-management in Yugoslavia, but I think that such opinions are often much too idealistic. In reality, that so called self-management system was controlled and coordinated by political bureaucracy and I think it is wrong to even call it self-management. It was certainly not a classless system and there certainly were authoritarian decision making. However, even self-management with those malfunctions was a much better system than this one. Anyway, self-management, real self-management, must come from people and it can't be imposed on them. We can learn from mistakes of the old so called self-management system and reinvent it and improve it.

It is a bit hard to summarize all social protests against dismantling social security system that occurred during transitional years. They are best described by slogan created in Slovenia during demonstrations in which more than forty thousand people participated: "For the maintenance of the welfare state." I have to mention the workers of the Serbian pharmaceutical factory Jugoremedija from the town of Zrenjanin, who have been engaged in an ongoing struggle to run their workplace themselves, who became "symbol of resistance to neoliberal capitalism in Serbia." They have fought the privatization of their factory for over three years. They have occupied factory and fought with police and private army. Recently, students of Belgrade University occupied the building of the philosophical faculty for seven days, until the University agreed to support demands of students against tuition fees and against the government. Those rebellious students, now and during occupation, functioned in accordance with a direct democracy decision-making.

So far, most of the rebellions are mainly reaction to the already imposed "structural adjustment" program of the IMF. I think that Serbia lacks an organized prevention of those impositions. People haven't expected such a disastrous consequences of the transitions and believed in politicians' lies about better future. There are anarcho-syndicalists and few anarchist-inspired collectives that struggle against neoliberal measures and offer anti-authoritarian vision of future society, but certainly there is a necessity of creation of united movement against capitalism.

Although a few members of Marxist-Leninist organizations from Serbia gave very important contribution during some social protests, I think that their political principles and visions are run over by time and that they don't, for the time being, give acceptable vision of society. They say that their main goal is a seizure of state power and that, for me, is not acceptable. There are other anarchist collectives, for example, anarcho-syndicalists from Serbia that are now maintaining Secretariat of the IWA. Their educational syndicate gave significant contributions to recent student demonstrations. There are few valuable people gather around *Kontrapunkt* magazine, collective Zluradi Paradi, SPK, etc. There is no printed magazine for radical Leftists and Freedom Fight movement, in coordination with Global Balkan network, will try to overcome that failure by editing and printing *Z Magazine* in our language.

AG: What about the Serbian Roma? Roma people are Europe's ubiquitous underclass and its most marginalized and oppressed citizens. An open letter presented to the European Union by the European Roma Rights Center on International Roma Day two years ago reminded us of the fact that "anti-Gypsyism continues to be rife, is rarely punished and is often used as an acceptable outlet of racism in mass media as well

as in every aspect of life," stressing "the persistent reality of extreme poverty and systemic human rights frustration or active abuse in the Roma ghettos which requires urgent concrete action." On a much more optimistic note, a friend of mine, Bill Templer, sees Roma communities as a "laboratory for self-management beyond borders." In his recent inspiring article in New Politics, he hopes that "their experience in the self-organization of a supranational identity in localized communities can help point certain directions over the longer haul for a denationalizing of Europe's political structures from the bottom up: decentralized nodes of community within a transnational frame of inventive federation."

FF: According to Mr. Paul Polansky, an activist working for the rights of the Roma people, the NATO bombing of Yugoslavia and the violence in its aftermath have destroyed the homes and lives of the Roma of Kosovo. Albanian nationalists have thrown the Roma out of Kosovo in even greater proportional numbers than the Serbs. Of the 150,000–200,000 Roma of Kosovo, less than 20,000 remain there when the NATO's "peace-keeping" forces took control of Kosovo. Fifteen thousand Romani homes have been destroyed. Mr. Polansky also claims that most international aid agencies in Kosovo discriminate against all minorities, especially Gypsies.

Those remaining Roma are living in UN-built refugee camps in the most degrading circumstances. Paul Polansky claims that the UN built the camps on toxic wasteland. In his book *UN-Leaded Blood* he stated: "At three camps built by the UN High Commission for Refugees, some sixty Gypsy children under the age of six have been exposed to such high levels of lead that they are highly likely to die soon or to suffer irreversible brain damage. This number represents every child born in the camps since they were built five and a half years ago."

The Roma people are in little less extent also discriminated in Serbia. They are usually beaten by police or skinheads and their entrance into certain object is forbidden. They usually have more problems with local authorities than with ordinary citizens. They have difficulties with finding jobs because of the color of their skin and they are usually allowed only to work some hard labor jobs.

But I have to mention my hometown, Raca Kragujevacka, a small town of about four thousand, where everybody knows everybody else, where in the summer of 1999 some four hundred Roma refugees from Kosovo found shelter in the big building of my old school located in the downtown. Most of them have never heard of my town before. They were well accepted by local population and there are more and more marriages made by people of different nationalities.

AG: Here, in the United States, the myth of Serbian OTPOR still persists. According to the liberals, but also a number of radical Leftists, they were the grassroots, directly democratic and non-violent force behind the Serbian "Black Revolution" of 2001. Could you tell us what OTPOR really is?
FF: In fact, organization OTPOR was a U.S.-aided and -trained organization. Its purpose was to overthrow Milošević's regime and to establish a government that would be obedient to imperialistic demands. After fall of Milošević in 2000, remains of that organization became a political party and after failure to become a part of Parliament, OTPOR merged into the Democratic Party. If you look at the official ideological declarations of OTPOR, (such as its own 1999 Declaration), you'll see that it was a nationalist, neoliberal organization which advocated "the restructuring of economy, creating the conditions for a free market, the inevitable privatization and opening of the economy to foreign investment backed by legal guarantees that would facilitate safe investment."

AG: What about that other seductive myth, the one of the "friendly civil society"? Are NGOs friends or foes in the process of building anti-authoritarian, Left-libertarian social movements in Serbia today? My impression is that the "friendly civil society" and the "advocates of human rights" have been

transformed into intellectual commissars of the "modern," neoliberal political forces.

FF: People from NGOs and those who represent the so-called civil society allow themselves to criticize certain aspects of the system, but never the system itself. They are part of the system and, as such, they are for changes that would never endanger the system. They are most welcomed guests of the American embassy. They are well paid, but they are useless. As reformist organizations, they assume system maintenance and if you start questioning the system, you'll have them on your back defending the system.

AG: But how do you see the recent elections? It seems that they will effect the final decision of the status for Kosovo. The Finnish fireman, Marti Ahtisaari (in the best tradition of Balkan colonial governors, after introducing his "plan" for Kosovo's "future"), declared that he is not really interested in what local politicians in Serbia and Kosovo have to say about his proposal. What would be an anarchist response to the artificial dilemma of nationalism or neoliberalism, which denies a possibility for another, horizontal and grassroots approach in this Serbian province? Is there an anarchist proposal for Kosovo?

FF: The international community now wants to solve problems that escalated after its "humanitarian interventions." There is an analogy with Iraq: the United States bombs a country promising establishment of democracy and freedom and after the bombing, the attacked country ends up in chaos. UN peacekeepers did nothing to prevent ethnic cleansing of Serbs and Roma in March of 2004. The special negotiator nominated by the UN, Marti Ahtisaari, strives to "monoethnic independence" which is opposed by Belgrade officials. They will probably be forced to accept it, but any forced agreement won't do any good. In exchange for Kosovo, Serbia will probably be granted a membership in European-Atlantic alliances.

As Chomsky has suggested, the partition of Kosovo must be seriously considered and that seems to me most appropriate for the time being but it should be, of course, just a temporary solution. Partitions and ethnic borders, although at the moment inevitable, are failures of humanity and mutual understanding.

However, a multiethnic society can't be imposed from above. It and ethnic division could be avoided if we recognize that the main problem is not territory and to whom it belongs, but unsolved essential social problems such as poverty, housing, refugees, and privatization. If society is shaped from below by social movements, through actions based on solidarity and inclusive democracy, we'd be witnessing the end of ethnic divisions and conflicts.

AG: And what about Montenegro?
FF: After the referendum in May 2006, Montenegro became an independent country. Montenegro's prime minister of that time, Milo Djukanović, was a former ally of Slobodan Milošević but in 1997 Western powers used him to dismantle the Federal Republic of Yugoslavia and to remove any obstacles to their interests in the Balkans. In return, Montenegro was bankrolled by Western financial support. Unemployment and poverty are very huge, and the country is ruled by ordinary criminals and cigarette-smugglers. There were many irregularities during anti-independence campaigns. Many people were forced to vote for independence and Montenegrins living abroad were allowed to vote whilst those living in Serbia were barred.

AG: In one of my recent essays, I tried to describe the phenomenon I called the Belgrade Consensus, or the political argument which is composed of three parts: neoliberalism, nationalism, and the politics of the so called civil society (civilizing the "uncivil one"). The protagonists of this unusual consensus of elites suggest that there could be no alternative beyond mutually dependent nationalist and neoliberal discourses. In this atmosphere, the people of Serbia are deprived of a genuine alternative. They are condemned to becoming depolit-

**icized, to the loss of "political illusions," to a crisis of politi-
cal activism, and worse still, to being receptive to those of the
populist extremism of the extreme Right.**

FF: Neoliberalism and nationalism are two sides of the same
coin. Nationalism, as terrorism, is just a symptom of a capitalist and colonial society. They are not opposed to each other.
Capitalist society itself creates the enemy it fights against. The
United States won't win the war against terrorism even if it
manages to exterminate all Al-Qaeda cells. As long as exploitation and imperialism exist, there will be those extreme sorts
of resistance. The United States should lead a "war on terror"
within its own borders—that is, it should change its own foreign policy that is the main inciter for terrorist activities.

In the Balkans, nationalistic impulses were stirred up
by imperialistic states in order to weaken those who might
oppose imperialistic plans through internal civil wars. Besides
that, neoliberalism and nationalism here are both ideologi-
cally rooted in liberalism. Between those two options, differences are almost irrelevant. Both options advocate privatization, dismantling social security system, etc.

**AG: Do you think that ideas such as participatory economics,
and other proposals for a participatory society, that we here
at Z like to advocate, make any sense for the Balkans? Are
visionary, participatory politics, which would rest on alternative political designs, and an invitation to think collectively
and seriously about the life after capitalism and hierarchy,
something that people in Serbia and the Balkans can relate
to? In 19th-century Russia and Serbia, revolutionaries used
to talk about "going to the people." Do you think that going to
the people with the ideas of participatory economy and participatory politics would encounter constructive responses?**

FF: Well, the idea of parecon is strictly opposed to the neoliberal dogma so as long as advocates of neoliberalism have
power of manufacturing opinions parecon won't be accepted
and familiar to ordinary people. I am sure that most activists are not acquainted with idea of parecon. Ideas that advo-

cate that everybody have a proportionate participation in the decisions that affect people's lives must have a stronghold in part of population for whose benefit those ideas are designed. They have to be closely connected with social movements that would advocate them and establish them in practice and in reality. There is an open space for these ideas, maybe especially in the Balkans. People lost faith in representative democracy and in political parties. They want to build their future and their lives on their own. I am sure they would recognize parecon as a proper alternative.

The Kosovo Question: Some Radical Perspectives

By Dragan Plavsic

March 2007

Andrej Grubačić provides an interesting perspective on the apparently intractable question of Kosovo. What is his perspective and how should we evaluate it?

Andrej offers a self-avowedly "utopian program of transformation" based on grassroots movements agitating around common social issues that foster cross-ethnic "organic solidarity" as a counter to interethnic conflict, leading to a "participatory society" from below as the ultimate answer to "the separation of Albanian and non-Albanian populations." In this way, Andrej argues, ethno-nationalism will retreat in Kosovo and we will, at last, be able to transcend the bloody and divisive logic of "new ethnic border lines."

This sweeping vision is indeed a captivating ideal to which every radical should aspire, and be inspired by, as it is the ultimate answer to the social question in the Balkans, as elsewhere. But it is nevertheless the case that ideals, however captivating, too often fail to guide us adequately or sufficiently when, as radicals, we are faced with the pressing need to provide concrete answers to concrete questions, such as those raised by the national question in Kosovo. This is arguably the central weakness of Andrej's perspective.

The national question in Kosovo, like all national questions, is a pre-eminently political question. Of course, it is inextricably intertwined with deeper economic and social issues, which need to be addressed and ultimately resolved. But the most concrete, the most immediate and the most pressing expression of any national question is invariably to be found on the level of politics, and so it is also on this level that we have to provide answers.

It is precisely here that Andrej's "utopian" perspective proves unsatisfactory; indeed, it would be more accurate to say that, by socializing the national question, his perspective represents an avoidance of politics and thus an avoidance of the national question in its proper sense. To offer a captivating social ideal as the answer to a pressing political problem is akin to drivers whose eyes are so intently fixed on the horizon that they cannot adequately negotiate the immediate obstacles that lie in their path.

It is these immediate obstacles that a radical politics has to negotiate when it comes to the question of Kosovo. There are not a few that need negotiating. Should we oppose or support Kosovo's right to self-determination, the right to form an independent state in its current borders? Should we oppose or support the UN regime that the United States bequeathed the province after its 1999 war against Serbia? Should we oppose or support Serbia's refusal to give up its claim to sovereignty over Kosovo? And should we oppose or support the territorial partition of Kosovo with Serbia? These are the concrete, immediate and pressing questions to which we, as radicals, should be able to provide concrete, coherent, and reasoned answers. Andrej's perspective is ultimately unsatisfactory because he fails to do so.

There are two other perspectives that radicals have offered on Kosovo which are also worth examining.

The Balkan Federation Idea

The first is one that is often proposed by much of what Andrej himself calls the "old" Left in the former Yugoslavia, particularly in Serbia: the idea of a Balkan socialist federation, an idea with a long, progressive political heritage rooted in the 19th century. This idea holds that the only way of transcending ethnic conflict is to do away with the squabbling, petty statelets of the region that have perennially used nationalism to further their ends and whose mutual animosities have so often been exploited by the imperial powers to impose their own "solutions" in the area. A Balkan Federation, the argument goes, would unify the region and serve as a protective bulwark against both imperial intervention and interethnic conflict.

Like Andrej's perspective, this too is a captivating ideal to which every radical should aspire, and be inspired by, as it is the ultimate answer to the national question in the Balkans. But it is also unsatisfactory because, while it is certainly an attempt to address the national question on the level of politics, it provides an abstract answer rather than a concrete one to the central political issue that needs addressing: the right of Kosovo to self-determination, to its own independent state.

Instead, this perspective is too often presented at best as a tacit avoidance of that central issue (a Balkan Federation is the best answer to the Kosovo question) or at worst as an explicit rejection of it (no to another statelet in the Balkans, yes to a Balkan Federation). Such an overriding emphasis on the idea of a Balkan Federation at a time when the dominant political trend is still in the direction of independent statehood, is unlikely to have the kind of daily political purchase on individuals and movements that radicals should seek.

Yet, in other ways, the Balkan Federation idea certainly has the potential to offer answers to the other pressing political questions that come up: no to UN colonial rule in Kosovo, no to Serbia's claims to Kosovo, no to partition. Nevertheless, all these answers are in the end fatally vitiated by the failure to answer concretely and directly the one central question that currently dominates any political discussion of the Kosovo question: the question of the right to self-determination.

Chomsky and Partition

The other answer to the Kosovo question that has emerged from a radical source is that of territorial partition, to which Noam Chomsky, in an interview last year with Radio Television Serbia, has given his support. Chomsky stated:

> My feeling has been for a long time that the only realistic solution is one that in fact was offered by the President of Serbia I think back round 1993 [Chomsky is referring to the proposal of former Serbian president of Yugoslavia, Dobrica Ćosić], namely some kind of partition, with the Serbian, by now very few Serbs left, but what were the Serbian areas being part of Serbia and the rest be what they called "independent," which means it'll join Albania.

While Chomsky's view certainly has the virtue of providing a concrete answer on the level of politics, it is nevertheless highly questionable whether it represents an adequately radical solution to the Kosovo question. There are two main reasons why this is so.

First, Chomsky proposes by partition precisely what Andrej opposes: the drawing of yet another set of ethnic borderlines in the Balkans. The consequences of doing so are not difficult to envisage. Even if partition were limited to Serbia gaining the three northern districts of Kosovo where Serbs are clearly in a majority, such partition, and the rancorous negotiations it is bound to entail, are certain to inflame still further the already inflammatory state of Albanian-Serb relations. Not only could this lead to yet another war over new ethnic borderlines, and to yet another round of ethnic cleansing of Albanians from majority Serb districts and vice-versa, but it would also, as a consequence, leave the remaining Serbs elsewhere in Kosovo even more vulnerable. In short, partition is likely to lead to immeasurably worsened ethnic relations and even to war.

Secondly, and no less importantly, the interethnic strife between Albanians and Serbs that is likely to intensify in the course of the partition process would very likely derail the most positive and significant political development in Kosovo since the 1999 war—the recent emergence of a Kosovan anti-colonial movement.

The Kosovan Anticolonial Movement

On February 10 of this year, a mass demonstration of three-thousand-strong in Kosovo's capital of Pristina demanding immediate independence from Serbia and an end to UN rule of the province was dispersed by UN and Kosovan police using tear gas and rubber bullets. Two demonstrators were shot dead and eighty-two received hospital treatment. That evening, the premises of the Movement for Self-Determination (MSD), which organized the demonstration, were raided, and its leader, thirty-one year old Albin Kurti, was arrested. A further demonstration on March 3 demanded Kurti's immediate release, but at the time of this writing he continues to languish in prison.

MSD's opposition to UN rule marks nothing less than the birth of a Kosovan anticolonial movement. Its activists, regularly arrested and harassed by the authorities, condemn the UN for being an "absolute ruler" whose "colonial occupation," based on "force not justice," prides itself "on being here to build democracy [but] is itself completely undemocratic." They lambaste the UN for not even ending Kosovo's drastic electricity shortages seven years after the 1999 war. Moreover, UN rule has been conspicuously unable with its privatizing neoliberal programs to alleviate Kosovo's desperate levels of poverty, or to resolve Albanian-Serb hostilities with its notoriously top-down approach to this critical issue.

At the same time, despite its uncompromising demand for independence from Belgrade, MSD is not Serbophobic. In 2004, its leader, Albin Kurti, opposed the mass Albanian attacks on Serb civilians and churches, leading one newspaper to condemn him for being "anti-Albanian." Kurti rightly understood that such attacks were a bloody diversion from the struggle for decolonization he wanted to wage.

MSD has also led opposition to the new Kosovo Peace Plan, the immediate cause of the Pristina demonstration, which the UN's envoy, Marti Ahtisaari, announced in February. Proposing that Kosovo should have the right to join the UN and to its own flag and anthem, he stopped short of calling for independence. Instead, he offered rule by an EU governor, supported by an EU-led police force and NATO troops. UNMIK becomes EUMIK, Kosovo remains a colony, and nothing changes. The refusal to call for independence was motivated by one overriding geopolitical fear—that an alienated Serbia might turn to Putin's Russia, which would then secure a foothold in the Balkans.

MSD's appearance therefore marks a shift in Kosovan politics from a destructive focus on Albanian-Serb hostilities to a focus on the struggle against the autocratic neocolonial power the UN currently wields over Kosovo. It is not difficult to see that partition, and all it would entail, would derail this movement because it would bring back the focus on Albanian-Serb hostilities that MSD has been assiduously shifting in an anticolonial direction.

Some Concrete Radical Perspectives

It is therefore important that radicals today support Kosovo's right to self-determination, to an independent state within its current borders. This is neither a distant dream nor an abstract solution; on the contrary, it is politically concrete, but it is also radical not least because the demand for Kosovan independence today is assuming an anticolonial character as the struggle to free Kosovo from autocratic UN or EU rule begins to gather steam.

As for Serbia's claims to Kosovo, it is critical that the Serbian radical Left fulfils its internationalist duty by opposing these nationalist claims. This can best be done if coupled with support for Kosovo's right to self-determination, the right to determine its own future free of UN or EU colonial rule.

It is through such concrete political acts of internationalism by Serbs who support Kosovan Albanian national rights, that agitation around social issues of common interest which Andrej points to (such as opposition to neoliberal privatization) can fruitfully begin. In this way, too, it is possible to begin to build the kind of basic political trust between Serbs and Albanians that will make the idea of a Balkan Federation a more feasible topic for mutual discussion.

One thing is certain, however: it is only by first giving concrete political support to Kosovo's right of self-determination that Left radicals in Serbia in particular will be able to cross the bridge that leads to genuine solidarity between Albanians and Serbs on the wider economic, political, and social issues they have in common. If they fail to do so today, then the national question will be used against them to derail any common initiatives they may try to undertake.

No State, No Nation: Balkan Federation

March 2007

It is the barbarians who now represent faith in human destiny and future of civilization, whereas the "civilized people" find their salvation only in barbarism: the massacre of the Communards and the return of the Pope.
—Mikhail Bakunin, *Protestation of the Alliance*, 1871

If in order to win it were necessary to erect the gallows in the public square, then I would prefer to lose.
—Errico Malatesta, *Pensiero e Volonta*, 1924

Does such an environment exist? It does not. It follows, then, that it has to be created.
—Mikhail Bakunin, *Integral Education*, 1869

A few days ago, the famous British integrated intellectual, Timothy Garton Ash, invited us to "tell our Kosovo." "Kosovo is many things to many people," asserted Ash, "tell me your Kosovo and I will tell you who you are." Allow me then, to start by telling you my Kosovo, and my Balkans. I advocate another Balkans, neither capitalist nor bureaucratic-socialistic: a transethnic society with polyculturalist outlook that recognizes multiple and overlapping identities and affiliations based on voluntary cooperation, mutual aid, a direct democracy of nested councils and a self-managed economy with participatory planning, framed within a regional frame of a federation.

I believe that the Kosovo question can only be answered in a regional framework, and I believe that the Balkans can provide a model for another Europe, a balkanized Europe of regions, as an alternative to both transnational European super-state and nation- states. The Balkanization of Europe would be premised on the politics of autonomous regions and plurality of cultures. I see the region, an entity once eroded by the centralized nation-state and capitalism, as the basis for the regeneration and reconstruction of social and political life of Europe. My Balkans is the Balkans of regional units rather than nations, recuperating their culturally diverse, regional polycultural identity, which had been lost in its incorporation into nation-state frameworks. For these reasons, I do not advocate the support for a new, mono-ethnic, Kosovo nation-state.

The Kosovo movement Verodonstovje has, as its motto, a catchy phrase: "no negotiation: self determination." The motto that I would like to offer is very different: no state, no nation: Balkan Federation. The project of Balkan Federation is a project of radical decolonization, polyculturality, social change from the bottom-up, analogous to and in active communication with such contemporary projects as the politics of *zapatismo* in Mexico and Argentine *horizontalidad*.

Regional experiences of the Balkans, such as its historical experience of self-organization, could balkanize and denationalize Europe's political structures. You will notice that I use the term Balkanization in a different way than it is being used by pundits and Euro-American balkanologists. Balkanization is, one might say, an invention of political balkanologists. This term is a fantastic abuse of language. One could even make a little joke and suggest that Euro-American politics in the Balkans was, historically, guided by three Bs: balkanization, barbarity, and bombs. People in the Balkans are barbarians, or so this Euro-imperial line goes; they tend to balkanize, and the only way to prevent that is to bomb them (or to sell them bombs so they can do it themselves).

Before examining, at the end of this reply [to Dragan Plavsic, see previous article —Ed.], your interesting and constructive arguments, I want to broach discussion of a few more general presuppositions and then try to contribute a few elements for a political reflection on Kosovo question.

Political balkanophobia

If we take a historical view, I think that we could identify a phenomenon, or rather, a whole complex of elite reactions that I propose to call "political balkanophobia": an elite fear of autonomous spaces. The European state system of the 17th and 18th centuries arose as a result of successful fights for the formation and territorial unification of a regional identity. The state-architects of Europe of that time were, in fact, obsessed with the demon of the Balkans, balkanization being taken here in the sense of an alternative process of territorial organization, decentralization, territorial autonomy and federalism. Balkanization, a process of constant fission and fusion, has been a remarkably threatening alternative for the emerging large, centralized, coercive systems. Debalkanization became a name, and an excuse, for a process of eliminating the threat of autonomous political spaces that lack any specialized and permanently constituted coercive authority separated from the society, as well as of eliminating the region's memory of its anticolonial and anti-statist struggles.

Today, in this new era of integration, the Balkans, and balkanization, are presented and projected to the world opinion as nothing but historical residue of "primitive nationalisms," again poses the threat to delirious European bureaucratization, just like in the era of the Absolutist State at its very base. The European Union is unsettled by the prospect of a politically rebellious (unstable) region, inside and against the imperial agglomeration. Listen to the words of the Hungarian prime minister: "The problems of the Roma are not locked on the territory of the individual EU member states, because the free movement of people means free movement of social problems." Debalkanization, in a sense of a pacification of "social problems," is essential for the future integration, in this new era of European history. It signals the need of the European elites, and local oligarchies, to neutralize any potential non state-nationalist alternative political design.

More dramatically put, the real choice of our times is the one between barbarism and balkanization.

To say that Balkan nationalisms are somehow not real would be dishonest, even ludicrous, and in any event very irresponsible. But to say that inter-national and ethnic strife determine Balkan identity is to play into the hands of dominant Euro-imperial discourse. I would even advance a thesis that the Balkans, as a region, is much more courageous, even if sometimes tragically unsuccessful, in its attempts to discover ways to confront the ethnic and religious differences. It is enough, I think, to remember the courageous example of former Yugoslavia and to compare it to Euro-American massacres of Jewish and Arab people, Amero-Indians, and historical legacy of feudal wars, colonialism, slavery and genocide. Who are the real barbarians? One of the crucial aspects of balkanophobia is the particularism of the European universalism. Eurocentric universalism was forged as an ideological balkanophobic response—even before the colonization of the Americas—as a process of "othering" of the Balkans, in the struggle to "break the heavy, mute spell of wilderness," where the Balkans had became a symbol of everything mysterious and threatening in European culture. The Balkans became a "wild" Europe, an entangling, intricate labyrinth inhabited by the creatures of sin and insolent nations incapable of governing themselves: a place in the heart of European darkness where an evil thought will carry a good man out of the light; a place outside, if on the doorstep, where people need to be evangelized in the name of civilizing missions, human rights, and civil society.

Where are we now?

Allow me to sketch, for readers who are not familiar with our Balkan peculiarities, something of a background. So what is this situation in which Kosovo, formally still part of Serbia, finds itself today?

Berlin's Institute for European Politics has just issued a 124-page report written on the behalf of the German Army. According to this interesting document, multiethnic society does not exist outside the bureaucratic pronouncements of the international community (in Trujillo's memorable description, the international community is a "Greek chorus of contemporary politics. No one has ever seen it, but it is singing in the background and everyone is playing to it"). The mission of the European Union, suggested by Ahtisaari, is not sustainable in either a conceptual or analytical sense, say the authors of the document. Kosovo is to be made destitute by bad management, corruption, and organized crime that involve not only Kosovo politicians but also members of European administration. The role of the United States, the document reads, is also counter productive: the United States is aiding the members of organized crime groups, giving training to former members of the Kosovo Liberation Army, and spoiling European efforts to investigate war crimes. According the 2005 analysis by German's foreign intelligence (BND), former Prime Minister Ramush Haradinaj plays a "key role in a broad spectrum of criminal, political and military activities that significantly affect the security situation throughout Kosovo. The group, which counts about one hundred members, is involved in drug and weapon smuggling, as well as illegal trade in dutiable items." The so-called "system Haradinaj," writes *Der Spiegel*, is supported by the regions de facto rulers from the West, represented by a string of envoys from the UN, NATO, EU, and OSCE. At the same time, we can read in the European Stability Initiative Report that the average annual income is 1,200 euros. Unemployment estimates range from 28 percent to more than 40 percent, with remittances from family members abroad comprising the second largest source of income, and accounting for 13 percent of household income. This rate has been dropping as Kosovo émigrés are returning home.

The Holbrooke option

There are quite a few options on the table: one colonial and two nationalist. Serbian nationalists insist on "autonomy without independence." Albanian nationalists insist on "independence and autonomy." The European Union and the United States are imposing, under the so-called Ahtisaari Plan, an "independence without autonomy." Russian politicians talk about the possible use of their veto in the General assembly if the wishes of Serbian nationalists are ignored. Serbian and Albanian nationalist politicians are in the process of long and unsuccessful negotiations.

I think that we can safely assume that the future of Kosovo has already been decided. The so-called negotiations are a charade with the sole purpose of giving some illusion of legality. In an interview given with the Balkan Investigative Research Network, Richard Holbrooke, America's former Balkan negotiator, says that independence, is inevitable now or next year: Serbia has lost the "moral rights to rule Kosovo." "The Russians don't give a damn about the Serbs. They care about Georgia. They are incredibly angry at Saakashvili. They want to overthrow Mikheil Saakashvili ..." "History is on the side of the Kosovo Albanians for the first time in 800 years. The horrible events of 1912 and 1989 are in the process of being reversed. Albanians are very understandably impatient [and] I share that impatience." He does admit that "The whole area is full of organized crime ... But our goal is not to fix every problem in the universe." Then he goes on to ask: "Where is the Kosovar Nelson Mandela?"

His Hannibal Lecter-style cynicism and his exquisite subtlety aside, I think that Holbrooke is right, and that Russia does not intend to interfere for the sake of Serbia. That is also the opinion of Fodor Lukjanov, editor of one of the leading foreign policy magazines in Russia (*Russia in Global Politics*), who, in an interview given to Radio Free Europe, says that Russia is not going to use her veto power, but will support some version of the Ahtisaari Plan. I am not at all convinced that Georgia is what is at stake here. As is usually the case, the truth is simpler. Kosovo and Metohija have the largest deposit of lignite in Europe. According to the web magazine Energy Observer, Russia is very interested in these reserves. The fact that much of the province's wealth lies in minerals is an advantage because Kosovo's mining tradition ensures a pool of skilled workers, and mineral investors are not as likely to be scared away by Kosovo's economic chaos, as it says on the website. In my opinion at least, Russia is using the opportunity to negotiate better terms for the privatization of Kosovo's minerals. To put things very simplistically, as Zbigniew Brzezinski likes to say.

It is, at the same time, painfully obvious that United States will not allow anything short of supervised independence of Kosovo. In a letter-report of the German conservative politician Willy Wimmer to the former German Chancellor Schroder, we can find the outlines for the U.S. policy in the Balkans: the purpose behind the Kosovo war was to enable the United States to correct an oversight of General Eisenhower's in the World War II and to establish a U.S. military presence in the Balkans with the perspective of controlling the strategically important peninsula. The American aim was to draw a geopolitical line from the Baltic Sea to Anatolia and to control this area as the Romans had once controlled it; for all this, the United States needs a speedy recognition of Kosovo, the exclusion of Serbia from Europe, and the prioritization of self determination before all other regulations or rules of international law.

The Radical Left and Kosovo question

This complicated situation presents a very difficult dilemma for the radical Left, and it frames the complex and sensitive nature of our conversation about Kosovo's future. It poses complex, deep, and unpleasant questions.

Let me try to address some of your [Plavsic's] criticisms, which I find very inspiring and constructive in their tone. It seems to me that you propose a very European solution to our Balkan problems. Your answer to the Kosovo question is to establish new states, built on seemingly unavoidable ethno-nationalist principles. You object to my self-avowed utopian approach, and see it as not political enough. It seems that we have different ideas of what politics is. This is probably related to the differences, and concrete disagreements, inscribed in our respective political traditions: anarchism and Marxism-Leninism. By politics I mean an organic, dialogical, shared, and participatory activity of the self-governing public. What you call politics I would call state-building or statecraft, a set of operations that are premised on the seizing the State power, and which are realized through a political party, or political movement; a miniature State, that replicates the State in its organization. For me, this approach intimates precisely what you reproach me for, and that is an abdication of a genuine politics, with a grave concomitant and related symptom of atrophy of political imagination. It prevents critical and political reflection on the social change, the meaning of which would lie in the attempt to bring into being other possibilities for human existence.

I do not avoid the national question, in proper or any other sense. But I do reject the nationalist (as opposed to polycultural) and statist solution, Serbian and Albanian, in every sense.

The radical Left should not worship the status quo, and should not adore *faits accomplis*. What we need in the Balkans, where daily papers are rarely our morning prayer but rather our brutal colonial farce, is a conquest of a point of view beyond the given—a work of a new, restored politics that separates recognition of people's creativity from adoration of power of facts. For the resurgence of the radical decolonization project, new political objectives and new intellectual attitudes are required.

Your solution is support for the right of Kosovo to self-determination, to its own independent state. This is, of course, a very legitimate position to take, but it leaves us with two major problems.

First, I do not see how this proposal is real. It seems to me that it is (even) more utopian than my own. You reproach

Noam's advocacy of partition on the grounds that it would inflame "still further the already inflammatory state of Albanian-Serb relations," and maybe even "lead to yet another war over new ethnic border lines, and to yet another round of ethnic cleansing of Albanians from majority Serb districts and vice-versa." I agree with you. But something does not work here. Your proposal is vulnerable and open to criticisms for the precise same reasons. In my opinion, the future of Kosovo has already been decided in the gentlemen club of Europe, United States, and Russia. So what can we do? If our intention, the most fundamental one, is to care about actual human lives, not for dead principles and if Kosovo becomes independent, as it almost certainly will, the fate of Roma and Serb civilians is sealed. They will be ethnically cleansed. The ones who manage to get out of the Kosovo alive, that is. The UN refuge commission is already preparing for this. Even the former Ambassador to Serbia, William Montgomery (certainly not a Serbian nationalist), warns in his weekly column in the Serbian weekly Danas that "Serbs in Kosovo cannot trust the international community and the guarantees given are no more worthy then paper on which they were written." If the radical Left decides to support the state-ethnic solution, it will have to support the right of Serbs and Roma to secede. Once the right for Albanians to secede from Serbia is established, no one will be able to deny the same right to the others, including, perhaps (or even very probably), to Republika Srpska, the Serbian part of Bosnia. And that will take us right back to Noam's solution of inevitable partition.

My fear of inevitable ethnic violence is supported by a recent proclamation of Hisen Durmisi, one of the leading activists of Vetënovedosje (Movement for Self-Determination, or MSD) to Balkan Insight: "Decentralization means secession and secession means war" ... This will be people's war for freedom, and Vetëvendosje movement will be there to lead it."

This brings us to another weakness of your position. You maintain that MSD is an anticolonial movement. Perhaps so. The question is if we should support this movement.

I like their sense of political humor. Twice they surrounded the UNMIK building with a yellow tape saying
"Crime scene—Do not cross." And they have a skilful sense of
euphemism: "UNMIKistan," "UNMIKolonialism," playing with
words like "F-UN-D" for "the end," or "T-UN-G" for "goodbye"
in Albanian. While I completely support their fight against
"autocratic neo-colonial power," I am very skeptical as to the
other part of your argument, or your belief that MSD is not
Serbophobic. They appear to carry the flame of a very traditional Albanian ethno-nationalism. The leader of MSD is
Albin Kurti, whom I have had an opportunity to meet back in
the days when he was a student representative of the Kosovo
parallel University. Kurti was, at that time, despite his dread-
locks, a fervent Albanian nationalist, advocating the legitimacy of the Great Albanian project, and of a very particular rural nationalist utopia. I had not heard anything about
him until the moment when he became a political adviser to
the KLA (UCK), a narco-guerilla group with a rather limited
political imagination. I have read the manifesto of MSD and
this document does not mention, in a single word, the idea
of cohabitation or of an internationalist society. A journalist
friend of mine who lives and works in Kosovo tells me that
among the many colorful and intelligent stickers and graffiti of MSD, you can also find things like "Smite the Serbs."
He also mentions the relationship between MSD and Balli
Kombetar (a Nationalist Front, right-wing group that advocates the monoethnic project of Great Albania). I do not have
enough information, but this is more than enough to make
me uncomfortable.

In some of my writings on the Balkans, I have tried to
demonstrate that the case of Croatia, Slovenia, Serbian parts
of Croatia and Bosnia, and Kosovo, is significantly different
from the history of anticolonial independence struggles in
the other parts of the world. We would be making a serious
mistake if we would try to apply, or rather to impose, in a
mechanic fashion, the same analytical and political framework. To use a very local joke, OTPOR does not always trans-

late as "resistance." The reality on the ground is very complex and very nuanced; it defies tailor-made solutions, reflexive angelology and demonology of particular struggles, and recognition of this nuanced reality demands from us to patiently tolerate regional complexities.

You further say that, "as for Serbia's claims to Kosovo, it is critical that the Serbian radical Left fulfils its internationalist duty by opposing these nationalist claims." I could not agree more. But I also think that it is critical, in the very same way, for radical Leftists to oppose Albanian nationalism. How can we oppose one nationalism and support another? We must refuse both. We should refuse all the above-mentioned balkanophobic alternatives for Kosovo, however "utopian" this might sound. What we can do is to lend our concrete support to the projects of mutual aid, mutual solidarity, poly-cultural identity, and politics of freedom.

I was always allergic to demands, expressed sometimes by other socialists, that anarchists need to come up with a position on the national question or imperialism. Anarchism is not a political party or a single political line, and there are as many positions as there are anarchists. But, this being said, I do believe that there is one fundamental common premise. Let us call it a prefigurative promise. We cannot create a future that we want by supporting, in the present, those projects and those movements that contradict our vision of future. As Malatesta has said, "if in order to win it were necessary to erect the gallows in the public square, then I would prefer to lose." Or to not choose between imposed balkanophobic solutions, to refuse the rationalization of the real, rationalization of the imposed alternatives, colonial and state-national.

We, the people of the Balkans, need to go back to and build upon the most precious part of our history: a polycultural vision of multiethnic, indeed transethnic, anti-authoritarian society. We need to understand the scandal borne by the word "Balkans" and rediscover the trenchancy of its idea. This kind of society is possible only in the framework of a

Balkan Federation, with no state, and beyond nation: a world where many worlds fit. If this is not our reality today, it follows that our duty, our only duty, is to fight to make it our reality tomorrow.

Parecon as a New Path
for the Balkans?
An Interview With Michael Albert

August 2007

The following interview was prepared for *ZMag Balkans*, a new print magazine, produced by Freedom Fight collective for Balkan audiences, modeled on *Z Magazine* U.S. and utilizing its content as well as local content bearing more directly on the Balkans. The interview was done, more specifically, at the request of the workers in a pharmaceutical factory Jugoremedija in Zrenjanin (Serbia) for an issue of *ZMag Balkans* focusing on participatory economics. The workers are running the plant, having taken it over, and are looking for information and ideas about how to rearrange their workplace to escape the ills of both capitalism and the market socialism they experienced in Yugoslavia. The interviewer was Andrej Grubačić, who is working with both the new magazine and the workers in the plant.

Andrej Grubačić: What is participatory economics?
Michael Albert: Many of its advocates call participatory economics parecon for short, and it is a vision of doing economics differently than under capitalism and what has been called socialism. Participatory economics elevates certain values, such as solidarity, equity, diversity, self-management, and efficiency to central organizing principles, and then proposes a set of institutions that can foster those values while accomplishing economic functions.

The key institutions of parecon are workers and consumers councils using self-managing decision making procedures that put all influence into the hands of those who are affected by decisions: income for how hard people work, how long they work, and the onerousness or harshness of the conditions under which they work; a new division of labor called balanced job complexes that gives each participant a mix of responsibilities such that all people's overall work allotments are comparably empowering in their implications for those involved; and a new way of determining economic inputs and outputs—or allocation—that allows the population to self-manage without class divisions and completes economic functions consistently with people's needs and capacities.

Succinctly: in capitalism, owners, together with about a fifth of the population who have highly empowered work, decide what is produced, by what means, and with what distribution. Of course, the owners and the more empowered fifth of the workforce get far more income than others, dominate choices and, in all critical respects, rule the economy. The latter group doesn't monopolize property, like the owners do, but instead monopolizes the tasks, conditions, and circumstances that facilitate influencing outcomes. I call them the coordinator class. Nearly four-fifths of the population, in contrast to owners and coordinators, monopolize neither property nor empowering positions. These workers do largely rote labor, suffer inferior incomes, obey orders, and endure boredom, all imposed from above. As John Lennon put it, "As soon as you're born they make you feel small, by giving you no time instead of it all." This is the working class.

Capitalism destroys solidarity, reduces variety, obliterates equity, and imposes harsh hierarchy. It is top heavy in power and opportunity. It is bottom heavy in pain and constraint. Indeed, capitalism imposes on workers a degree of economic obedience beyond what any dictator ever dreamed of imposing politically. Who ever heard of citizens asking governors permission to go to the bathroom—a commonplace occurrence for workers in many corporations.

Capitalism's ills are not due, however, to antisocial people. Instead, capitalism's institutions impose horrible behavior even on its most social citizens. In capitalism, as a famous American baseball manager quipped, since you have to benefit at the expense of others and keep climbing oblivious to their pain and suffering, "nice guys finish last." More aggressively: "garbage rises." Witness Washington's White House.

Participatory economics, or parecon, is an alternative way to organize economic life. Parecon has equitable incomes, circumstances, opportunities, and responsibilities for all participants. Each parecon participant has a fair share of control over their own life and over all shared social outcomes. Parecon eliminates class division. Parecon produces solidarity. Even an antisocial individual in a parecon has to account for social well-being, if he or she wishes to prosper.

Parecon diversifies outcomes and generates equitable distribution that remunerates each participant for how long and for how hard they work, as well as for harsh conditions they may suffer at work. Parecon conveys to each person a say in what is produced, what means are used, and how outputs are allocated, all in proportion to the degree he or she is affected by those decisions. Parecon, in other words, has completely different values than capitalism and to further its different values parecon incorporates different institutions. For example, parecon has workers' and consumers' councils where workers and consumers employ diverse modes of discussion, debate, and democratic determination to attain true self-management. In parecon, there are no corporate owners and managers deciding outcomes from the top down.

Parecon has "balanced job complexes" in which each worker does a fair combination of empowering and rote labor, so that all participants have comparably empowering circumstances instead of 20 percent of the workforce monopolizing all the empowering tasks and 80 percent doing only subordinate labor. In a parecon, there is still expertise. There is still coordination. Decisions still get made. But there is no minority monopolizing empowering information, activity, and access to decision making positions while a majority is made subservient by doing only deadening daily tasks with no decision making component.

In parecon, each and every job—which means each and every person's work—involves a mix calibrated so that each participant has comparably empowering conditions to all others. A parecon has no owning class. It has no technocratic, managerial, or coordinator class. A parecon has only workers and consumers cooperatively and creatively fulfilling their capacities consistently with each participant having a fair share of influence.

Parecon has remuneration for effort and sacrifice, which translates to remuneration for the duration, intensity, and harshness of the work people do. Parecon rejects remuneration for power, property, or even for output. Instead of gargantuan disparities of income and wealth, parecon has a just distribution of social product.

Parecon also does away with markets that pit each actor against all others; destroy solidarity; impose class division; misprice all public goods; ignore collective effects beyond direct buyers and sellers; violate ecological balance and sustainability; and have many other faults as well. In place of markets, parecon utilizes a system of workers and consumers self-managing councils cooperatively negotiating inputs and outputs for all firms and actors in accord with true and full social costs and benefits of economic activities.

In an interview like this, even with me abusing your patience with long answers, it is still impossible to make a compelling case for an entirely different economic system. I can only offer a brief list of parecon's values and institutions, as above. I know such brevity is vague and hard for unfamiliar readers to give substance to. But in an interview like this we have no room for detailed clarification, supporting argument, or discussion. My apologies.

What I hope, however, is that readers who know from their own experience that capitalist economies routinely cause us to fleece each other, deny us a say over our own lives, force us to dominate the lives of others, distribute massive outputs to those who do the most pleasurable or even who do little work at all and distribute meager outputs to those who do the least pleasurable and the overwhelming volume of work, will hope that parecon is a real alternative. I hope, in other words, that instead of quietly accepting rich people's mantra that "there is no alternative," we will all seek something better, beyond capitalism, and that, moved by our aspirations we will carefully consider parecon on its merits. One place you might begin, if you don't believe that humanity is forever doomed to suffer gross inequality and hierarchy via capitalist ownership, corporations, and markets, is at http://www.parecon.org.

AG: You seem to maintain that parecon is not only more just but also more efficient then capitalism. Is that your view?
MA: Yes, but that is partly because of how I use the word efficiency. I suspect what you mean by your question is: if we have some resources and equipment, and a bunch of people to do work, will parecon generate outputs comparable or greater in volume in a given time as what capitalism would deliver with the same resources, people, and time? And assuming we mean outputs that benefit people—as compared to useless waste, redundancy, policing and cleaning ecological messes that were created needlessly, and so on—then yes, I think parecon would be more efficient, even in terms of just gross but useful output per hour, by quite a large margin.

Among other reasons, this is because in a parecon huge swaths of labor are no longer given to wasteful or destructive production: parecon avoids redundant output, much packaging and advertising, much control, cleaning up messes in the environment that won't be created in the first place, war, and so on. So all that productivity is put to more socially beneficial outcomes and, therefore, output that is useful to humans—per hour of labor expended and per volume of resources used—will on these accounts be far greater than it is now. Additionally, there is every evidence—insofar as we have admittedly limited examples to judge—that increasing workers say over the activities they engage in, reducing alienation, etc., increases productive intents and capacities.

But I would suggest that an even more important step than seeing the above is to think about what we actually mean by efficiency. The word means, in a dictionary, accomplishing what you seek without wasting assets that you value. Clearly, with that definition, only a lunatic would be against efficiency, since that would mean either not accomplishing what you seek or doing it in a way incurring unnecessary costs.

So why do so many of us, at least in my experience, get nervous when we hear the word efficiency intoned—as if it were a kind of prayer or mantra consistently employed right before kicking us in the head? I think we get nervous because in capitalism, in actual practice, efficiency means accomplishing what owners seek, not all of us, without wasting assets that owners value no matter what the rest of us value. In other words, capitalist efficiency is about maximizing profits for the owners and if a firm wastes resources or trashes the environment or subverts or restricts people's lives in the process, that is no problem, since the owners care only about themselves not about those who suffer those effects.

So with this larger understanding of efficiency, there is simply no comparison between capitalism and parecon. Capitalism is horrendously inefficient in that it wastes resources, energy, and human labor on vast quantities of inhumane output and doesn't even try to meet needs and develop potentials as a high priority, much less to protect the rights and well being of workers. Parecon, in contrast, produces and allocates in light of full social costs and benefits of all citizens and in pursuit of all people's well-being and development. In capitalism, it is efficient to mess up the environment and then clean it up, if one is making profits while doing so. Likewise, in capitalism, to use up the lives of workers while making profits is again efficient. In a parecon, in contrast, the environment is valued, workers lives are valued, and messing up either is a cost to avoid. And this isn't because people in a parecon are somehow biologically different in their preferences. It is because a parecon's way of organizing work, making decisions, and apportioning benefits all foster these outcomes.

AG: But isn't your aim what we have already had to endure here, in the Balkans, under the name of "socialism"?

MA: No. Socialism has come in two shapes, either with markets or with central planning. You had the former in Yugoslavia, but the latter also existed, of course, for example in the Soviet Union. This system that has called itself socialism has also included remunerating labor for its output and for its bargaining power. And it has included the familiar corporate division of labor in which about 20 percent of the workforce, whom I call the coordinator class, had a monopoly on the empowering tasks and the rest were stuck doing only rote and obedient labor. As a result of these institutional commitments, socialism as you and others have known it, has been not a classless economy, but an economy in which about 20 percent ruled over the workers below. There have also been other flaws—including political, cultural, social—but the basic problem with what has been called socialist economics has been that it has eliminated one boss (the owning class or capitalist class) only to enshrine another boss, whom I call the coordinator class.

AG: So how exactly is this new system different from Yugoslav self-management?

MA: Yugoslav self-management had markets, the old corporate division of labor, and remuneration for bargaining power and output. In place of these, parecon has participatory planning which is a kind of cooperative, horizontal, negotiation of inputs and outputs; balanced job complexes in which each worker gets a combination of responsibilities so their overall work load is comparably empowering to what other workers enjoy; and remuneration for how long people work, how hard people work, and the onerousness of the conditions under which people work.

These are not minor but are instead centrally important differences. They yield very different motivations, in turn generating very different outcomes. The core institutions of Yugoslav self-management, with the exception of doing away with private ownership of workplaces, are rejected by parecon for being class biased and antithetical to equity, solidarity, and self-management. In their place, parecon adopts classless institutions favoring real self-management, solidarity, equity, diversity, efficiency, etc.

AG: Do you think that working people in Serbia, who used to live under state socialism and now live in transitional capitalism, would be able to find parecon attractive and persuasive?
MA: I can't see why not. Would working people in Serbia like to control their own destiny? Would they like a fair share, a truly fair share, of the social product? Would they like to have no rulers above, and no obedient passive people below? Would they like an economy that treats the environment—and people too—with respect and with dignity? I can understand why Serb citizens might be skeptical that an economy can deliver such benefits, but once a compelling case is made that parecon can do just that, even coming out of the disastrous experiences you have endured, I don't see why advocacy wouldn't follow.

The ills of market socialism that people in Serbia have experienced and rejected are what induced the design and advocacy of parecon. It is precisely because the market system was so flawed that a new vision was needed and created. Your distaste for that old system should not reduce interest in parecon, but should instead foster it.

AG: What would a participatory workplace look like?
MA: A participatory workplace will look different, in some respects, depending on the industry it is in, its size and technologies, the history and preferences of the workforce, etc.

That is, most features of a workplace are contextual, worked out by workers in context of their own desires and consumer desires, and in context of relations with other workplaces, available technologies, etc. Some features, however, are central to what a participatory economy is. These are what make a workplace pareconish. These are what will recur in case after case.

So, a participatory workplace has a workers' council and also diverse subcomponents of that, including divisions, teams, little groups, etc. The workers' council is the main venue of decision-making. Within the workers' council (and also the component divisions, teams, groups, etc.), decisions are taken so as to foster and enact self-management. How much discussion and preparation there is before any particular decision is reached; what the norms are for delaying or conducting a vote or for reconsidering one later; and what the actual procedures of the votes are (for example, majority rule, or consensus, or perhaps a different total needed for a positive result such as two thirds, etc., or any other possibility) depend on what best conveys self-management case by case. But the aim in all cases is the same: that each worker should have a say in workplace decisions in proportion to the degree the worker is affected by them (and likewise for consumers, for that matter), while also getting the jobs done.

A participatory workplace also has payment for labor that people do, of course. But the rate of payment is very different than under capitalism, or under what has been called socialism. No one gets income for owning property—that idea, the idea of profits, is simply gone. But also no-one gets paid for credentials, or for bargaining power, or even for the volume or value of their output. Instead, each worker gets paid for how long they work, how hard they work, and how onerous their work is, so long as the work is socially useful and desired. You get more for working longer, harder, or under worse conditions. Pretty much the opposite of what you can see all around, now. You don't get more for ownership, or for being strong enough to demand more, or even for producing something more valuable, or for being able to produce more quickly (as long as you are producing well enough to be socially valuable).

A participatory workplace also has what are called balanced job complexes. This takes a bit longer to explain. Imagine a list of all the tasks done in a workplace, a very long list. The typical way to currently create jobs out of this long list of tasks is to combine a set of tasks that are rather similar in their "empowerment effects" and lump them into a job. Some jobs combine mostly empowering labor—labor that conveys information, skills, social habits, access to options, and even a degree of personal drive essential to participating in making decisions. Other jobs combine mostly rote, repetitive, disempowering labor—labor that diminishes overall awareness and knowledge, that reduces skills, that isolates and denigrates and exhausts the worker, leaving him or her poorly prepared to participate in decisions and even disinclined to do so. This is called a corporate division of labor and it yields a class difference between so that about 20 percent of the workforce is empowered and dominates choices, and 80 percent is disempowered and endures boredom while obeying orders. The former group I call the coordinator class, the latter group I call the working class. What follows immediately from this is the realization that in what have been called market socialist and centrally planned socialist economies it hasn't only been horrible that the governments were authoritarian. Additionally, these economies elevated the coordinator class to ruling economic status. Out with the old boss—the capitalist owners—and in with the new boss—the coordinator decision maker. Parecon is about getting beyond that kind of trade

With balanced job complexes (in contrast to corporate divisions of labor) in a participatory workplace still have a long list of tasks that need doing. The list c... es quite a bit. You no longer seek to maximize the gain few owners, but now you seek to operate as an effectivucer of items needed by society in light of the desires workers and consumers. Still, the list of all tasks noss remains long.

But in parecon, instead of combining tasks to impose jobs arrayed in a hierarchy of empowerment, we combine tasks to achieve a classless workforce. That is, we combine tasks so that each worker has a fair (balanced) share of empowering and disempowering tasks composing their overall work responsibilities. It isn't that everyone does everything. Not only is that ridiculous, in that people don't want to do everything and are not well suited or even suited at all to doing everything but also everything is way too much in any case. There are hundreds, even thousands, of tasks done in a complex workplace. Any one person can do only a relatively small bunch of different things as part of their job. So the idea is that we each do a mix of tasks we are able and suited to do, but the list is a mix of empowering and not so empowering and also disempowering work, so that on balance our workplace experience is like that of all our co-workers in this one crucial way: we are each comparably empowered and thus comparably prepared by our position in the economy to participate fully and effectively in the decision making life of the workplace.

AG: You mean that with balanced jobs, there would be no managers?

MA: A managerial function remains in many workplaces, in many aspects. Think of a symphony orchestra. Someone still conducts, but that person doesn't only conduct. Rather, they also do some other functions, and the overall mix is such that their work is comparably empowering to the work others do. The same holds for the hospital, say. There is still brain surgery and there is still cleaning of bed pans, but there are not people who do only the former or who do only the latter. And the same holds for the factory. Engineering still gets done. Design is done. Maintaining good social relations also involves various tasks. And so does assembly, and so on. What no longer happens is for one person to be doing overwhelmingly empowering work and another person to be doing overwhelmingly disempowering work.

In a publishing house where I worked that was parecon-ish, everyone did editorial work on the grounds that if you weren't doing that, you weren't really publishing. Everyone shared in the rote tasks like answering phones, taking mail, and cleaning the place. Everyone did production, which in those days was overwhelmingly typesetting the books, then a very debilitating and exhausting kind of labor. Then each person also did some other work, maybe designing and producing catalogs, or working on keeping records, or whatever. Overall, however, we each had a fair mix of things to do. When we met to make decisions, there was no one person or small group or people who were by their work better able and more attuned, over and over, to setting an agenda, providing key information, knowing overarching circumstances, having more access to skills or information or assets, and so on. We could thus have self-management, with everyone able to have their fair share of informed influence over choices.

AG: How would people measure each other's effort to decide incomes?
MA: There is no single right answer, as different workplaces would likely differ partly due to different conditions and types of work, and partly due to different choices by the workers' council. What will recur, case to case, if the model proves valid, is that the workers' council will settle on a way of determining how long people work, how hard they work, and how onerous their work is, compared to average. It is important to realize, however, that in the model it is critical that people are doing socially valued labor. I can't work incredibly hard for long hours under harsh conditions, doing something that no one values and expect to get paid for it. I can't be a brain surgeon or a football goalie, because I am just not able to do those things well enough to provide socially valuable product.

So how might different workplaces choose to determine worker's remuneration levels for jobs they are able to do? Some may feel that actual differences, averaged over time, will be rather modest and won't matter too much so there is no point in constantly closely evaluating differences. I actually tend to think that. If a workplace had that view, it might have average pay, above average pay, extreme pay, below average pay, and low pay. Another workplace, feeling instead that people will want to vary more often and more consistently and caring greatly about the differences, may prefer a much tighter set of levels, say, in 5 percent steps, or even 2 percent steps. So how does a workplace decide that I should get average pay, or above average pay, or below average pay, in some amount according to its pay levels?

The workers will report their time, their intensity of work. Most likely, an evaluation will hear that self-assessment and then include a look at a person's output to see if the person's time is being productively spent. This is not remunerating output, by the way. If I do surgery for an hour, and I am dysfunctional, I won't keep getting paid for it as if I was doing a socially valuable hour of labor. But if I do it acceptably well, then I will. The rate of the payment per hour has nothing to do with the volume or value of the output, but the volume of the output does tell us if time spent was spent well or frivolously and therefore if it should be remunerated at the going hourly rate. You can't claim ten hours of above average high-intensity labor for work that produced what ten hours of below average or average intensity labor, given your abilities, should have yielded, unless there is some good explanation for the discrepancy.

Workers may decide, in a small workplace, to have collective, periodic meetings about distribution of income. Or, more likely, in a larger workplace, evaluation will be by people with this evaluative task as part of their balanced job complexes—including collating claims about duration, intensity, and onerousness of work, reporting to the council, preparing for votes, etc. It is important to realize that no one has anything to gain by denying others their true incomes or anything to lose by granting them.

Mostly, all this and much more is the case because this is a new kind of workplace with real participation, classlessness, and with motives that make sense, and because there are balanced job complexes that greatly diminish differences in overall onerousness of work or even eliminate them for all practical purposes so that remuneration is just for duration (which is easy to assess) and for intensity, which is also pretty easy for workmates to evaluate.

Without going too far into details, it is important to note that in a full parecon, a workplace agrees to certain outputs as part of the cooperatively negotiated social plan. It can't fall short of that and yet claim that everyone is working well, socially usefully, etc., unless there is a good explanation for the shortfall, other than that people weren't working well, or hard, etc. In other words, the workplace's overall output has to match up, in terms of hours claimed and intensity claimed, with total remuneration for the workforce.

AG: But how would this company, or a workplace, function outside of a market? How would they sell their products? Or relate to other, non-parecon workplaces? Is "parecon in one factory" even possible?

MA: I think the harder question is probably how would they operate within a market, assuming we set up a pareconish workplace though the rest of the economy is still capitalist. In a full parecon, to first answer your question as posed, the workplace functions without market allocation, which is replaced but with cooperative planning, or what I call participatory planning. There is much written about this new approach to allocation, but the essence is that it is a set of procedures and structures that allow workers and consumers councils to express their desires for both production and consumption, and to then refine and otherwise alter their preferences in light of options and possibilities revealed by others until a plan is arrived at. It is self-managing decision-making applied to inputs and outputs throughout the economy. The pareconish motives and incentives generate output that is consistent, however, with meeting needs not only of consumers but also of workers. There is no drive to accumulate for the sake of competition, nor to sell things that aren't needed, nor to dominate other workers or workplaces. There is a drive, consistent with conditions and options, to meet needs and develop potentials, which includes needs for free time, for learning, and so on. The problem with all this is getting there, but once there, the absence of markets is not a problem at all— it is instead a major achievement. In the old Yugoslavia, the persistence of markets imposed on people motives contrary to their values: to get ahead at the expense of others; to produce for the sake of competitive advantage; to divide the workplace into coordinators and workers so that the former could impose cost cutting measures on the latter; and so on. That is all left behind, precisely by leaving behind market allocation.

AG: But what about now, under capitalism? What about trying to have a pareconish workplace while having no choice but to operate in context of the still existing market?

MA: I spent some time in Argentina meeting with a group of representatives from about thirty workplaces, each of which was taken over by its workforce, collectivized, and then run in accord with their desires but also within a capitalist context of market allocation. These representatives went around the room describing their experiences before I was to speak. People became very forthright, and it was incredibly instructive. These were worker-run firms, typically called co-ops. They ranged in size from just a few workers to hundreds and it would not have been different had they gone larger as well. The workers, upon taking over, first sought to make wages equitable, generally by making them all equal. They sought also to incorporate real democracy, even real self-management, by creating a workers' council and giving it decisive power. But they retained, in most cases, the old division of labor. And they also operated within the market context, which still persists in Argentina. Person after person described the great hopes and feelings of solidarity and accomplishment they shared at the outset of their factory occupations, but then also the steady deterioration of hopes and feelings of solidarity that they suffered over time. They reported, many of them crying while doing so, that though they were intent on establishing worthy workplaces, they felt their experiments were going bad, and more exactly, that they were falling back into old patterns. They wondered if maybe, despite their best intentions, there really was something about human nature or about social organization of all kinds that made it that there was no way other than the familiar—however debilitating—way of doing economics.

Then I spoke and talked about how their attachment to the old division of labor and their having to operate in a market context were what was undoing their gains. These particular old institutions had implications—in this case imposing motives, behaviors, divisions of labor, and hierarchies of power and income that they didn't want—and it only felt to them like these bad trends were coming from within themselves, but really they were coming from these institutional holdovers. The old corporate division of labor guaranteed that about 20 percent would dominate meetings, decide results, and in time see themselves as more deserving and raise their own pay, while 80 percent would be alienated at meetings, have little to contribute, feel less valuable, and in time accept lower pay, even drifting away from decision-making entirely. This is precisely what they had experienced. Other outfits that did alter the division of labor said, however, that they too were reverting to old ways, albeit more slowly, so it couldn't only be due to the division of labor. I discussed with them how operating within a market context meant they had to cut costs, having to decide in essence to oppress themselves with speed up, with bad conditions, and to do alienated advertising, and to avoid cleaning up their pollution, thereby hurting others as well, all to outcompete other firms so as to maintain themselves in business, and therefore to maintain an income at all. The drive to make such horribly antisocial and alienating decisions (I offered by way of explanation of their depressing experience) leads to pressures to insulate a set of people from those decisions, a set who is well trained to decide outcomes that hurt others while not enduring the costs themselves. This ensues the hiring of managers and giving them air-conditioned offices, better hours, etc., so they will make the cost-cutting decisions affecting other workers.

The answer to your questions about being pareconish while functioning in a market situation, in other words, is that we can set up workplaces with equitable remuneration and self-managed decision making and balanced job complexes, but if they have to operate in a market setting, those gains that we have fought to construct will be very unstable, constantly feeling heavy pressures to revert to more familiar old ways of doing things so as to be able to deal with banks and other old style institutions, and so as to be able to compete. So, yes, it can certainly be done, and is certainly a good thing to do, both to enjoy the benefits locally and to provide a model and explore its features, but it is a continuing struggle against outside pressures.

And finally, yes, one can also imagine that as there are a number of pareconish firms, they can begin to operate not solely inside the market's dictates, but also as they choose, perhaps cooperatively negotiating their exchanges rather than settling for market prices. This is not unknown now in the world, even at the national level. Thus, when Venezuela and Bolivia trade, at least in some items, they don't use market prices, but they instead cooperatively negotiate the terms of the exchange. The idea is that the poor nation, in this case Bolivia, should garner more of the benefits of the exchange so that the wealth gap between the countries diminishes, rather than the richer nation getting still richer at the expense of the poorer nation, as, say, occurs with neoliberal market trade relations.

AG: Here, in the "transitional" countries of the European East, local "experts" usually claim that "there is no alternative" to the rule of free market capitalism. Is this really true? Is neoliberal capitalism, which our experts call inevitable, different then past capitalisms? And are there any other examples of

alternative economies, outside and against capitalism in the world today?

MA: No, the depressing claim isn't true at all. It is a bit like a dictator saying there is no alternative to dictatorship. Or like a criminal mob saying that only they can patrol the streets. Participatory economics is not just a workable alternative, however; it is a workable alternative that eliminates class rule and generates equity and self-management, among other virtues. In other words, it is workable and it is also worthy. Neoliberal capitalism, in contrast, is overwhelmingly just capitalism with the owners powerful enough to reduce concessions that were previously won by working people. In the same way that social democracy is just capitalism with workers as more powerful and thereby able to moderate the harshest features, neoliberalism is just capitalism with capitalists as more powerful and able to intensify the harshest features.

But as to your other query, no, I am afraid at the moment there are no participatory economic economies in the world. There are many experiments and efforts, however, that are either explicitly or implicitly consistent with trying to attain parecon and classlessness. The fact that such an economy doesn't yet exist in full, however, is in no way an argument that one can never exist. This would be like saying, just a few decades ago, that the fact that there was no country that wasn't grotesquely patriarchal meant there never could be one. Such entreaties to retain horrible relations are nonsense expounded by those who benefit from those relations.

Put differently, a real argument that there is no alternative other than capitalism would have to show that there could be no institutions other than corporate divisions of labor, markets, and private ownership of resources and equipment that could accomplish production and consumption at all. No one has ever even tried to offer such an argument, though many claim it is the case. A more plausible argument might say that there is no alternative other than capitalism that is worth our attention, because there is no alternative that is more worthy. Someone proposing that would have to show that there were no other institutions that could do economics more justly, more equitably, more socially, more democratically, etc., than capitalism. But parecon can do all that and much more, putting the lie to the claims, which, again, are only trumpeted, but not soberly argued.

The reason, by the way, that your "experts" call neoliberal capitalism inevitable despite having zero evidence or argument for the claim, is because they work for capitalism, are paid by capitalism, enjoy capitalism's perks and benefits, see themselves as deserving of those perks and benefits, see others as inferior, etc. It is not due to them having great wisdom or knowledge, however, as you probably know well from your own direct understanding of the situation.

AG: Another catchword is the European Union. There is something of a mystical promise in the air, according to which every social problem will be solved upon the entry in this supra national structure. Do you find the European Union to be historically "progressive" and useful for the people in the Balkan countries?

MA: I don't know much about the European Union. But based on general understanding, I doubt it is of any significant consequence, beyond very modest implications, that is. It may change some things a bit for the better, or a bit for the worse, of course. But my intuition would be that it has absolutely zero to do with overcoming the most basic defining problems of current societies. Quite the contrary, my intuition would be it presupposes their continuation. The reasons for my having these expectations are because the European Union is a product of the interests of owning and empowered elites, not of working people.

AG: What would a hypothetical "participatory strategy," for the working people in a country like Serbia be like?

MA: I can't really answer specifically, not knowing nearly enough about Serbia. I can answer more generally, however, at least up to a point. I think that a strategy for attaining a parecon would have a few key components. It would involve building workers and consumers councils in existing workplaces and through those participatory structures fighting for short-term gains in both workplaces and communities which, however, would be sought in ways leading toward further gains. It would involve, as well, seeking diverse kinds of more general societal gains, such as laws for higher wages or better conditions, or the government and citizens doing participatory budgeting, and much else of that sort.

In essence, movements would fight for improvements in people's lives now, but in ways developing consciousness, desires, and means of fighting for still more gains in the future, all on a path leading to classlessness. If a pareconish movement fights for higher wages, it does so while developing awareness of remuneration for duration, intensity, and onerousness of work. If a pareconish movement fights for workers having more say, or for restraints on pollution, etc. it does so while developing awareness of the meaning and merits of self-management and participatory planning. And so on, for gain after gain.

A strategy to win a parecon, I think, would also be highly attuned to the three-class rather than two-class view of both capitalism and possible ways of going beyond capitalism. In wanting to incorporate into present activity values and means of operating that reflect and move us toward our future goals, it follows that with a three-class conception, we would not have our movement elevate coordinator class folks to rule. On the contrary, our movement would be classless and would incorporate equitable remuneration, balanced job complexes, and self-management for decision making. We won't want movements that lead toward coordinator class dominated economics, like what Yugoslavia had in the past, so we will need movements that elevate working people and foreshadow and develop the means for introducing a new division of labor.

There is much else to say, of course, but it is all rather general because serious strategy, beyond generalities, is so specific to particular contexts. But I guess that the key summary insight, at least in my view, is that we need movements that are aimed at classlessness and that operate with methods, values, goals, and structures leading toward true self-management and classlessness, not just by their caring and enlightened rhetoric, but by the very choices they make about their own organization and campaigns both now and into the future. Indeed, parecon's main value for the moment is probably the twofold one of overcoming cynicism about what is possible on the one hand, and providing guidance to avoid making movement choices that would attain something other than what we desire on the other.

Anti-Privatization Protests in Serbia: Global Balkans Interviews Milenko Srećković (Freedom Fight)

October 2009

The IMF recently concluded a one-week mission to Serbia, during which it extended the second tranche of a EUR 4.3 billion loan package to Serbia. However, it gave the government until late October to reign in public sector spending as a condition for disbursing the third tranche of the agreement (worth EUR 1.4 billion) by the end of the year. The tough negotiations come at a time when the incumbent government of Serbia is facing a 4 percent contraction in its economy and a determined workers movement that refuses to bear the burden of economic restructuring after years of corruption that has bound together key Serbian business and political interests in the squandering of public funds. The end of 2009 is also the self-imposed deadline set by the government for completing the sell-off of all "socially owned" (i.e. formerly self-managed) companies in Serbia.

There are currently over thirty strike actions throughout the country, many of which have taken-on radical forms in recent months, including factory occupations; railway blockades; city-hall and police-station takeovers; sleep-ins; boss-nappings, hunger strikes; even a case of self-mutilation. In these actions, workers are often seeking to prevent shady privatization deals from occurring, or trying to save their jobs and enterprises from bankruptcy (following such privatizations). The main concern of most workers in these actions is to ensure the continued payment of salaries, compensation, etc. upon which their survival and those of their communities depends. Many of these strikes have been organized at the factory level, with little input from the mainstream unions in Serbia.

In recent days, a number of Strike Committees have come together to form a Coordinating Committee for Workers Protests in Serbia (CCWPS). Currently five Strike Committees have joined the CC representing workers from three cities and five branches of industry (electrical components, pharmaceuticals, rail-products, food-processing, and confectionary products). One of the groups in the new Coordinating Committee, the workers of Zastava Elektro from the city of Raca, are currently in Belgrade in front of the headquarters of Serbia's Privatization Agency.

Global Balkans: The IMF was just recently in Serbia to negotiate the disbursement of a EUR 4.3 billion loan to the country. What is the current situation in Serbia with respect to the economic crisis? What makes 2009 an important year in Serbia's privatization attempts?

Milenko Srećković: The current economic collapse in Serbia would have occurred even without the "economic crisis." It's the direct result of a range of neoliberal economic measures. The privatization process in Serbia, which is a central component of the neoliberal project, brought about the ruin of many factories and the near total de-industrialization of the country. This process began in 2001, in its most extreme form, when the new "democratic" government of Serbia introduced a new Privatization Law. At that time, all socially owned property was confiscated and its privatization became mandatory. A deadline was imposed by state authorities for the completion of the privatization process. That deadline runs out at the end of this year!

However, following eight years of privatization, the general opinion is that privatization only served to ravage an economy that somehow managed to survive the sanctions of the 1990s and a (three month) NATO bombing campaign in 1999. Of course, it wasn't the most prosperous economy in Europe at the time, but it had the potential to develop and employ a large number of people given the right approach.

By 2002, a number of domestic development banks (i.e. Beobanka, Investbanka, Beogradska Banka, Jugobanka), which could have extended credits to industry at low-interest, were deliberately driven into bankruptcy by the government. With this move, the space was created to open branches of foreign banks (none of which had a developmental function). This [financial reform] was supported by the IMF and the World Bank and implemented by the IMF's domestic cadres. These cadres (like Mladjan Dinkić) have been permanent fixtures in every Serbian government since October 2000. Domestic industry, already shaken up by ten years of crisis n the 1990s, suddenly found itself without a source of favorable credit.

The state has shown little interest in maintaining production in those enterprises that employ a large number of workers. Receipts from the sale of factories were used to fill the state-budget and purchase social peace, while enabling a favorable infrastructure for foreign investors to be created so that they could engage in green-field investments in the newly opened "free zones." These "free zones" are characterized by working conditions that offer minimal pay, thereby allowing foreign investors to use cheap labor (which is cynically called our "comparative advantage" by local neoliberal economists).

Currently there is a marked increase in labor protests largely due to the non-payment of wages and benefits, or because of layoffs, etc. Workers are increasingly demanding from the [Serbian] Privatization Agency put an end to a spate of bad privatization deals. In fact, this agency is the best evidence that the new "democratic" authorities totally retained the model of a centralized state from the communist period, since they now need this apparatus to introduce neoliberal reforms. That is to say, this type of agency is an integral part of the state wherever such massive privatizations occur. Such a powerful state agency has never existed in Serbia (regardless of which empire ruled in the region!).

Of course, it was precisely such a strong Privatization Agency that was needed to secure the ultimate goal—to allow new private owners to purge these newly acquired assets of their workers, while retaining ownership over all the plant, capital and land of these factories. They could then either sell or rent this newly "freed" space to other businesses. In this way they were able to create a high-rate of unemployment, creating an important precondition for "green-field" investments. Workers have taken to pointing out the persistent involvement of the Privatization Agency's functionaries in such criminal activities that have driven many factories to ruin often in direct violation of the stipulations regulating their privatization. However, the legal system is set up in such a way that the agency is always right, and even when it has clearly failed to uphold the law everyone knows that nothing will happen. This is because a good portion of the proceeds from privatization has gone into the financing of political parties (both among those in the current government and for those in the oppositions ranks).

GB: How has the workers' movement responded?
MS: The independent, grassroots workers' movement in which we're participating draws on the experience of the workers' struggle in the city of Zrenjanin from recent years. This is a model that we're trying to spread to other cities in Serbia. Zrenjanin, which was one of the industrial centers of both Serbia and the former Yugoslavia, suffered a total collapse of local industry. The current unemployment rate there now stands at 35 percent.

However, in Zrenjanin, there were also factories where workers offered strong resistance, like in the Jugoremedija pharmaceutical factory where they succeeded in removing the new owner who was leading the company into bankruptcy. These workers recently succeeded in installing their own management, restarted production, and saved their jobs.

Having solved their own existential problems, they continued to struggle in solidarity with their local community, establishing a working-class political party known as Ravnopravnost (Equality) and extending their solidarity to workers from other factories in Zrenjanin, which were caught-up in similar struggles. The movement has received the support of the local community, as well as many organizers and public figures from outside Zrenjanin, including some engaged intellectuals like Nebojsa Popov (the editor of *Republika*) and Ivan Zlatic, an activist from the Freedom Fight movement, etc.

The movement we're building is based on the right to work, or I should say more precisely, the right of workers to decide on the fate of the factories in which they're employed and from which they themselves, along with their families and their local communities, live.

Another important stronghold of this movement is in the city of Raca, near Kragujevac. Raca has become the site of one of the most determined and most radical workers' struggles for the preservation of their workplaces. During the past month, we managed to link together the representatives of Strike Committees from several enterprises and suggested that, in moments where there's a real possibility and need, they could coordinate their efforts and struggle for their rights together. On this basis we founded the Coordinating Committee for Workers Protests in Serbia (CCWPS).

GB: Tell us about the new Coordinating Committee?
MS: During the recent August 11 Zastava Elektro workers' protest in front of the Privatization Agency in Belgrade, during which the workers spent the night in front of Agency, we invited workers from similarly affected enterprises that we've been working with to join us. The intention was to extend the solidarity that existed between workers in a given city to workers from other cities that might be at quite a distance from each other. It was in this way that we created the basis for a Coordinating Committee that was established by the representatives of workers from the Zastava Elektro [electri-

cal components] factory in Raca, the Srbolek [pharmaceuti-cal] factory in Belgrade, as well as workers from Sinvoz [rail-car production] and BEK [food processing] plants in Zrenjanin. We put a callout for other Strike Committees in Serbia to join us.

A few days later, workers from the Ravanica [confection-ary] factory in Cuprija joined the Coordinating Committee. We're expecting more Strike Committees to join us in the coming days. The plan is to be prepared for the fall when an escalation in worker discontent and rebellion is expected throughout Serbia. The main aim is to struggle in solidarity with one another against the collapse of our factories and the protection of our jobs. The government has already put together its team for the suppression of workers' protests, with the aim of silencing our concerns. Now we must dem-onstrate that we're strong, united and organized, because oth-erwise the entire democratic potential of the workers move-ment will disappear into case-specific negotiations with the government working group.

GB: What concrete successes has this Committee already had?

MS: We are struggling to ensure that the government's work-ing group accepts the [democratically elected] representa-tives of the Strike Committees as their interlocutors in any future negotiations. The government has already chosen its own partners in carrying out the so-called "social dialogue," which was obviously chosen from the leadership of the main-stream unions. The workers in Serbia are deeply disillusioned with the behavior of the big unions, especially in the course of the past year—and especially since the onset of the eco-nomic crisis—because they've shown themselves to be allies of the government in attempting to slow down the current strike-wave. In some cases, they were even directly involved in sabotaging some actions by workers. It is for this reason that we're asking that the government's main interlocutors on the side of the workers be a coordinating body that represents the interests and demands of the actual workers' Strike Committees [at the factory level]. We've put some real pressure on the government, and we'll continue to do so. We're hoping for positive results.

However, if this question is hinting at the success achieved in light of the recent offer by the owner of Zastava Elektro, Ranko Dejanovic, to return the factory to the ownership of the workers (following six months of radical strike action) ... I have to let you know that we've rejected the owner's offer. The negotiations with the government are always tied-up in avoiding a number of traps that they're trying to set for us. This offer [from Dejanovic] is one of these traps, even though the media presented it as a big victory for the workers. In fact, all they're giving us is a factory that the current owner has overburdened with serious debts and mortgage issues. It would be only a matter of days before such a factory faced bankruptcy. It would be hard to resume production so long as the state refuses to cancel all the debts accumulated by Dejanovic—debts accumulated in partnership with functionaries from the Privatization Agency, which allowed him to retain ownership for so long—even though he was clearly violating his obligations [under the terms of the privatization agreement].

The struggle for the future of Zastava Elektro continues to this very moment. Today, workers will again hold a protest in front of the Privatization Agency (unless, of course, the police again try to prevent bus-companies from driving the workers from Raca to Belgrade). If this happens, we'll again have to blockade the communal police station, the city council, or the main railway-line near Raca.

GB: What is the position of women and minorities in the workers movement?
MS: There is no exclusion in this movement of anyone on the basis of their gender or nationality. Every well-intentioned person is welcome to join this workers movement, regardless if they're male, female, or belong to an ethnic minor-

ity group. In fact, I'd draw your attention to the fact that the workers collectives in which women are in the overwhelming majority are more steadfast in their struggles. In the cases of Jugoremedija and Zastava Elektro, more than 70 percent of those employed are women.

GB: What are the strengths and weaknesses of this movement?
MS: The greatest strength of this movement is the mutual trust that exists within it. This trust is invaluable and it took years to build. The biggest problem that we're confronting is the fact that Serbia and the former Yugoslavia have a long-standing legacy of authoritarian intelligence agencies which, in the current context, aren't able to carry out their repression against people in the open. Instead, in the interests of the powerful, they attempt to sabotage the resistance to injustice and exploitation through manipulation and corruption. Many people had their lives completely destroyed when they decided to say enough is enough to the authorities. Its depressing when you see a government calling itself democratic, but as soon as it feels its hold on power slipping, resorts to all kinds of provocations, intrigues, bribery, sophistry, blackmail, and threats. However, people have really had enough of everything.

GB: Is there a danger of the Right capitalizing on popular discontent as a result of this crisis as it has elsewhere?
MS: The Right has, for the most part, profited during elections as a result of popular discontent. Their demagogic approach to social policy is convincing to many. The biggest opposition party at the moment is close to the extreme Right. On the other hand, the so-called "pro-European" and "democratic" parties are corrupt and are loyally implementing neoliberal policies, while their social policy is catastrophic. Workers are increasingly recognizing the need for their own party, which we've already seen happen in Zrenjanin. I firmly believe that we'll soon see the current political scene filled with authentic working-class parties, so that the workers' discontent will

no longer be misused by either the right or the false champions of "social justice."

GB: What can folks from the outside do to support local resistance to neoliberalism?
MS: The most important thing is that information about our struggle be disseminated in an accurate way. Even though the problem of workers and oppressed groups in society are similar throughout the world as a result of globalization, every context also has its own specificities, which we must come to know in detail before making any conclusions. These specificities can often be the source of misunderstandings, since everywhere one can find opportunists and grandstanding individuals among Leftist activists who do things only to impress their friends on the international scene. Such activities may not be related to the local context in which they operate in any way, but they'll still take such actions. Such opportunists in fact can bring real harm to actual struggles occurring in their local context. For this reason it is important that the situation in Serbia is understood and transmitted in a precise way, so that there is no room for manipulation.

New Rounds of Enclosure and Resistance: Fighting Notes from "Transitional" Serbia

Interview with Pokret za Slobodu (Freedom Fight)

May 2010

Andrej Grubačić: Let me begin by asking about the last round of privatization in Serbia. What used to be called in the state-socialist system of former Yugoslavia, "socially owned property," is being enclosed and privatized. How advanced is this process of "privatization through bankruptcy" at the moment? And at the risk of sounding legalistic, how legal is this process of accumulation by dispossession?

Freedom Fight: The privatization of socially owed property is almost completely done. The few big structures that remain are now turned into state enterprises, like the Bor complex (mines and mining industry) or the arms industry in Čačak, Užice, Kragujevac, and so on. There are also some mid-level and small socially owed companies that are still not privatized, and last year the government decided simply to liquidate them. This liquidation is not based on economic reasons—it is a completely political decision to shut down all the remaining socially owed companies. The Ministry of Economy calls it "privatization through bankruptcy." The decision is absolutely illegal. Serbian law on bankruptcy proscribes the causes for starting the liquidation process, and the government's order to kill an otherwise well-doing company just because it is socially owed is not one of them. This decision was a cause for several protests last year, and the strongest group of workers who are still fighting is the one in Ravanica from Ćuprija. Last summer, its workers blocked the factory to prevent the government's people from taking over the management. The protest gained strong public support, especially after the newspapers published the fact that Ravanica is not only the last factory in Ćuprija up for privatization, but also the only one that still works, and works very well. Ćuprija used to have several well-known factories, and literally all of them were closed down or went bankrupt in the privatization process. The government feared this would initiate further debate about the success of the privatization process in Serbia, so they retreated from Ravanica and confirmed the old management as the official one. At this point, Ravanica is the last remaining socially owed company in Serbia that remains in operation.

As far as the state owed companies, the government is planning to sell the pharmaceutical factory Galenika, Telekom Company, JAT Airways and Elektrodistribucija. They decided to sell Telekom this year, which caused very strong public protest. Both big unions of Telekom are against privatization, and they are supported by lots of intellectuals, some media (Republika and Balkan online magazine) and a former telecommunications minister. We can expect big fight over the issue this summer.

AG: Freedom Fight collective, or Pokret za Slobodu in Yugoslav, is a member of the Coordination Committee of Workers' Protest in Serbia. What is the news from below? One of the goals of Freedom Fight, of Pokret, is to help create a horizontal, prefigurative, self-managed structure that would allow for a genuine workers self-activity—solidarity unionism. What is the reality of rank and file workers resistance, and what is the relationship with the old, vertical union structures?

FF: Last year's wave of protests was caused by the results of the privatization process. Privatization failed to provide promised economic development, and after this problem was further emphasized by the global economic crisis, people began holding strikes and protests. Lots of privatization contracts were canceled (Zastava Elektro, Vršački Vinogradi,

Ikarbus), and several of these workers groups formed the Coordination Committee of Workers' Protests. Pokret za slobodu is also a member of the committee. Forming of this committee was not only a reaction to the government's policies, but also on the policies of the big unions. It was previously the union's job to connect the workers groups that are protesting, but they instead choose to take the government's side. During the protest of the Zastava Elektro workers, we witnessed the union actually sabotaging the workers' plan to organize demonstrations in front of the Privatization Agency's (PA) building in Belgrade. Then Pokret za slobodu called Zrenjanin and Belgrade workers to help them—they organized demonstrations together, and that was the beginning of the Coordination Committee. The Zastava Elektro protest was successful. The PA was forced to cancel the privatization contract, but two months ago they sold Zastava Elektro again to the Yura Company from South Korea. Yura officials banned union organizing, and most of the old workers who were in last year's protests left the factory. They feel that the new sale of the company is a kind of revenge by the government for the protest. Furthermore, the pro-government press is now attacking them by saying that they are lazy—that last year "they were protesting for their jobs, but when Korean company offers them jobs, they refuse to work!"

On the other hand, the protest of another group from the Coordination Committee, Trudbenik gradnja workers, was unsuccessful even though they proved that their boss was severely breaking the privatization contract. The PA accepted their evidence, and it released the official hundred-pages detailed report on how the boss was breaking the law, but then they said, "OK, you guys were right, he is robbing both you and the state, it is outrageous, but we won't break the contract." Just like that. Why? Because this was a clear message for all the other workers what would happen if they rebel, and especially if they are doing it outside of the union structures. The cost of this for the workers was very high—more than two hundred Trudbenik workers were sacked by the boss because of the protest. At the beginning of the strike in August last year they knew what would happen if they turn it into a protest against the privatization contract. But they took the risk, knowing that the canceling of the privatization contract was their only chance to get the jobs back. It was him or them, and they proved that the law is on their side, but now they are out, not the boss. At the same time, Zastava Elektro workers are punished for their last year's successful protest as well. The Coordination Committee is still far from being strong enough to help them, besides holding more protests, so at this point the situation doesn't look good. However, we are expecting a new wave of protests this summer, and that would be the chance for our organization—Coordination Committee of Workers' Protests in Serbia—to grow stronger.

AG: So is this the new focus of your current activity? Are there any efforts to document the experiences of last year and your struggle for solidarity unionism against the long theft we know as privatization?

FF: Besides our work within the Coordination Committee, Pokret za slobodu is now trying to broaden the network. We are now establishing contacts with peasants associations. They are the group completely repressed by the government because they don't have a level of organization strong enough to fight radically against either the government's measures that are destroying their economy, nor against the private monopolies trading with the agricultural products that are the fruit of their labor. This is very important issue here, since over two million people in Serbia depend only on agriculture for their livelihood.

We are currently working on a film and a book about last year's protests, because we believe it is important to analyze what really happened—it's continued significance—and to give our side of the story. The Serbian press is writing about workers' issues only form the perspective of big politics or big unions, and we want to show the perspectives of the people who were in the protests. These protests are not just another subject of somebody's political agenda, they are coming from the people, and what we are doing is trying to help these people be heard.

AG: In my view, one of the truly "balkanopolitan" elements of the Balkan and Serbian society are the Roma: their struggle against hierarchical, state-imposed authority and regulation, against the market economy and systems of both state socialism and capitalism, along with their culture, are a powerful inspiration for dreaming another Balkans. On the other hand, and for this very reason, they were and remain to be the single most oppressed group in the Balkan states.

FF: Roma are the only group in Serbia that is completely left to its own fate. It is a desperate, catastrophic situation. The number of itinerant poor is now even larger due to exclusion mechanisms of the neoliberal state. Roma live in the streets, they collect trash and paper in order to survive. Some estimates put the number of Roma in Serbia at 600,000, although the 2002 census only registered 102,193 people as Roma. According to the UNICEF report on the condition of Roma children in the Republic of Serbia (2006), almost 70 percent of Roma children are poor and over 60 percent of Roma households with children live below poverty line. Children are the most imperiled, living outside of cities in households with several children. Over 80 percent of indigent Roma children live in families in which the adult members of the family do not have basic education.

AG: And in the meantime, the activist scene in Serbia is, in my opinion, very disconnected from these realities—or at least it was when I lived in Serbia. I hope that some things changed for the better since then, and that there is now at least an attempt to bring about a relationship of active solidarity, radical community organizing, and "accompaniment" towards the situation of Roma in Serbia and the Balkans as a whole.

FF: The activist scene in Serbia is still weak and without influence, but there are some signs that this might change. Since the "transition" process started in 2001, the biggest problem of the Serbian Leftist community wasn't the fact that it was small, weak, outnumbered by Nazis and so on, but that it was incompetent and ignorant about local problems. Lots of energy was wasted on activities that had little to do with the actual problems of Serbian workers in "transition." And those problems were huge—too huge not to be seen and confronted. For that reason, we can say now that it was almost lucky that most of the activities of the Leftist collectives in the past decade went virtually unnoticed by the broad public. It was pretty embarrassing to have some self-proclaimed anarcho-syndicalist leaders preaching against privatization from the ideological point of view but without a clue about the local context, as if they just fell in from another world. For years, we were practically the only collective that was working with the actual people on the ground in strikes. But since last year, this has started to change: there are several Belgrade collectives now that are trying to support different groups of people in strike or in some other kind of protest, which is very significant because only by broadening our movement will the current Leftist scene begin to make an influence, even though for the time-being it is still small.

Don't Mourn, Balkanize!
A Vision for the Balkans

May 2010

A decade or so ago, during the European humanitarian adventure in the Balkans, Michael Nicholson, an eminent British journalist, wrote in his *Natasha's Story* that "The ferocity of the Balkan peoples has at times been so primitive that anthropologists have likened them to the Amazon's Yanamamo, one of the world's most savage and primitive tribes. Up until the turn of the present century there were still reports from the Balkans of decapitated enemy heads presented as trophies on silver plates at victory dinners. Nor was it unknown for the winners to eat the loser's heart and liver."

I was born into a good communist Balkan family where we have never enjoyed such delicacies. Perhaps naively, I suspect that most of my fellow tribesmen have never tasted them either. So, the question emerges: how is it possible that this distinguished British gentleman is able to produce such an appallingly disturbing description?

No less disturbing, for want of a better term, is a sociological analysis that another eminent man of letters, Simon Winchester, offers in his *The Fracture Zone: A Return to the Balkans*, where he observes that "Just as the peninsula—these strange and feral Balkans—is outlandish and unlike the rest of Europe, for its inhabitants, the wild peoples of the Balkans, who evolved into something that varies substantially from whatever is the human norm."

Somewhat more recently, on the other side of the ocean, Michael Ignatieff, self-taught political theorist and (as Tamara Vukov observes not without some consternation) quite possibly a future Prime Minister of Canada, announces, with quite remarkable honesty, a prospect of "Nation-building in Bosnia, Kosovo, and Afghanistan because they are laboratories in which a new imperium is taking shape, in which American military power, European money and humanitarian motive have combined to produce a form of imperial rule for a post-imperial age." That is, in these ungovernable barbarian frontier zones of failed states and ethnic conflict, a "temporary imperialism," in the form of limited occupation is necessary. "Bosnia after Dayton offered laboratory conditions in which to experiment with nation-building," he continues, as "the reconstruction of the Balkans has not been an exercise in humanitarian social work, it has always been an imperial project ..." because "nation-building is the kind of imperialism you get in a human rights era."

How do we account for statements like these? Where is this perverse attitude coming from? Who are these people to think they can come and "build our nations?" In this brief essay, I will offer two analytically interrelated explanations. One is political and the other one is structural. The political explanation resides in two different meanings of the word "balkanization." The first is what I will call "balkanization from above." This form of balkanization is, one might say, an invention of European colonial modernity and its balkanologists. One could even make a little joke and suggest that Euro-American politics in the Balkans was, historically, guided by three B's: balkanization, barbarity, and bombs. People in the Balkans are barbarians, or so this Euro-imperial line goes, they tend to balkanize, and the only way to prevent that is to bomb them, or sell them bombs so that they can do it themselves.

If we take a historical view, I think that we could identify a phenomenon, or, rather, a whole complex of elite reactions, that I propose calling "political balkanophobia": an elite fear of autonomous spaces. Balkanization from above came into existence as an elite response to autonomous processes from below. European colonial modernity arose, in no small part, as a result of successful fights for the formation and territorial unification of a regional identity. The state-architects of Europe of that time were, in fact, obsessed with the demon of the Balkans, balkanization being taken here in the sense of a "balkanization from below," an alternative process of territorial organization, decentralization, territorial autonomy, and federalism. Balkanization from below, a process of constant fission and fusion, has been a remarkably threatening alternative for the emerging large, centralized, coercive systems. With the modern invention of Balkanity, Balkanization (from above!) became a name, and an excuse, for a process of eliminating the threat of autonomous political spaces that lack any specialized and permanently constituted coercive authority separated from the society, as well as of eliminating the region's memory of its anti-modern and anti-statist struggles.

I believe that the invention of "Balkanity" as a political and geocultural concept should be located within the historical landscape organized by the 1878 Congress in Berlin. It is my argument that the modern history of the Balkans properly begins in the Berlin Congress—home to "carve-up of the Balkans," "the Great Game" in Central Asia, and the "Scramble for Africa"—after which, as Maria Todorova suggests, the adjective "Balkan" ceased to be "a vague geographical concept and was transformed into one of the most consistently pejorative epithets in Western political discourse."

It is interesting to note that this is the same period in which Bram Stoker writes his famous gothic novel, *Dracula*. Here, as Vesna Goldsworthy shrewdly observes, we are introduced to a new and strange world: "Dracula's world represents everything that is anathema to the Victorians—passion, sex, unrestrained violence ... Dracula must not simply be killed but completely destroyed by the united representatives of the West—an Englishman, a Dutchman and an American ... Their mission to restore order in the Balkans represents a fictional expression of the attempts in the late-19th and 20th centuries by the Western powers to impose peace on the peninsula." The next steps in defining balkanization from above emerged during the First and Second Balkan Wars of 1912 and 1913, widely believed to "offer definitive proof of 'medieval' behavior on the part of Balkan warriors." Reading contemporary documents it is easy to see how the supposed violent nature of the Balkans was used as an alibi for the future interventions of always-benevolent European powers.

However, the crucial moment of development of balkanization from above was a courageous action by Gavrilo Princip and his comrades in 1914. Misha Glenny quotes John Gunther's popular book *Inside Europe* (1940) which

> summarized feelings on this side of the Atlantic: "It is an intolerable affront to human and political nature that these wretched and unhappy little countries in the Balkan peninsula can, and do, have quarrels that cause world wars. Some hundred and fifty thousand young Americans died because of an event in 1914 in a mud-caked primitive village, Sarajevo. Loathsome and almost obscene snarls in Balkan politics, hardly intelligible to a Western reader, are still vital to the peace of Europe, and perhaps the world.'

The colonial imagination of Stocker lived on with the queen of mystery novels. In *The Secret of Chimneys*, Agatha Christie depicted a "Herzoslovakian" peasant, Boris Anchoukoff, with "high Slavonic cheekbones, and dreamy fanatic eyes." He is, we learn, "a human bloodhound from a race of brigands."

It is interesting to note that the term "Balkans," with its "race of brigands," was barely used during the Communist period. Four of the countries were subsumed into the phrase "Eastern Europe" while Greece and Turkey were "NATO's southern flank." It is no accident that when Yugoslavia collapsed in 1991, the term Balkans came back. At the same time as the "savage Balkans" was reintroduced, the propaganda myth of the artificiality of now former Yugoslavia, and its "dark Balkan origins," emerged from the woodwork of metropolitan academia.

Today, in this new era of integration, the Balkans, former Yugoslavia, and balkanization are presented and projected to the world opinion as nothing but the historical residue of "primitive nationalisms," and once again pose a threat to delirious European bureaucratization—just like in the era of the Berlin Congress—at its core. The European Union is unsettled by the prospect of a politically rebellious region, inside of, and against, imperial agglomeration. Listen to the words of the Hungarian prime minister: "The problems of the Roma are not locked on the territory of the individual EU member states, because the free movement of people means free movement of social problems." This is balkanization from above, the pacification of "free movement of social problems."

It is my contention that both the late-19th-century Europe and the neoliberal bureaucratic Europe were built against and in the opposition to the Balkans. There is a historical continuity between Berlin and Lisbon. The road to both leads through the Balkans and, most crucially, through the former Yugoslavia and mud-caked village of Sarajevo, today once again under the occupation of the ever watchful "international community."

The second explanation for the particular attitude of modern/colonial Europe towards the Balkans cuts much deeper. What I termed "invention of Balkanity" lies at the very heart of European universalism. The modern/capitalist European universalist project, included, as its "other side," the invention of the Balkans, where the Balkans was discovered as a symbol of everything mysterious and threatening in European culture. The Balkans became a "wild" Europe, an entangling, intricate labyrinth inhabited by creatures of sin, insolent nations, incapable of governing themselves, a place in the heart of European darkness. A place outside, if on the doorstep, where people need to be evangelized in the name of civilizing missions, human rights and civil society. This is the Balkans as a self-destructive hole in world history, an endless reservoir of violence and negativity, as a chaotic gap in world time. This cultural element cannot be overstated.

In recent years, a group of progressive and radical balkanologists initiated a serious theoretical attempt to correct the epistemological centrism of European scholarship. Milica Bakic Hayden, drawing from Edward Said's conceptual world of *Orientalism* and situating the Balkans in this category of historical explanation, introduced a new heuristic of "nesting orientalism" as a variation on the orientalist theme. Maria Todorova further recognizes different traits in the constructed identity of the Balkans, not "merely as a subspecies of orientalism," but as a "specific rhetorical paradigm." There is an independent trajectory in defining the hegemonic representation of the peninsula, which she terms "balkanism." Even more perceptively, Tamara Vukov recently made an intervention in this debate in her useful analysis of "neo-balkanism," in which she locates the Balkans within the historical reality of global capitalism.

While welcoming this epistemic change of perspective, and acknowledging the value of aforementioned research, my inclination is to relate the particular historical time/ space of the Balkans to the processes of global capitalist coloniality that Anibal Quijano describes as "coloniality of power." Coloniality of power, according to Quijano, presupposes a new model of global power, an inauguration of the first modern/colonial/capitalist world-system, which was structured around a notion of race. While it might be possible to understand the history of European interpretative violence inflicted upon "European Turkey" as one of "nesting orientalisms," it seems to me impossible to understand the history of the Balkans, after its invention in the wake of the Berlin Congress, outside of the new global hegemonic model and technology of power, in place since the Conquest of the Americas, that articulates race and labor, space and peoples, according to the needs of capital and to the benefit of European peoples. It is important, in my view, to take into more serious consideration Enrique Dussel's distinction between "two modernities": one that is "Eurocentric, provincial, and regional," and the other which is world-oriented and includes the "other side," that which "was dominated, exploited, and concealed." Dussel insists that we need to "deny the innocence of modernity," because "by affirming the alterity of the other (which was previously denied), it is possible to "discover" for the first time the hidden "other side" of modernity: the peripheral colonial world, the sacrificed indigenous peoples, the enslaved black, the oppressed woman, the alienated infant, the estranged popular culture: the victims of modernity, all of them victims of an irrational act that contradicts modernity's ideal of rationality." He calls this project "transmodernity," a "worldwide ethical liberation project in which alterity, which was part and parcel of modernity, would be able to fulfill itself." The alterity and "exteriority" of the Balkans, and its "white but not quite" inhabitants, should not be thought about as a pure outside, untouched by the modern. It refers to an outside that is precisely constituted as difference by hegemonic processes.

I hope that all these approaches can help introduce a fresh conceptual framework for the understanding of recent and not so recent historical intertwining of "balkanist" and nationalist discourses. In order to change the Balkans, we need to start thinking otherwise about and from the Balkans. Here, I would like to suggest that such an understanding requires its own collective and emancipatory research project, a project of thinking otherwise from the interior exteriority of the border, and that might be called "balkanology from below." This emancipatory research program would contribute developing, from this side of "the other side of modernity," what Arturo Escobar calls "an other way of thinking, *un paradigma otro*, the very possibility of talking about worlds and knowledges otherwise." Radical balkanologists, organized in such a community of argumentation, could benefit greatly from the intellectual work of the so-called modernity/coloniality group, represented by Quijano, Dussel, Mignolo, and other activist scholars. It would be an unfortunate mistake to see the impressive work of this group as a paradigm for Latin America, rather than as an "other way of thinking that runs counter to the great modernist narratives (Christianity, liberalism, and Marxism); a narrative that "locates its own inquiry in the very borders of systems of thought and reaches towards the possibility of non-Eurocentric modes of thinking." At the same time, in unlocking the radical potential for thinking from difference and towards the constitution of alternative local and regional worlds, and taking seriously the epistemic force of local histories and thinking theory through from the political praxis of subaltern groups, radical balkanologists would do well to follow in the steps of Peter Linebaugh, Marcus Rediker, and other historians from below who have been adventuring for traces of the "many-headed hydra" of rebels and revolutionaries, and hidden stories of popular struggles across the proletarian Atlantic. The beautiful, dazzling history of anti-authoritarian Balkans is replete with struggles of pirates and land pirates; *hajduks, uskoci*, and *klephts*; *bogumils* and partisans; heretics; and agrarian rebels of all kind, all misunderstood by communist and nationalist historians alike. This project, of balkanology from below, could be imagined as a unidisciplinary (Wallerstein) or undisciplinary (Escobar) program, with members coming from many different fields, "undisciplining the disciplines," and establishing a single field of study. This might help us learn how to free our past and our future from "the Eurocentric mirror where our image is always, necessarily, distorted."

I have already described balkanization from below as a narrative that insists on social and cultural affinities, as well as on customs in common resulting from interethnic mutual aid and solidarity, and resulting in what can be termed an interethnic self-activity, one that was severed through the Euro-colonial intervention. In the Balkans, the many-headed hydra has its own political program and vision. The name for this vision is Balkan Federation. There are two principal manifestations of this program, one that I will call federalism from above, based on the idea of federated socialist states, and another that rests on a horizontalist principle of an "organic commonwealth," of a specific "community of communities," that I will call federalism from below.

One of the first expressions of Balkan federalism is mentioned by a Greek historian Loukis Hassiotis, who reminds us of early efforts of Balkan radicals who, in 1865, established the Democratic Eastern Federation with "its syncretic mix of democratic, socialist and national ideas." From this moment onward, the history of Balkan federalism diverges. One line of development will lead to the established political and cultural elites of the Balkan states who were always receptive to the ideas of federalism. Hassiotis writes that "Conservative and liberal politicians, even kings (like King Otto of Greece and Milan Obrenović of Serbia), briefly and randomly presented themselves as supporters of some kind of federalism." Likewise, federalism from above is expressed in the politics of communist parties. Almost all communist parties before the war had a Balkan Federation (a federation of socialist states) as a part of, or even a centerpiece of, their respective programs. In this vein, the most important federalist efforts can be found in the Balkan Conferences of the interwar period, and in Tito's federalist plans right after World War II.

There is another, far more interesting line to follow in the development of Balkan federalism. It is also well know that many anarchists took part in the revolts of Bosnia-Herzegovina and of Bulgaria (1875–1878). Malatesta was not successful in his attempt to enter Bosnia, but his comrade Stepniak was and he left us an important testimony about the struggle against the Ottomans. Moreover, writes Hassiotis, "socialists participated in the movement for Macedonian autonomy (Boatmen, Revolutionary Macedonian Organization), as well as in the anti-Ottoman revolts in Crete, even the interstate Greco-Turkish war in 1897." Some of the anti-authoritarian socialists, like Svetozar Marković or Botev, supported a Balkan Federation built from below, a stateless federation that would establish itself as the result of social revolution and not interstate arrangements and would be based on the confederationist organizing of traditional Southern Slavic agrarian communities. In the anarchist newspaper *Νίον Φως* (new light) from Pyrgos we read, in an article on Crete, that "we, the revolutionaries of the future, should not be patriotic and religious revolutionaries, we should be social and international revolutionaries. Our only enemies are the economic and authoritarian tyrants of any religion. Enough with fighting for flags and symbols. It is time we fought for our political, economic and social freedom in general."

These lines of Greek anarchists were almost forgotten after the World War. But so was the reality of federalism from above, as the Cold War and the breakup of the Stalin-Tito alliance, and finally destruction of Yugoslavia rendered it practically unthinkable. Today, after the horrors of bureaucratic socialism, after many episodes of ethno-nationalist violence, and in the ruins of Eurocentered neoliberalism, I believe it crucial that we revive horizontal federalism. We stand in a long and magnificent tradition.

Before I am accused of painting too bright of a picture, let me just say few words about another painful dichotomy inscribed in the history of the peninsula, the one between nationalism and regional interethnic self-activity. The history of the Balkans is not only a history of interethnic cooperation. It is also a bloody history of nationalist atrocities that we are responsible for, that are self-inflicted. Not more than anywhere else in Europe, perhaps, and not without encouragement from outside, but nevertheless very real. The authoritarian Left in the Balkans, with its stubborn insistence on "national sovereignty," and support for nation-state form as a necessary stage in social liberation, played a negative role in defining a position on nationalism. I would not like to be misunderstood here. When I say that I advocate regionalism and pluriculturalism, or that I criticize a Jacobin model of a monocultural state, I do not mean to say that we can evade the violent aspects of our brutal nationalist past. We have to confront in the same breath the terror visited upon us by Euro-colonial violence and our own self-inflicted brutalities. For the past to become a principle of action in the present, we have to stop living in the past and instead integrate it into the present in an emancipatory way. In order to build a pluricultural Balkans, the present has to be liberated from the past. It should be clear that I am not advocating an erasure of the past, but a work of remembrance as part of the work of freedom. This cannot be done by embracing any form of particularism, ethnic or regional. Following Achille Mbembe, I would like to borrow a term for this always incomplete project, riddled with tensions and contradictions, which both embraces and transcends the question of specificity, and call it balkanopolitanism—a way of being from the Balkans articulated through an openness to difference and a transcendence of nationalism. Balkanopolitanism, as a regional project, actively seeking out new experiences, rejecting "the confines of bounded communities and their own cultural backgrounds," would transcend Balkan nationalisms through curiosity for the foreign and an openness to hybridity, "embracing, with full knowledge of the facts, strangeness, foreignness, and remoteness, the ability to recognize one's face in that of a foreigner and make the most of the traces of remoteness in closeness." If Arturo Escobar is right when he suggests that being place-based is not the same as being place-bound, then Balkanopolitanism would be a precious gift to the project of global universalism, where, in words of Senghor, the world becomes a meeting place of giving and receiving (*rendez-vous du donner et du recevoir*).

But how can a national issue be dealt with in a more programmatic sense? I believe that nationalism can only be answered within a regional framework, and I believe that the Balkans can provide a model for another Europe, a balkanized Europe of regions, as an alternative to both transnational European super-state and nation-states. A balkanization of Europe would be premised on the politics of autonomous regions and a plurality of cultures. I see the region, an entity once eroded by the centralized nation-state and capitalism, as the basis for the regeneration and reconstruction of the social and political life of Europe. I agree with the optimism of Kropotkin when he anticipates "a time when in Russia each component of a federation, a free federation of rural communities and free cities, will make the free commonwealth, and I believe too that Western Europe will also move in this direction."

So what would this Balkan Federation, with no states and no nations, be like? I think that new Balkan revolutionaries should embrace and defend the project of a contemporary Balkan Federation as one of radical decolonization, pluriculturality, social change from the bottom-up, analogous to and in active communication with such contemporary projects as the pluricultural politics of the indigenous people of Andean Federation, Anarchists Against the Wall in the Middle East, or grassroots movements from Africa who chant that "we are the poor."

This Balkans, neither capitalist nor bureaucratic-socialistic, would be a transethnic society with a balkanopolitan, pluriculturalist outlook, an outlook which previously existed but was lost in its incorporation into nation-state frameworks, an outlook that recognizes multiple and overlapping identities and affiliations characterized by proliferation and multiplicity, an outlook that recognizes the unity produced out of difference. This would be a Balkans based on voluntary co-operation and mutual aid, direct democracy of neighborhood assemblies and city federations, free associations that "extend themselves and cover every branch of human activity," with a self-managed economy with participatory planning, structured within the regional frame of a state-dissolving federation.

To build such a world, we would need a new type of politics from below. It should be clear that by politics I mean an organic, dialogical, shared and participatory activity of the self-governing public and not a statecraft, a set of operations that are premised on the seizing of State power and which are realized through a political party, nor any political movement that replicates the State in its organization. I am talking about an anti-authoritarian politics that is utopian, in the sense that it celebrates political imagination and attempts to bring into being other possibilities for human existence—one that conquers a point of view beyond the given, and refuses the rationalization of the real, the rationalization of the imposed colonial and state-national alternatives. I am talking about a new, restored politics of mutual aid, mutual solidarity, pluricultural identity, and freedom.

Translated into practice, this comes very close to Uri Gordon's description of Anarchists Against the Wall and the cooperative transethnic village of Neve Shalom, both examples of "radical peace-building" in the Middle East:

> The point, however, is the grassroots grounding of the process itself. Realistically speaking, then, we are looking to the activities of groups and communities that can contaminate the statist peace process with a more thoroughgoing agenda of social transformation. What grounds such an agenda, from an anarchist perspective, is the argument that the creation of genuine peace requires the creation and fostering of political spaces which facilitate voluntary cooperation and mutual aid (between Israelis and Palestinians).

Moving from the Balkans of nationalism and exploitation to the (federated) Balkans of solidarity and struggle is possible only in the context of interethnic accompaniment and concrete struggles that prefigure a "no-state solution" of regional federalism. The Freedom Fight movement in Serbia, anti-authoritarian movements and migrant groups like Clandestina in Greece, and Bulgarian anarchist federations are some important cases in point. But we need many more.

We, "the revolutionaries of the future," need to go back and build upon what is the most precious part of our history, and that is a pluricultural vision of multiethnic, indeed transethnic, anti-authoritarian society. We need to understand the scandal borne by the word "Balkans" and rediscover the trenchancy of its idea. The kind of society we are talking about is possible only within the framework of a Balkan Federation, with no state, and beyond nation. A world where many worlds fit. If this is not our reality today, it follows that our duty, our only duty, is to fight to make it our reality tomorrow.

About the Author:
Andrej Grubačić is a dissident from the Balkans. A radical historian and sociologist, he is the co-author of *Wobblies and Zapatistas* and editor of *The Staughton Lynd Reader*. He is a fellow traveler of Zapatista-inspired direct action movements, as well as The Industrial Workers of the World (IWW or the Wobblies), and a co-founder of Global Balkans Network and *Balkan Z Magazine*. He is currently a lecturer at San Francisco Art Institute.

About Roxanne Dunbar-Ortiz (Foreword):
Roxanne Dunbar-Ortiz is a historian and professor in the Department of Ethnic Studies at California State University, Hayward. She is the author of *Red Dirt: Growing up Okie*, *The Great Sioux Nation*, and *Roots of Resistance*, among other books.

ABOUT PM PRESS

PM Press was founded at the end of 2007 by a small collection of folks with decades of publishing, media, and organizing experience. PM Press co-conspirators have published and distributed hundreds of books, pamphlets, CDs, and DVDs. Members of PM have founded enduring book fairs, spearheaded victorious tenant organizing campaigns, and worked closely with bookstores, academic conferences, and even rock bands to deliver political and challenging ideas to all walks of life. We're old enough to know what we're doing and young enough to know what's at stake.

We seek to create radical and stimulating fiction and non-fiction books, pamphlets, t-shirts, visual and audio materials to entertain, educate and inspire you. We aim to distribute these through every available channel with every available technology — whether that means you are seeing anarchist classics at our bookfair stalls; reading our latest vegan cookbook at the café; downloading geeky fiction e-books; or digging new music and timely videos from our website.

PM Press is always on the lookout for talented and skilled volunteers, artists, activists and writers to work with. If you have a great idea for a project or can contribute in some way, please get in touch.

PM Press
PO Box 23912
Oakland, CA 94623
www.pmpress.org

FRIENDS OF PM PRESS

These are indisputably momentous times — the financial system is melting down globally and the Empire is stumbling. Now more than ever there is a vital need for radical ideas.

In the three years since its founding — and on a mere shoestring — PM Press has risen to the formidable challenge of publishing and distributing knowledge and entertainment for the struggles ahead. With over 100 releases to date, we have published an impressive and stimulating array of literature, art, music, politics, and culture. Using every available medium, we've succeeded in connecting those hungry for ideas and information to those putting them into practice.

Friends of PM allows you to directly help impact, amplify, and revitalize the discourse and actions of radical writers, filmmakers, and artists. It provides us with a stable foundation from which we can build upon our early successes and provides a much-needed subsidy for the materials that can't necessarily pay their own way. You can help make that happen – and receive every new title automatically delivered to your door once a month – by joining as a Friend of PM Press. And, we'll throw in a free T-Shirt when you sign up.

Here are your options:
- **$25 a month** Get all books and pamphlets plus 50% discount on all webstore purchases
- **$25 a month** Get all CDs and DVDs plus 50% discount on all webstore purchases
- **$40 a month** Get all PM Press releases plus 50% discount on all webstore purchases
- **$100 a month** Superstar — Everything plus PM merchandise, free downloads, and 50% discount on all webstore purchases

For those who can't afford $25 or more a month, we're introducing **Sustainer Rates** at $15, $10 and $5. Sustainers get a free PM Press t-shirt and a 50% discount on all purchases from our website.

Your Visa or Mastercard will be billed once a month, until you tell us to stop. Or until our efforts succeed in bringing the revolution around. Or the financial meltdown of Capital makes plastic redundant. Whichever comes first.